D0098537

HOMEGROWN

HOMEGROWN

HOW THE RED SOX BUILT A
CHAMPION FROM THE GROUND UP

ALEX SPEIER

wm

WILLIAM MORROW
An Imprint of HarperCollinsPublishers

HarperCollins books may be purchased for educational, business, or sales promotional use. For information, please email the Special Markets Department at SPsales@harpercollins.com.

FIRST EDITION

Library of Congress Cataloging-in-Publication Data has been applied for.

ISBN 978-0-06-294355-2   33614081494584

19 20 21 22 23   DIX/LSC   10 9 8 7 6 5 4 3 2 1

To Alyssa, Max, and Gavin
There is no *Homegrown* without home.
I love you all.

CONTENTS

CHILLS RAN THROUGH MEMBERS OF the Red Sox as they watched the familiar, lanky figure emerge from the bullpen door. The sight of Chris Sale jogging across right field and to the mound with a chance to close out the World Series vanquished any lingering doubts, replacing them with an elated sense of anticipation.

The Dodger Stadium night had been overtaken by Red Sox fans, volume rising with each strike of the ninth. Red Sox players hugged the front railing of the dugout, waiting to leap onto the field in the most sought-after event of a baseball lifetime.

As Sale mowed down two straight Dodgers, Justin Turner and then Kike Hernandez, with devastating sliders, it became clear that the Red Sox ace would not leave his teammates waiting long—certainly not in comparison to the years that had been spent building to this place and time. Just one batter remained: Manny Machado, a potentially perfect final obstacle for the 2018 season given the charged role played by the Dodgers third baseman in the Red Sox' joyless 2017 campaign.

With the count at one ball and two strikes, Sale unleashed the ultimate wipeout slider, a pitch that swooped across the plate in such devastating fashion that Machado lost his footing while swinging over the top of it. Christian Vazquez—ten years removed from being drafted out of high school in Puerto Rico, the longest-tenured member of the Red Sox organization on the World Series roster—corralled the historic pitch and set in motion a race to the mound, where he'd encounter more than a few familiar faces.

As members of the Red Sox converged on the night of October 28, 2018, it seemed almost immediately necessary to look beyond the mere fact of what they'd just accomplished in search of context and meaning. Somehow, "champions" seemed inadequately understated in describing the exploits of a juggernaut.

With a franchise-record 108 wins in the regular season and an unrelenting blitz through three postseason series in October during which Boston won eleven of fourteen games—losing just one game each to the Yankees in the American League Division Series, the Astros in the American League Championship Series, and the Dodgers in the World Series—the 2018 Red Sox stood as a twenty-first-century baseball leviathan. Only one team in baseball history, the 1998 Yankees, finished a championship season with more victories than the 119 accumulated in the regular season and playoffs by this Red Sox team.

Yet the magnitude of the accomplishment was not foremost on the mind of Mookie Betts as he approached the growing celebration in the middle of the field. Instead, as the twenty-six-year-old face of the franchise approached the throng, a single adverb accompanied him.

"Finally," Betts thought.

For Betts and many of his teammates, the championship represented not just the culmination of a single great season but of a far more textured history—and one that had been anything but singularly joyous.

Roughly five years before he experienced the game's pinnacle, Betts had been so discouraged by the undistinguished start of his professional career that he'd contemplated quitting the sport altogether. Alongside Xander Bogaerts—"really like a twin brother," Betts said of a player who'd been born four days before him—he'd been part of two of the worst seasons in modern Red Sox history, including one where he felt so unwelcomed in the big leagues that at one point he was relieved for his demotion to the minors.

He'd spent time feeling like the world was pitting him against his career-long friend, Jackie Bradley Jr., making their futures a competition only one could win. And even when he'd experienced both individual and team success in the 2016 and 2017 seasons, those years ended in disappointment, with early dismissals from the playoffs.

That past played into the sweetness of that Southern California night, as Betts converged with fellow 2011 draftee Bradley and 2015 first-rounder Andrew Benintendi behind the infield dirt before taking off on the weightless sprint to the infield scrum.

There, they encountered Bogaerts, the twenty-six-year-old shortstop who'd been in the Red Sox organization since signing out of Aruba in 2009, and who represented the lone active holdover from the team's previous championship in 2013. Third baseman Rafael Devers, signed out of the Dominican Republic as a sixteen-year-old in 2013 and who had turned twenty-two years old during the World Series, ran over from his position to join the growing mob.

Those six players represented a remarkable confluence. The Red Sox became the first American League team since the 1984 Tigers with at least six homegrown players under thirty years old on the field or in the lineup at the moment that they clinched.

That group formed, in the words of assistant GM Eddie Romero, "the heartbeat of the club," one that represented not just greatness in that moment but a sometimes painful but ultimately triumphant trajectory over the decade.

They weren't alone, of course. The contest that secured a title had been started by David Price, a pitcher who came to Boston on a record-setting $217 million contract. Another high-priced free agent, J. D. Martinez, had launched a home run. And it was Sale, a player imported via a blockbuster trade, who unleashed the final pitch of the season.

Those imported players made clear that the Red Sox had benefited not just from a phenomenal group of players who'd been scouted by the organization as amateurs but also from remarkable resources, the most expensive World Series winner ever. Yet while there was an undeniably immense investment made by the Red Sox in the 2018 team, payroll alone could not form the basis of a championship.

Indeed, in many ways, the team's considerable financial assets were less valuable—and certainly less scarce—than another kind of resource that featured prominently on the field at the time of the final pitch of the 2018 season. That yield of six players on the field for the final pitch was the end result of a remarkable distillation process that connected so many members of the organization to the triumph.

Since 2011—the year that Betts and Bradley were drafted and made their professional debuts—a total of 907 players had stepped onto the field as Red Sox minor leaguers. They'd been supported during that time by seventy-one uniformed coaches in the farm system, sixty-three athletic training staffers, twenty-five strength and conditioning coaches, and six mental skills instructors. The group had been assembled by dozens of domestic and international scouts with an unhealthy number of miles on their cars or in their frequent flyer accounts, and dozens more front-office members who'd devoted themselves to finding players who would one day, they hoped, have the chance to help deliver a World Series title to Boston.

And now, they had done just that—finally. As Betts met with his teammates, years funneled into a triumphant instant.

"I've been with these guys for so long," Betts thought. "It's just . . . it's a long time coming."

CHAPTER 1

THE BOILER ROOM

Chaos and possibility coalesced in the hours, minutes, and seconds leading up to midnight on August 15, 2011, creating the conditions for an organizational Big Bang. One night would shape the Red Sox for years to come.

Roughly fifteen members of the Red Sox baseball operations department were barricaded in the basement of Fenway Park, anticipating a frenzied rush to that night's deadline to sign their 2011 draftees. They'd been there all day—not an unusual development, even when, as with that August 15, there wasn't a Red Sox home game.

The subterranean setting for this looming landmark seemed at once baffling and entirely appropriate. Baseball ops resided year-round in this space with almost no natural light, the only windows to the outside so close to the ceiling that the view to the outside world rarely afforded more than a glimpse of some feet of passersby.

The Vegas-like separation from the world's natural clock made it almost impossible to have a sense for the time of day. But that blurring of the day's structure seemed fitting for a group whose long days and nights often defied standard schedules.

In many ways, the basement was perfect for this particular cast and the peculiar way that it operated. The baseball operations department was a world unto itself, separate from other parts of the team's organization—particularly its business interests. The sequestration had a Thanksgiving vibe, with proper behavior among the well-attired grown-ups upstairs, and mischief among the more casually attired occupants of the basement.

A number of cubicles and desks filled the main working area; on the perimeter, the few enclosed offices still felt connected to that main area due to the large windows along their entry walls. The space had a large, open feel, not only conducive to the broad group conversations that shaped the Red Sox big league roster, farm system, and draft efforts—among other topics—but also allowing for team-building of a very different sort under Red Sox GM Theo Epstein.

At times, the basement resembled a surreal reimagining of *The Office.* One time, Epstein grabbed a golf club and ripped a drive with an intended trajectory away from his coworkers. Instead, the ball caromed off a pillar and into the office of director of player development Ben Cherington, whose head had been tilted down as he worked at his desk.

The ball struck Cherington, and when his coworkers heard a scream and ran in to see blood gushing from his face, they initially feared that he'd lost an eye. He hadn't; 'twas merely a flesh wound, and when Cherington emerged unharmed, the incident became part of the working area's lore.

Cherington wasn't the only one to emerge bruised from the setting. In front of Epstein's office, the relative absence of furniture created an agora of sorts, where staff members gathered for meetings and regular shenanigans. Often two employees donned boxing gloves and headgear and went at it—not quite *Fight Club,* but certainly close enough to make clear that this was not the typical workplace.

The most popular sparring partner was amateur scouting director Amiel Sawdaye, whose five-foot-eight stature made him something of the little brother of the group. Yet Sawdaye was described affectionately by some colleagues as the "front-office Pedroia" for his self-confidence and leadership that belied his size, and for the immense impact he had on the organization through the draft.

As the clock advanced toward the midnight deadline on that memorable night, Sawdaye was in for a different sort of fight. He'd been put in charge of organizing a potentially transformational day in Red Sox history—one that would help shape the legacies of both Epstein, whose tenure in Boston was nearing its end, and Cherington, who would soon take over as the Red Sox general manager.

FROM THE MOMENT HE WAS hired as the GM in November 2002, Epstein had a vision for the Red Sox. The Brookline native had grown up celebrating the accomplishments of incredible talents who'd come through the team's farm system—Jim Rice, Roger Clemens, Dwight Evans—to lead the Red Sox to the ultimately heartbreaking precipice of a title in 1986. He'd also seen missteps, as when the team gave up future Hall of Famer Jeff Bagwell, then in the minors, in exchange for middle reliever Larry Andersen. Epstein knew which of those directions he wanted the Red Sox to follow.

Before his introductory press conference, he thought for a while about how to describe his own view of organization-building—a model that would not just involve the pursuit of a single championship, but that would create an infrastructure, a talent pipeline to fuel perennial postseason ambitions.

"One of the points I wanted to be clear on was that we were really going to focus on building through young players, building through scouting, building through player development, and just as importantly, get away from the notion that we had to please the media in November and December, make a big splash, and build for the immediate future," said Epstein.

In that first press conference, Epstein settled on a single phrase for that vision: a "scouting and player development machine"—meaning an amateur scouting department that would draft potential stars, and a minor league system that would help those players realize their fullest potential. Yet that ambition wasn't without challenges.

All draft picks are, at their heart, lottery tickets with differing likelihoods and sizes of payoff. None comes with guarantees; all carry risk. Even the first overall pick can be a bust. Through 2019, the No. 1 overall pick had produced more players who'd never reached the big leagues before retiring (three) than Hall of Famers. A single big league regular from a team's entire draft represents a strong yield; a second impact player is an organizational watershed.

Moreover, talent isn't concentrated exclusively in the first round of a draft. Because of the difficulty of seeing a high school player's future in a crystal ball, it's entirely possible that the best player in a draft might not be taken until long after the first round. Most famously, catcher Mike Piazza was taken in the 62nd round of the 1988 draft—a round so low that it had been eliminated due to its typical irrelevance by 2011—but went on to a Hall of Fame career.

Still, all things being equal, teams would rather pick earlier than later, and the Red Sox, by dint of their success, usually didn't get to compete for the players taken at the top of the draft who—even with a real risk of flopping—offered the best chance of a jackpot.

But while the structure of the draft meant that the very best players were usually off the board by the time the Red Sox picked, the team identified ways of diminishing its disadvantage. Under the system that existed through 2011, teams willing to ignore Major League Baseball's recommended bonus amounts for each pick in the draft—"slot recommendations" or, more casually, "slot"—had a chance to spend their way to the acquisition of additional elite talent in the draft.

Slot is dictated by where a player is taken in the draft. The higher the pick, the higher the recommended slot value, meaning the top pick in the draft is supposed to get paid the most and the last pick of the first round is supposed to get more than the first pick of the second round.

But the Red Sox hadn't been shy about disrupting that structure. Starting in 2006, they invested hundreds of thousands of dollars above slot for numerous players taken outside of the top five rounds. The team's owners fielded scolding phone calls from the MLB Office of the Commissioner about their supposed excesses, but they remained undeterred. As one opposing general manager noted enviously during that time, "We have to convince our owners why we want to spend on the draft. [The Red Sox] don't. They get it."

By that night in August 2011, Epstein had been in his job for nine years that had transformed the identity of the franchise. In 2004, the team's first World Series triumph in eighty-six years ended the days when the mention of the organization was synonymous with Sisyphean futility. A second title in 2007 offered evidence of dominance, if not quite a dynasty. Still, the team wanted more, and recognized that the draft provided a way to sustain championship contention for years to come.

Both Red Sox principal owner John Henry and chairman Tom Werner had come to Boston after time spent in charge of small-market teams—the Marlins for Henry, and the Padres for Werner. There they had focused on trying to build around young players by necessity. Now they had the luxury of one of the highest payrolls in the game, but did not ignore the lessons of their prior career stops.

"We were aware that the draft was as good a place to spend your money as any," said Werner. "Every year, teams say, 'We just need that one piece.' That's foolishness. It's too important to have a core of talent. In basketball, LeBron James can play forty minutes a game. He could be a difference-maker. But in baseball, you need to have six or eight difference-makers. You've got to have that core."

As the brain trust huddled in the basement with the signing deadline approaching, members of the Red Sox believed they faced perhaps their last opportunity to build such a group.

THAT YEAR'S JUNE AMATEUR DRAFT was considered one of the best, deepest classes in decades. In the summer of 2010, the quality of players seen on the high school and college Team USA baseball squads suggested a potential bonanza in the summer of 2011.

"It was flush with talent," said Sawdaye, a key voice in the Red Sox amateur scouting department from 2003 to 2016, including as the head of the department for the 2010 through 2014 drafts.

The Red Sox were poised to take advantage. Under the Collective Bargaining Agreement (CBA) that was scheduled to expire after the 2011 season, teams received two compensation draft picks for the departure of premier free agents; signing a free agent meant the loss of one first-round pick. To Epstein, the potential advantage of what he called "more bites of the apple" was clear.

Epstein also noted an ancillary benefit to attaching great value to those compensation picks: The willingness to see the benefit of walking away from free agents helped the team to build around players still in their primes, rather than concentrating resources on veterans who were more likely to be entering decline phases.

"More bites of the young, ripening apple," he noted, "and fewer bites of the older, rotting apple."

The Red Sox, during Epstein's tenure, accumulated more compensatory draft picks than any other organization, a practice that was significant in 2011. Though signing Carl Crawford to a soon-to-be-regretted seven-year, $142 million contract the previous December had cost the Red Sox their original first-round selection, the team's willingness to let Adrian Beltre and Victor Martinez walk stocked the Sox with four compensatory picks among the first forty selections of the 2011 draft.

Beyond those first four picks, however, the Red Sox could still spend aggressively on later-round picks. The slot recommendations by MLB in 2011 were just that—recommendations that could be ignored with a wag of the finger but without penalty. That created opportunity.

Invariably, some extremely talented high school players slipped in the draft over concerns that they wouldn't sign unless they received a bonus well in excess of the slot recommendation where they were drafted. Those players represented intriguing targets for the Sox, who weren't shy about opening their wallets.

But with the CBA governing the sport in the process of renegotiation, the Red Sox recognized that their enthusiasm to pursue top-shelf talent later in the draft likely was going to be constrained. There was a good chance that by 2012, the ability to blow past slot recommendations to land extra talent would face significant restrictions.

And if the roulette table was about to close, the Red Sox didn't want to miss a last chance to spread some chips in 2011. There was a standout group of players as well as the ability for the team to choose its budget rather than have it be mandated by Major League Baseball.

"That year was certainly the perfect storm in so many different ways," said Tom Allison, one of the team's regional crosscheckers in the draft that year.

Sawdaye and Epstein wanted to make sure the Sox were poised to take advantage of the confluence of circumstances by putting as many sets of eyes as possible not just on the players who were in consideration for the top four picks but also on those who would be available deeper in the draft. The team created a sizable scouting infrastructure to do just that.

In 2011, the Sox employed twenty-four full-time scouts dedicated to the draft: eighteen area scouts, who were responsible for anything from a multi-state region such as the Northwest to those who covered just a fraction of a state in baseball hotbeds Florida and California to one who covered the entirety of Canada; four regional crosscheckers, who followed up on the reports of a handful of four to five area scouts in a larger coverage region (Southeast, Midwest, Central, and West); one hybrid scout with coverage of the Northeast area and crosschecked in Canada; and one national crosschecker, who jumped around the country to gain firsthand, apples-to-apples perspective on top prospects. The six crosscheckers employed by the team that year represented, according to data from Major League Baseball, the most of any organization entering 2011. The team also had two special assignment scouts and a special assistant to the GM who was heavily involved in amateur scouting. That departmental architecture was no accident for a team that considered multiple looks essential to strong evaluations—particularly when considering players for whom the Sox might be willing to bust past slot recommendations.

"It was the last chance to do this," said Michael Rikard, the national crosschecker in 2011 who eventually became Sawdaye's successor as amateur scouting director. "We really tried to make it an emphasis to ramp up our coverage on the types of guys who, in the coming years, we wouldn't be able to get anymore."

LIKE MOST TEAMS, RED SOX scouts use a 20 to 80 grading scale—at least when examining specific traits. So, for instance, a player might feature an average fastball (50, the midpoint of the scale), a plus curveball (60), and a below-average changeup that, based on the player's evident feel for the pitch or general aptitude on the mound, might one day play up to average (45 present value, future 50).

But once the specific attributes are graded, the team wants its evaluators to step back and offer a big-picture assessment of a player's potential upside ("ceiling," in the preferred nomenclature of scouting) using eight designations:

A1—Hall of Famer

A2—Perennial All-Star position player or a front-of-the-rotation starting pitcher

B1—Consistently above-average everyday position player (perhaps an occasional All-Star), a No. 2 or No. 3 starting pitcher, or a perennial All-Star reliever

B2—Average everyday position player; above-average utility player; No. 4 or No. 5 starting pitcher; above-average reliever

C1—Platoon player or versatile reserve; depth starting pitcher; middle reliever

C2—An up-and-down player who shuttles between the big leagues and the minors to provide depth

D—A player who represents a credible option for a call-up of no more than a couple of days, usually due to adequate defensive ability

NP—Non-prospect, never expected to reach the big leagues,
   but potentially still valuable to filling out a farm system

In addition to those letter/number grades, the Red Sox also
had their scouts evaluate the probability that a player would
reach that identified ceiling, asking them to determine whether
a player had an excellent, good, fair, or poor chance of hitting
on his high-end projection.

The value of even a B2 player in the big leagues is immense.
The Red Sox sought to select—and, hopefully, sign—a wealth of
players who were worthy of such a ceiling, even if it meant spending heavily on them (bonuses are often commensurate with upside rather than probability) and taking some risks. High school
players, for instance, almost never get graded as anything above
fair, and more often get pegged as having a poor probability of
reaching their ceilings, a nod to the statistical reality of how few
actually fulfill the pre-draft daydreams that they inspire.

Each year before the draft, the amateur scouting department
and the rest of the front office would convene for more than a
week of meetings. By the time the 2011 gathering kicked off,
the organization had accumulated a staggering amount of information. On most players, they had at least a year of reports
from area scouts followed by visits from regional and national
crosscheckers. They had player statistics, of course, plus medical
and often psychological data.

The question, as always, was how to sort through it. As Steve
Sanders, then a front-office intern who would go on to become
the director of amateur scouting for the Blue Jays, recalled of
the pre-draft meetings, "There was a sense of enormity. It was
almost controlled chaos—so much information, so many names
to get through."

In the roughly ten days in late May and early June 2011 leading up to the start of the three-day, fifty-round draft, the most

intense debates as the Red Sox lined up their draft board focused on college pitchers. That year's draft class was strikingly deep in quality college starting pitching. The Red Sox anticipated that they'd be selecting from one of three options with their first pick, the nineteenth overall: Matt Barnes, Sonny Gray, or Alex Meyer.

There were strong differences of opinion. Gray was the most successful of the three as an ace at an elite college program at Vanderbilt, but the Red Sox had concerns related to his size and lack of a clear third pitch. Barnes had been overlooked and undrafted out of high school but emerged late in his college career at the University of Connecticut. He had a passionate advocate in Northeast area scout Ray Fagnant, but there were questions about why he hadn't been more dominant throughout his career. Meyer, meanwhile, was someone the Sox knew well; they had drafted him out of high school in 2008, but he had rebuffed their offer of roughly $2 million. After three years at Kentucky, he had electrifying stuff, but potentially significant command issues.

To organize its debate, the team entered "The Matrix"—or at least an exercise by that name. On a whiteboard, the team listed an array of categories and argued about the order in which the three pitchers ranked in a number of constituent categories, including their fastballs, deliveries, and breaking balls. The team then took the sum of those rankings to see who came out ahead.

After the lengthy debates, Barnes received a B2/B1 grade with good probability of reaching a mid-rotation ceiling, putting him ahead of Gray (B2 good) and Meyer (B1 fair). Gray was taken by Oakland with the eighteenth pick of the draft, one spot in front of the Red Sox. With a choice between Barnes and Meyer, the Red Sox chose Barnes.

With their second pick, the Sox considered high school players with significant upside: a player with a seemingly strong commitment to the University of Texas—athletic catcher Blake Swihart—along with right-hander Taylor Guerrieri. Ultimately, despite significant questions about whether he could be signed away from his commitment to the University of Texas—Swihart's entire wardrobe, noted one high school coach, was burnt orange, a nod to the Longhorns—the Red Sox went with Swihart, a potentially elite offensive and defensive presence.

With their third pick, the No. 36 overall selection (as with the pick of Barnes, compensation for the Tigers' signing of Victor Martinez), the Red Sox zeroed in on tall, rail-thin left-hander Henry Owens. Based on the enormous bust rate of high school pitchers in the draft—especially left-handers—the Red Sox had to go through a lengthy checklist before considering someone from that demographic with a top pick, but felt that Owens—a potential B1 with poor or fair probability—had too much potential to ignore.

Finally, with the No. 40 pick, the team targeted an outfielder whom it never expected to be available with its first pick in the 2011 draft, let alone its fourth. In 2010, Jackie Bradley Jr. had been so brilliant as a sophomore—winning Most Outstanding Player while leading the University of South Carolina to a College World Series title—that he seemed destined to go near the top of the next year's draft when he became eligible for it, following his junior season. For a team like the Red Sox, whose typical success meant such picks were unavailable, devoting scouting resources to covering him as a junior seemed almost wasteful.

But Bradley's performance unraveled as a junior. As the team prepared for the 2011 draft, he became a possibility. The Sox debated the relative merits of Bradley—who, even if he didn't hit at all in the big leagues, had a remarkable defensive profile; George Springer, Barnes's teammate at UConn who had shown enough as a junior that the Red Sox recognized he would probably be taken well before any of their picks (he went with the eleventh pick to the Houston Astros); and Mikie Mahtook, a junior at Louisiana State University who was having a phenomenal season.

In the days leading up to the draft, members of the Red Sox scouting department achieved a measure of clarity as they went through a "too high/too low" exercise they frequently employ—a good way to break the monotony over days of meetings while also helping the team to sift through its preferences.

On a main board, the team lined up the magnetized names of roughly one hundred or so prospects in order of preference, divided into five to six columns of fifteen to twenty each. That approach allowed the group to revisit and sharpen its ranking order.

During the too high/too low process, the Sox identified Bradley, by virtue of his defense, as having the better top-end ceiling and baseline floor than Mahtook. The team viewed Bradley as either a B2 or, in the eyes of some of their evaluators, a B1 with good probability to hit on that potential. Moreover, thanks to his struggles as a junior, he had a better chance of sliding a bit deeper in the draft.

Indeed, Mahtook was taken by the Rays with the No. 31 pick—one of Tampa Bay's ten selections in either the first or supplemental first rounds. Bradley got to the Red Sox at No. 40.

The Sox' first-round work was done. But in the subsequent rounds, they made a number of key selections. Of particular note, the Red Sox took two players from the area of scout Danny Watkins. In the fifth round, the team grabbed a diminutive but extremely athletic shortstop out of Overton High School in Nashville, Markus Lynn "Mookie" Betts, and in the eighth, they took Senquez Golson out of Pascagoula High School in Mississippi.

While discussing Betts, special assignment scout Mark Wasinger, one of the evaluators who'd parachuted into Tennessee to see him, took stock of the player's ability to hit the ball hard to all fields and how his instincts played in both the field and as a baserunner in a way that might allow his performance to surpass his raw physical tools. Wasinger offered a frame of reference for such a player.

"Derek Jeter came up," recalled Jared Banner, the Red Sox amateur scouting coordinator that year. "You don't hear comps to Hall of Fame players very often. It jumped out."

Wasinger wasn't saying that Betts would have a career like Jeter. But like Watkins, he saw a potential championship-caliber contributor, one who the Red Sox believed had a solid chance of emerging as a B2 player—a solid everyday regular—and maybe something beyond that, depending on his future physical development.

Golson's ceiling was even higher, even if there was less likelihood that he'd reach it, and more uncertainty about whether he'd sign. The star cornerback had a scholarship offer to play football at Ole Miss, but his athleticism was unrivaled. If the Sox could sign him, it would qualify as a coup. Both Betts and Golson represented exactly the sort of high-upside, hard-to-sign players to whom they might not have access again.

With that group, along with some interesting college performers whom the team viewed as relatively straightforward to sign (notably including fourth-rounder Noe Ramirez, a right-hander from Cal State Fullerton, and ninth-rounder Travis Shaw, a corner infielder with what seemed like a made-for-Fenway swing out of Kent State)—the Red Sox believed they had the makings of a great draft class. Now they just had to sign the players.

THE THIRTY MAJOR LEAGUE TEAMS weren't the only ones who recognized the 2011 draft as a closing window of opportunity.

Draftees and their agents likewise saw a chance to hold out for signing bonuses that surpassed slot recommendations, at a time when clubs weren't restricted from such expenditures. In the years leading up to 2011, a growing number of draftees received bonuses that vastly exceeded those recommendations—a path accelerated by the Red Sox, whose aggressive spending on later-round picks starting in 2006 had contributed to something of an arms race in the draft.

Between the June draft and mid-August in 2011, almost none of the top picks signed—either with the Red Sox or other teams. In the final days leading up to the deadline, there was a growing awareness that the final day before the draft deadline could prove chaotic.

Technically, the signing deadline was on August 16, but just barely: any bonus agreements had to be submitted to MLB's central office in New York by email by 12:00:59. Entering August 15, seven key Red Sox draftees' fates were unresolved—the four first-round picks, fifth-rounder Betts, seventh-rounder Cody Kukuk, and eighth-rounder Golson.

Different front-office members were assigned to negotiate with different advisors so that movement toward a number of deals could advance simultaneously. On top of that, a support structure was designed. While Banner, the amateur scouting coordinator, would serve as the point person to send in the deals to Major League Baseball, in case either his computer crashed or there were too many deals getting done at once, other office staffers were assigned to each negotiator to send in terms by either computer or BlackBerry to ensure that the necessary information would transmit before 12:01 A.M., when any unsigned picks would turn into pumpkins.

With virtually no other dialogue with players or their advisors on August 15, the team had the opportunity to focus its attention on a one-of-a-kind conversation. When the Red Sox drafted Senquez Golson, they understood the risk that he might not sign and would instead fulfill his two-sport college scholarship at Ole Miss. The allure of playing SEC football in front of packed houses in Oxford for a player with legitimate NFL ambitions was considerable.

"I was kind of surprised when they drafted me," said Golson. "I just wasn't sure if I was ready to give up football. I had my heart set on Ole Miss so much. If I was going to give it up, it was going to take a lot."

Still, the Sox saw an athlete with shoot-the-moon potential. Though his two-sport background had limited his time on baseball fields and made him cruder than other amateur baseball prospects, it wasn't hard to see upside as great as that of any player in the draft. Golson's exceptional speed would play everywhere—center field, on the bases, out of the batter's box—and his physical strength suggested a player with massive power potential despite a five-foot-nine frame.

Moreover, despite Golson's lack of refinement, Danny Watkins saw a player who kept improving virtually every time he stepped on a field. And when Sawdaye saw Golson do a backflip running off the field, he also recognized someone with exceptional coordination—the type of athlete who is capable of figuring out how to do just about anything in any sporting context.

"You could look at Senquez and go, 'Man, what if this all comes together?'" recounted Watkins.

The Sox recognized that there was a lot of risk in Golson's profile—both in terms of whether he'd realize his potential (though given a B1 ceiling, the Sox pegged his likelihood of reaching it as poor) and, even before that, whether he'd sign. The team thus viewed him as a Hail Mary of sorts. In the days leading up to August 15, the club doubted it would sign him, even with a bonus offer of more than $1 million on the table.

Although Golson had started football scrimmages in August,

the Red Sox took one last shot at persuasion. A team official went to chat with him after a practice. Golson found himself sufficiently intrigued by both the Red Sox and a seven-figure signing bonus that he agreed to fly to Boston to take a physical and continue his conversations.

The red carpet awaited. Red Sox manager Terry Francona picked up Golson, his mother, and his girlfriend at the airport and chauffeured them through Boston.

Boston was an unseasonable mid-sixties and rainy when Golson arrived (the eighteen-year-old had to buy a jacket upon landing), a stark contrast to the swelter of the practices he'd left behind. Still, he was undeterred upon arriving at Fenway Park, readily accepting an invitation to sprint onto the field—a personalized welcome message on the scoreboard—in the rain and sign his name inside the fabled Green Monster while touring the ballpark.

"Maybe," he thought, "I can see myself playing center field in the big leagues."

But Golson still felt conflicted about the idea of giving up Saturdays at Ole Miss for the long bus rides of the minors. To make that jump, he needed more money from the Red Sox.

The Red Sox thought they'd offered enough. But perhaps the money was too abstract. Dave Finley, the special assistant to the GM, had an idea.

"I remember telling Theo, 'Hey, in the old days, the scout would come into the kid's home with a briefcase full of money. If he put ten thousand dollars in hundred-dollar bills in front of you, it looked like a lot more money,'" said Finley.

Finley wondered: Could the team get $1 million in cash from a bank and put it on a desk in front of Golson?

The team, Finley thought, could then pull out stacks of cash and place them on the table for illustrative purposes: "This will buy your parents' house; this will buy you a house down the street; this will be your cash, this is how much will be left over . . ."

That plan never came to fruition, but the team did all that it could to try to persuade Golson of the dimensions of the money and opportunity it wanted to offer him while he spent the day in a conference room by the team's offices. A succession of officials went in to make the case for him to sign.

Good cop, bad cop?

"Every cop," corrected Brian O'Halloran, the director of baseball operations, who was among those to talk to Golson, his mother, and his girlfriend.

The team bumped up its offer; Golson recalled the team eventually reaching a $1.35 million bonus. But over the day, the Red Sox sensed little movement from him during the roughly eight hours he spent in the office. At one point he told Epstein directly that he wouldn't sign—yet still he remained in the team's offices in the hours and minutes leading to midnight, a faint light sneaking past the jamb of a mostly closed door. Golson just couldn't walk away.

By mid-evening, the Red Sox had reached an agreement with Kukuk.

Still, six prospects—five if not counting Golson—remained. Day, afternoon, evening, and night had passed with almost no contact between the team and the players or their representatives. The Red Sox were eager to engage their counterparts, yet didn't want to betray their growing urgency—while also recognizing the risks associated with posturing.

"If this is a game of chicken that everyone really wants to win," one team official noted at the time, "everyone may lose."

Finally, with roughly a half hour left until the signing deadline and the four first-rounders along with Betts still requiring resolution, the silence ended.

THE DESKS AND CUBES OF the amateur scouting department were tucked in the back of the Fenway Park basement. Near them, Sawdaye sat in his office, where he'd handle the negotiations with Swihart, viewed as the most difficult player to sign. Finley, responsible for Bradley and Owens, set up residence in an office that had been taken over by an unused exercise bike and elliptical machine as well as boxes of merchandise and giveaways. Epstein would conduct talks with Barnes from his office, and VP of player development and amateur scouting Mike Hazen was in charge of Betts.

No one had left the premises during the daylong wait—not that such a scenario was that unfamiliar to the inhabitants of the basement.

"I take my vitamin D pills," said assistant director of amateur scouting Gus Quattlebaum. "We don't see the sun very often."

But with midnight no longer distant, there were signs of daylight in the negotiations.

Finley was the first to establish contact with an agent, around 11:30 P.M. Though Bradley was represented by Scott Boras—the legendary agent with a long history of getting top dollar for his clients while negotiating down to the final moments of deadlines on draft day—it was one of his top assistants, Scott Chiamparino, who reached out to Finley.

The development wasn't unexpected. Boras had bigger fish to fry on August 15, as he also represented No. 1 pick Gerrit Cole, No. 4 selection Bubba Starling, No. 5 pick Anthony Rendon, Alex Meyer, and Josh Bell—none of whom had signed, all of whom would wait until almost midnight. Chiamparino, meanwhile, had been a minor league teammate of Finley.

Throughout the summer, Bradley had been unsure whether he'd sign. In mid-August, he'd returned to the South Carolina campus, prepared to reenroll for his senior year and finish his degree if an agreement couldn't be reached. As midnight neared, he was running through a workout program, not sure if or when he'd hear from his advisors.

But negotiations with the outfielder proved relatively simple once they finally began. Save for players taken at the very top of the draft, college juniors had little leverage and rarely signed for more than the slot-recommended bonus. It took about fifteen minutes for Finley and Chiamparino to identify middle ground at $1.1 million.

Bradley received a call at 11:47 P.M. to let him know the offer. He agreed, called his parents to let them know the good news, then resumed his workout.

Betts was next. In the weeks leading up to the deadline, the Red Sox had made a point of cultivating their relationship with the high schooler. Sawdaye, Rikard, and Georgia area scout Tim Hyers all spent time with the eighteen-year-old that summer as he played in a tournament in East Cobb, Georgia. Sawdaye also invited Betts to visit the Red Sox' Single-A affiliate in Greenville, South Carolina, where the scouting director was struck by the high schooler's sense of belonging and comfort among professionals.

"There was a calmness he portrayed. A lot of seventeen-, eighteen-year-olds don't talk. They're intimidated. Mookie wasn't. He was different," said Sawdaye. "It was, 'Hey, if I sign, I'm going to go out and try to be the best player I can be, and if I don't, then I'm going to school and I'll be the best player there. I understand the process. If it works out, it works out, but if not, I'll go to school. I've got a good option there.'"

Betts had been impressed by the Red Sox, but he and his family also had strong views about what it would take for him to pass on a scholarship offer at the University of Tennessee. The Sox had been around $350,000 for much of the summer. Betts sought more than twice that—$750,000.

He was on standby all day with Matt Hannaford, his advisor, though Betts did his best to distract himself. He went to play basketball with his friends, though he kept his phone nearby. Still, no news. By the time Betts got home that night, he was sufficiently skeptical about the possibility of an agreement that at eleven thirty he was packing for his dorm at Tennessee.

"We were dead set on going to school," Betts recalled.

The Sox thought there was a chance that they could bring Betts down into the range of an agreement for $500,000 if they pushed him till midnight—but also realized that trying to do so would come with an opportunity cost, at a time when other negotiations needed attention. The chance to land a player who'd inspired strong conviction as a potential B2 with what the team's scouts viewed as a fair likelihood of reaching that level was not one that the Red Sox wanted to lose.

With the hourglass emptying, Epstein delivered a blunt mandate to VP of player development and amateur scouting Mike Hazen: get the deal done.

"The fucking CBA is going to change. We're not going to have these opportunities to sign players, especially guys that we like, as fifth rounders," Sawdaye recalled Epstein saying. "If you guys really believe this guy is an everyday big leaguer, what are we holding back on? We have the money in the budget, just give him what he wants."

Betts and the Red Sox reached an agreement for $750,000.

At that point, the reality of the clock dawned on the front-office members. One front-office member recalled a shift in the tenor of conversations inside the Red Sox offices in the minutes that followed the Bradley and Betts agreements.

A roll call of sorts occurred to discern who had been talking to the other party in the assigned negotiations. The answer? Almost no conversations had occurred with any of the remaining players.

"Maybe we should do that soon," suggested one of the officials. "We only have ten minutes left."

What followed in those final ten minutes, he suggested, was "straight chaos . . . hell in a handbasket."

Finally, across the board, agents and front offices alike were ready to engage. Over the last minutes before midnight, the day of quiet gave way to the chaos of something that sounded like a trading room floor, numbers and names being shouted across the team's offices.

Tickticktickticktickticktick. Inaction gave way to frenzy. Three first-rounders—Barnes, Swihart, and Owens—remained, as did Golson, still sitting in the conference room with his mother and girlfriend.

"For a while, people forgot about [Golson] in there because everybody was focused on getting everybody else signed," said Raquel Ferreira, the team's director of minor league operations at the time, and among those transmitting contract details to the Commissioner's Office as midnight neared. "People were screaming their heads off. It was crazy. It was crazy. There will definitely never be another night like that again."

Barnes, like Bradley, was a college junior with minimal leverage. Still, his advisor, John Courtright—who was with Barnes and his parents at their Connecticut home—wanted to get his client as much money as possible in this last great cash grab before a new CBA.

Barnes appreciated that effort—to a point. Initial contact between Courtright and the Red Sox occurred around 11:48 P.M.

Barnes listened with growing concern as the negotiation continued.

"SIXTY SECONDS!"

Quattlebaum's voice, by default a mild shout, boomed across the basement. His calibration was faulty—he was a minute ahead of the actual clock—but under the circumstances, given the dire consequences of failing to get a deal submitted on time, too early was considerably better than too late.

"But," he later conceded, "it probably made it more dramatic than it needed to be."

Yet the drama wasn't limited to the Red Sox front office. In Connecticut, Barnes felt panic as his own clock moved inside the final minute.

"I was like, 'Listen, we're signing. I'm not going back to school, man. That's the last thing I want to do,'" said Barnes.

Epstein and Courtright agreed to a $1.5 million bonus for the team's top pick in the 2011 draft at 11:59 P.M. Incredibly, with the distance to the deadline being measured in seconds, two picks remained unsigned.

"FORTY-FIVE SECONDS!"

On the night of August 14, Swihart's agent, Greg Genske, had informed Sawdaye that the catcher wanted a $6 million bonus. Swihart had tremendous leverage—the option not just of going to college, but also, because he'd turn twenty-one during his sophomore year, a chance to reenter the draft in two years.

But based on the interactions Swihart had with the team in the buildup to the draft, Sawdaye entered his negotiations with Genske—which started about five minutes before midnight, with the agent starting at that massive initial number—with confidence that the number would shift significantly.

His number went to $4 million at about 11:57 P.M., with the Red Sox still sitting at $1.75 million inside the final minute.

Sawdaye and Swihart's advisor were screaming back and

forth by phone, trying to compress millions of dollars of movement into seconds of conversations.

"You don't understand—he's going to school!"

"THIRTY SECONDS!"

With about twenty seconds left, the two sides found common ground: Swihart would sign for $2.5 million.

Owens—whose negotiations were being handled by Finley—still remained. The pitcher sought $2.5 million; that night, he'd told his advisor, Joe Urbon, that he was prepared to go to the University of Miami if the Red Sox didn't hit his intended asking price of $1.5 million.

The movement was as much auction as negotiation, with Finley and the reps for Owens screaming numbers at each other in the last minute—$2.5 million, $2.3 million, $1.9 million, $1.7 million. Finley frantically signaled numbers to intern Steve Sanders, who was responsible for updating the figures in the email and filing the agreement with the Commissioner's Office when it was consummated.

The Red Sox offered $1.5 million—the target Owens had in mind entering the signing process. Informed of the bid by his advisors, Owens accepted—but with one problem: crappy cell phone reception in parts of the Red Sox baseball operations dungeon, particularly in the office/storage space where Finley was handling the negotiation.

With seconds remaining, Owens's advisors tried to call Finley but couldn't. The calls went straight to voice mail.

"FIFTEEN SECONDS!"

Epstein reached out: Would Owens do the deal for $1.55 million?

Owens's dropped call had earned him an extra 50 grand.

"TEN SECONDS!"

"DONE!" Epstein shouted in the office.

Sanders clicked send, and then . . . slowly, the negotiators emerged from their separate lairs to take inventory.

"We all came out like we just fought a twelve-round heavyweight fight," said Finley.

Betts? Done, Hazen affirmed. Owens? Yes, said Finley. Barnes? Yes, said Epstein.

Sawdaye didn't emerge from his office initially. But after about five minutes, during which he'd been sorting through a few final details about Barnes's agreement, he joined his colleagues.

Yes, said Sawdaye: Swihart had agreed for $2.5 million.

Subsiding adrenaline mixed with relief and joy. High fives were exchanged around the room with news that everyone—or, nearly everyone—had signed.

A subdued Golson and his contingent exited the conference room and walked away from Fenway Park. The clock had run out.

"Everyone was mad at me—my family, my agent, everyone was like, 'What are you thinking?'" said Golson. "Everyone from my town was like, 'What, how could you turn down a million dollars?'"

Golson went to Ole Miss, got taken in the second round of the NFL Draft by the Steelers in 2015, and by 2018 had made more as a football player than he'd turned down to be a baseball player. Still, years later, the road not taken remained clear in his mind.

"I think about it all the time," Golson said of that decision. "The Red Sox are still my favorite team. . . . I don't regret anything, but I think, 'What if I would have played?'"

The silence that hovered around Golson on the walk to his hotel stood in contrast to the sense of triumph among those in the baseball operations department, many of whom lingered while sipping whatever booze, including champagne—a remnant, Finley thought, of one of the team's 2007 celebrations on the way to winning a World Series—while hanging out until three in the morning, probably accompanied by a few bags of Doritos.

As much as the moment was one worthy of celebration, the prevailing excitement was about a sense of possibility rather than certainty or even likelihood. The Red Sox hadn't acquired polished diamonds but instead a coal mine that over time might—*might*—turn into precious gems.

Perhaps Swihart and Kukuk would be the prizes of the group; maybe it would be Barnes and Betts; perhaps Bradley and Owens. The front office had identified players worthy of significant financial bets, but without any clear way of forecasting what their futures might look like.

It was entirely possible that the Red Sox had just spent millions of dollars on players who would never make a meaningful big league impact.

But the moment when players are added to an organization is a shared moment of hope—a particularly alluring concept for a team that seemingly sat atop the sport's pinnacle.

The Red Sox had two championships in their possession from the prior seven years and had a major league club that, at that moment, was tied for first place in the American League East—appearing as one of the best teams in the majors for 2011 and perhaps even some years to come. The group of draftees the team had just signed looked like it had a chance to sustain the team's championship aspirations into the next decade.

"We just knew that with the guys we got, this was going to be a draft that the Red Sox would look back on for a long time and say, 'Man, what a night that was,'" recalled Finley.

Still, some reserve was in order. A couple of days after the draft signing deadline, Epstein was asked for his thoughts on the 2011 draft haul.

"Check back in five years," he suggested.

CHAPTER 2

THE NEXT GREAT RED SOX TEAM

ON OCTOBER 25, 2011, Ben Cherington experienced a Fenway Park coronation that marked the realization of a dream. The eleventh general manager in Red Sox history had earned the title toward which he'd spent his entire adult life working, while gaining the opportunity to fulfill that ambition for the team he'd loved starting as a toddler in New Hampshire.

Yet it's unlikely that the daydreams of one day running a baseball operation included thoughts of the firing-squad atmosphere that awaited Cherington as he prepared to enter the media interview room at Fenway Park just ten months later, nor of the complicated task that awaited him. Somehow Cherington had to define a credible vision of a more promising future at a time when his club was on its way to its most devastating on-field shipwreck in nearly half a century.

The backdrop was grim. By August 24, the Red Sox were 60-66 after a brutal 7-15 start to August. The lineup bordered on unrecognizable at a time when veterans David Ortiz and Carl Crawford as well as promising rookie Will Middlebrooks had endured season-ending injuries, and the rotation was a mess of injury and underperformance on the way to a 5.19 ERA, the worst by a Red Sox starting staff in eighty years. They were taking on water quickly enough that it had become readily apparent that the team would miss the playoffs for a fourth straight season.

Just three and a half weeks earlier, the Red Sox hadn't been ready to give up on 2012. The team was within arm's reach of a postseason berth at the July 31 trade deadline. A win that day improved their record to 53-51, three and a half games out of the second wild-card spot. It was far from a guarantee of contention, but not so hopeless a proposition as to lead Boston to the almost inconceivable strategy of selling.

Still, while the team hadn't abandoned all pretense of the postseason, it didn't look like a legitimate contender. For four months the Sox had wobbled around an axis of .500 ball. So many of the team's most talented—and highest-paid—players were performing so far below expectations that, even with the team technically in the hunt for a playoff berth, the roster felt fundamentally flawed. It was natural—and reasonable—to place much of the blame on Bobby Valentine. Yet in his first season as Red Sox general manager, Cherington was reluctant to scapegoat his manager. He knew he needed to take stock of the entire organization and map out a vision for the future.

"I'd spent a lot of time over the course of the summer trying to figure out who we were and reached the conclusion, I would say in early August, that it just wasn't working," said Cherington. "The crux of those conversations was, 'Let's not settle for a chance to be good. Our standard is higher than that.' As we got into August, I think we came to the conclusion that we couldn't be great in the way that we wanted to be great over a long period of time unless we made some more fundamental changes."

Yet as Cherington surveyed his team, he wasn't optimistic. He was saddled with a core of expensive, underperforming veterans, who were unlikely to appeal to many other teams. What sort of "fundamental changes" were possible?

An unexpected lifeboat appeared. Guggenheim Sports Management had bought the Dodgers in the spring for a reported $2 billion for the team and its ballpark. With the group in the middle of negotiating a TV deal that would be worth billions, Los Angeles was looking for stars—even at great cost, a fact driven home by an unexpected phone call from Dodgers president Stan Kasten to Red Sox CEO/president Larry Lucchino shortly before the deadline.

"Larry, I can't believe I'm making this phone call; in all my years of baseball, I've never made a phone call like this, but we have money to spend and we're looking to take on some high-priced, high-quality players, so if you're thinking of moving any of yours, don't forget us," Lucchino recalled Kasten saying.

Red Sox first baseman Adrian Gonzalez was bilingual, having been raised in Mexico and Southern California, and had emerged as one of the game's elite hitters over the previous half decade. Gonzalez, Dodgers GM Ned Colletti thought, would be an ideal target for a team looking to build around identifiable stars.

But he wasn't cheap. The Red Sox had acquired Gonzalez from the Padres in a blockbuster trade after the 2010 season, and he was now in the first season of a seven-year, $154 million extension he'd signed shortly after the start of the 2011 season. After he finished seventh in A.L. MVP voting in 2011, his 2012 campaign had been to that point in August a mild disappointment, particularly given that he'd hit just fifteen homers so far in the season.

Even so, the Dodgers trusted his track record and saw a star who seemed ideally suited to their market. While Cherington and Dodgers counterpart Ned Colletti exchanged ideas about a package that would include Gonzalez and other financially burdensome players leading up to the July 31 deadline, the idea seemed too complicated—and the Red Sox too close to at least some small hope of contention—to consummate anything. Perhaps, Red Sox officials thought, the conversation could resume in the winter.

That timetable accelerated with the Red Sox' woeful start to August, a sputter that ended any visions of a long-shot playoff berth and thus altered the context against which the Red Sox would determine the value of their players. Though the July 31 deadline to complete trades without restriction had already passed, the two teams conceived of a deal that would involve players who were owed such enormous sums of money that they might be able to pass through waivers without being claimed by any other teams—thus clearing the path for a rare August blockbuster involving players who went unclaimed through that process.

The Dodgers would add not only Gonzalez—a player whose production and stature still justified his contract—but also outfielder Carl Crawford, who'd just undergone Tommy John surgery in the second season of his seven-year, $142 million deal, and right-hander Josh Beckett, who was showing significant decline from his top-of-the-rotation status in the second season of a four-year, $68 million deal. Los Angeles would also take on utility infielder Nick Punto. In exchange, the Dodgers would send five players to the Sox, most notably hard-throwing right-handers Allen Webster and Rubby De La Rosa—though the prospects were secondary in significance to the bailout from just over $260 million in commitments.

A roster reconfiguration that seemed like it might require multiple years instead was accomplished in one dramatic hack of a Gordian knot. On August 25, 2012, the Red Sox transformed from a team with no financial flexibility to one that suddenly could reshape its team in dramatic fashion.

"Manna from heaven," said team chairman Tom Werner.

The move wasn't without massive cost. Early in the year, after a horrific loss to the Yankees, Valentine had posited, "If this isn't bottom, then we'll find some new ends to the earth, I guess." The Dodgers trade doomed the Sox to exploring those reaches. They would win just nine of their final thirty-six games.

But the newfound flexibility presented the Red Sox with an opportunity. Prior to a press conference to discuss the deal, Cherington met directly with several key Red Sox players to explain both why he felt compelled to make the move and what he was committed to building going forward. He then gave those goals public voice in a session with the media.

Cherington opened with an unvarnished acknowledgment that the Red Sox were "not who we want to be right now," something that forced openness to the drastic reshaping of the roster accomplished by the trade. As the team prepared to redeploy resources to start assembling a different team for 2013 and beyond, Cherington gave definition to those efforts.

"We're excited," he said, "about the opportunity this gives us to build the next great Red Sox team."

The next great Red Sox team. He would repeat the phrase, or some subtle variation thereof, in response to each of the initial three questions he took. Though Cherington would later say that he came up with the phrase on the spot, it began to take on the weight of a mantra, both within and outside the organization.

In his own mind and in his conversations with other front-office members and owners, he'd spent so much time discussing and thinking about a standard of greatness for the team that the aspirational notion naturally forced its way into his thoughts about nearly every aspect of the trade and the Red Sox' future.

"We were always thinking about not just how do we win every year but how do we win eleven games in October," said Cherington.

The trade—and the phrase—instilled a newfound sense of purpose and clarity in the Red Sox' plans.

Yet while Cherington's original concept of the phrase reflected a desire to restore the big league team to contention, others in the organization recognized that the term had implications for roots that ran much deeper than the major league roster.

"Building the next great Red Sox team, that's a long-term deal. That's not a one-year proposition," Mike Hazen, the Red Sox assistant GM under Cherington from 2011 to 2015, said. "The next great Red Sox team, at least in my interpretation, isn't in 2016, a great Red Sox team emerges and it's gone in 2017. When we're looking at building that, we're talking about having a core on the team—a significant core."

The team, Hazen said, would need a "young and controllable" core—players who emerged from the farm system to deliver elite production during their first six years of major league service time, before they became eligible to market their services to all thirty teams via free agency. If the team could assemble a group of high-impact young players who delivered incredible bang for the buck in the big leagues, the Red Sox believed that they could leverage their other resources to achieve a period of sustained success.

The idea of forging such a nucleus seemed a natural undertaking for Cherington to oversee.

IN OCTOBER 2011, CHERINGTON TOOK over as the general manager of the Red Sox at a time of organizational embarrassment. That fall, in the span of two months, the Red Sox had gone from a paragon of competitive stability—a team that seemed destined, at the time of the 2011 draft signing deadline, to cruise to its seventh postseason berth in nine years—to one that spiraled out of the playoffs with a 7-20 September implosion. Manager Terry Francona had been ousted, and a series of revelations of a factionalized, rudderless clubhouse followed.

GM Theo Epstein, meanwhile, felt that after ten seasons with the Red Sox, nine as general manager, he needed the reinvigoration of a new challenge, ultimately leaving Boston to become the president of baseball operations with the Cubs. On October 25, 2011, the same day that Cherington was introduced as his Red Sox successor, Epstein explained that he relished the idea of experiencing anew in Chicago the most satisfying aspects of his job in Boston: seeking a franchise's first championship in generations by rebuilding its scouting and minor league systems from the ground up.

Yet the architect of two championships in Boston also identified another reason for leaving. Though the embers from 2011's September explosion still smoldered, Epstein felt that the Red Sox organization was well positioned for the long haul both in the big leagues and especially in the minors, particularly given the players who'd joined the organization on the chaotic night of August 15. And Epstein believed that he would be leaving the Red Sox not only with the raw materials to succeed but also with the ideal person to help form the team's budding young talents into big league stars.

"Ben is more qualified than anyone in the game to take this job over," Epstein said on the day of his and Cherington's introductions to their new roles. "I wouldn't have left the Red Sox if he weren't the guy who was going to take over."

By his own admission, Cherington had been "uber-focused on baseball" dating to his upbringing in New Hampshire, but particularly once he enrolled at Amherst College. There, he was single-minded in the pursuit of a front-office future, to the point where he passed on the chance to study abroad because he didn't want to miss a practice.

Even when he'd blown out his shoulder while playing hockey in the winter before his junior season—an injury that ended his pitching career—he stayed with the team as, effectively, an

unpaid coach, a role that was natural for someone who was un-
commonly mature and serious about the game. At the conclusion of his college career, Cherington spent a year as his alma
mater's pitching coach while earning a master's degree from the
Sports Management Program at the University of Massachusetts. During a spring training trip through Florida, Cherington
roomed with an assistant coach with decades of college coaching
experience, Charlie Roys.

"How old is Ben, thirty-five?" Roys asked Amherst head
coach Bill Thurston of the twenty-two-year-old.

Cherington's career in baseball front offices had been equally
purposeful. Over fourteen seasons in the game and ten years in
which he'd worked closely with Epstein, Cherington had received a progressive apprenticeship that covered all aspects of
the baseball operations department. He'd been a video advance
scout for Cleveland in 1998, a domestic amateur area scout and
then an international scouting coordinator with the Red Sox
under GM Dan Duquette from 1999 to 2001, and then a farm
director, a vice president with oversight of both the farm system
and the amateur draft, and an assistant GM with significant responsibilities for the major league team under Epstein.

Cherington possessed universal respect inside the Red Sox
organization for his quiet leadership, tireless attention to detail,
and ability to consider every problem through virtually every
departmental lens. His commitment to surveying a wide range
of people for their opinions—he widely recommended James
Surowiecki's *Wisdom of Crowds* as essential reading for decision
making—empowered colleagues while cultivating admiration
and loyalty.

It was this broad range of experiences that made Cherington
the obvious choice to succeed Epstein.

"I could not at this point in Red Sox history imagine Ben
with any other organization and I have trouble imagining the

Red Sox without Ben Cherington," Lucchino said at Cherington's introduction as GM.

While Cherington had a diverse array of experiences throughout a baseball front office, there was little question about the aspect of team-building that seemed most deeply rooted in his baseball being.

"It's a huge part of his DNA, player development," said Raquel Ferreira, whom Cherington tabbed to oversee the organization's minor league administration in 2002. "He truly believed that every single player mattered. And Theo had the same notion. We all bought into it, we all thought it was true, that when you draft these guys, you have a responsibility to them, and not just to them, but to their family, to see everything through on the field and off the field. And we really developed this culture here."

Epstein was the one who had first given name to that effort, introducing publicly the idea of a "scouting and player development machine." But behind the scenes, it was Cherington, Epstein's selection as the director of player development, who was responsible for designing, constructing, and then maintaining that machine.

During organization meetings shortly after Epstein's appointment as GM, Cherington led a roomful of about one hundred Red Sox employees in detailed discussions of roughly one hundred minor leaguers. The discussion made clear the organization's intention to create a talent pipeline, with Cherington overseeing its flow.

"It was his passion," said Josh Byrnes, an assistant GM under Epstein at the time. "I think it was his determination to make the Red Sox the type of organization that could develop impact homegrown players."

Cherington likewise worked with Epstein to produce a three-hundred-page manual, "The Red Sox Way," to streamline and guide the organization's consistent, top-to-bottom phi-losophy and teaching of minor leaguers. Under Cherington, the Sox went from an organization that typically concentrated its at-tention on its best few prospects to one that would no longer let players slip through the cracks, with individualized development plans produced for each member of the farm system. As play-ers moved up the ladder, they would get consistent instruction, rather than suggestions that were sometimes at cross purposes from one level to the next.

In his one year in Cleveland in 1998, Cherington—as part of a front office that yielded numerous future general managers—encountered an organization that was forward-looking with its integrated approach to player development, focused not just on game performance but also on the broader view of players' medical, psychological, and training needs. In Boston, Cher-ington likewise worked to create a culture that extended beyond instruction on the field. He believed in a holistic approach to player development that encompassed on-field needs and also accounted for the strange and often bewildering world of minor league baseball.

Minor league players, many of them teenagers, had to make sense of living away from home for the first time in their lives while making tiny salaries—with the industry-wide minor league minimum salary set at less than $1,000 a month when Cherington was the Red Sox farm director. Particularly at the outset of their careers, those players were not only seeing com-petition that was better than any they'd faced in their lives but also trying to figure out how to feed themselves, manage their finances, and determine what it meant to be a professional both at and away from the ballpark.

This education often had to take place hundreds or thou-sands of miles from home, confronting players with cultural ad-justments and in some cases linguistic ones. The potential to be overwhelmed by any or all of those elements created easily overlooked impediments to a player's career advancement on the field.

Cherington recognized the dimensions of that challenge and during his time as Epstein's farm director, VP, and assistant GM, the Red Sox made several hires and implemented numerous programs meant to ease some of the jarring lifestyle transitions faced by their young players. The Red Sox were interested not just in smoothing edges of inexperience on the field but also in controlling environmental factors that could impact a player's growth, from mental skills to nutrition to cultural adaptation for players coming to the States from Latin America.

"We wanted to create a system that allowed each and every player to develop to his fullest, whether that meant a ten-year major league career or a player who topped out at A-ball," said Cherington. "We felt, first of all, that every player who signs deserves that opportunity. And from a business sense, each of those players is an asset to the Boston Red Sox. We have a responsibility to maximize the value of that asset."

Cherington wanted to look beyond the immediate present to understand the long view. As much as publications such as *Baseball America*—whose annual list of the top 100 prospects in all of baseball and the top 30 in each organization carried considerable influence—provided a meaningful sense of the industry's valuation of a minor leaguer, prospect status as popularly understood represented little more than a potentially misleading snapshot in time.

Reacting to that single snapshot could lead to faulty conclusions and bad personnel decisions, particularly for an organization that concentrated its developmental resources on just a few select talents while casting aside those who did not merit the "prospect" label. During Cherington's tenure as farm director, the organization became less driven by evaluations at specific moments than by the range of potential career directions for young players over the longer haul. Cherington derived particular satisfaction from seeing the success of someone like Kason Gabbard—a 29th-round draft pick in 2000 who withstood years of injuries, went 4-0 with a 3.73 ERA in seven big league starts for the Red Sox in 2007, and gained enough value to become a trade chip in that championship season. The Sox became an organization that rarely gave up on players only to see them flourish in new organizations.

When Cherington took over for Epstein as the general manager, he held true to character with a long-term vision for how the Red Sox would proceed over the next five-plus years, segmented into three stages that he outlined to the team's owners and baseball operations department.

Despite its September collapse, the major league team Cherington inherited remained stocked with talent, even if it lacked much flexibility. Three Red Sox players—center fielder Jacoby Ellsbury, first baseman Gonzalez, and second baseman Dustin Pedroia—landed in the top ten in American League MVP voting after the 2011 season. Designated hitter David Ortiz remained as a longtime team anchor. Third baseman Kevin Youkilis and starters Beckett and Jon Lester all had been All-Stars that year. There were, in other words, several players who gave the team the look of a short-term contender.

Below that surface, the Sox believed that they had a position player prospect wave taking shape on the horizon. Some players—most notably third baseman Will Middlebrooks—had reached the upper minors and appeared to be nearing a big league opportunity. Further away, the draft class of 2011 headlined at the time by Barnes, Bradley, Swihart, and Owens, along with shortstop Xander Bogaerts, showed significant potential.

With those assets in mind, Cherington outlined a three-phase path to championship contention.

In Phase One, from 2012 through either 2013 or 2014, the team would rely heavily on veterans who were with the Red Sox on long-term deals. Holdovers from 2011—some of them homegrown, like Pedroia, Ellsbury, Lester, and Youkilis—represented the basis of the team's competitive aspirations moving forward into the next two to three seasons.

"We believed that that core was good enough that if complemented the right way and with some breaks going your way that we could win in the short term," said Cherington.

The challenge was that given the long-term deals with Gonzalez, Crawford, Beckett, and John Lackey, the Sox had little available money to add talent via free agency. The team likely would have to execute trades in order to smooth the roster's edges in Phase One.

Phase Two, earmarked as roughly 2014 to 2016, would be a period of transition. Young players in the farm system would start graduating into everyday roles in the big leagues. The team hoped that prospects would come up to complement the three pillars whom the Red Sox hoped to extend with new deals: Pedroia (eligible for free agency after the 2014 season), Lester (also up after 2014), and Ortiz (a free agent after 2011 who returned on a one-year deal for 2012). The team also possessed long-term pieces who were signed beyond 2014 (Gonzalez and Crawford). The development of any single young player was far from certain, so Cherington anticipated that this phase would be turbulent. A precise mix of veteran additions would be necessary to create stability and sustain title ambitions during this period.

"It was the middle phase that we were all more concerned about," said Cherington. "I knew we'd have to hit on more things in free agency and trades to win but I thought we could do that."

In Phase Three, the young guns would take center stage. By roughly 2016, Cherington anticipated that a new foundation of prospects—both those already in the Red Sox farm system and future additions through the draft and international amateur markets—would serve as the basis for the team's long-term success over the rest of the decade.

"We really did believe we had and could continue to add high-impact young players and help them develop and help them become the next core," said Cherington. "That's how I was looking at it."

Cherington knew that getting too aggressive in Phase One or Phase Two—and weakening the farm system in the process—would jeopardize the entire plan. Meanwhile, Cherington's development-driven view of prospects—the embrace of the notion that the organization was capable of helping young players to realize their fullest potential—further convinced him to cling to what he viewed as the best young talents in the organization, even if he couldn't be sure which ones would hit and which ones wouldn't.

"I remember thinking [that] . . . to execute these three phases we're going to have to hold on to the difference-makers," Cherington said. "And I wasn't smart enough to know exactly who those players are going to be."

Most of his personnel moves were geared toward keeping as many of these promising lotto tickets as he could—though there were early exceptions, which he came to view as mistakes.

IN DECEMBER 2011, THE RED SOX needed a closer. Their longtime bullpen ace, Jonathan Papelbon, had just signed with the Phillies for more money than the Red Sox wanted to spend. Cherington identified two appealing replacements via trade in Mark Melancon of the Astros and Andrew Bailey of the A's. While neither could match Papelbon's track record, the addition of two pitchers who'd proven effective as closers—and who were still young and relatively inexpensive—offered the promise of a strong back end of the bullpen.

The price to acquire the two pitchers, at first glance, didn't seem intolerable: the Sox would send shortstop Jed Lowrie and right-hander Kyle Weiland to the Astros for Melancon, and a package headlined by outfielder Josh Reddick to the A's for Bailey.

Melancon pitched so poorly in his first four games with the Red Sox—allowing five homers—that he was demoted to the minors and was almost never asked to pitch again in meaningful situations before being traded the next winter to Pittsburgh. Though Weiland suffered a shoulder injury after three starts with Houston and never again pitched in the big leagues, Lowrie was a solid to above-average (if oft-injured) big leaguer for several years, even making an All-Star team in 2018.

If the Melancon deal was disappointing, the Bailey deal bordered on calamitous. The right-hander suffered a torn thumb ligament in spring training, a harbinger of a two-year stint in which he was rarely healthy and almost never a useful closer when he was. Reddick, on the other hand, emerged as an impactful outfielder for the A's almost immediately, hitting 32 homers in 2012 while playing standout defense that made him a well-above-average player for Oakland, which surged to an unexpected playoff berth.

The Sox had seen Reddick excel for much of 2011 after being called up from Triple-A Pawtucket, with the young outfielder carrying a .343 average and .958 OPS into early August. But a wrist injury that eventually required off-season surgery, along with the toll of the season, wore on his production down the stretch. After Reddick hit .208 with a .585 OPS over his final 42 games in August and September, the Sox staff lost faith in him. He wasn't on the field for any of the final five games of the team's 2011 collapse. To Cherington and his Sox baseball operations staff, Reddick had seemed expendable. Clearly, they had been wrong. Why?

In retrospect, Cherington believed the team fell prey to recency bias, staring at the late 2011 snapshot and focusing too much on flaws that had been magnified at the big league level. Moreover, at a time when both Reddick and another promising young outfielder, Ryan Kalish, had shown flashes of big league potential, the Sox had placed their faith in Kalish to be the more reliable player—even though he required both neck and shoulder surgeries in the months following the 2011 season, and never again in his career was healthy enough to match the considerable promise he'd shown as a big league rookie in late 2010.

The belief in Kalish over Reddick was justifiable, but ultimately wrong—a demonstration of what Cherington meant when he said (often) that he wasn't good enough to know exactly which potential difference-makers would become actual difference-makers capable of being Phase Two and Phase Three contributors.

The Red Sox hadn't done a good enough job of protecting their upper-levels prospects who could emerge as big league depth and potentially regulars. Cherington wasn't the only one who recognized that development by 2012.

"You have to have a strong system. You need strong evaluators. We've let too many young prospects go and have also paid a price for that," said principal owner John Henry that season. "I feel personally responsible for not protecting the farm system over the past few years. I knew better."

Yet while the team had made moves that by 2012 had compromised the organization's depth in the upper levels of its farm system, a strong base in the lower minor leagues offered signs that the future was bright.

•   •   •

Though the big league team sputtered, 2012 hadn't been a total loss. Third baseman Will Middlebrooks, summoned to the big leagues as a twenty-three-year-old, showed middle-of-the-order potential. He hit .288/.325/.509 with 15 homers in half a season's worth of games before a broken hand ended his year in August. Middlebrooks, left-handed starter Felix Doubront, and reliever Junichi Tazawa all graduated to the big leagues in 2012 and looked like long-term assets at the game's highest level.

Yet in the minors, there were signs of an even more impactful group that was starting to make its way through the farm system. Almost from the first day of that minor league season, it became clear that the previous Red Sox draft class—the one acquired at such great expense, and finalized with a frenzy—had a chance to shape the franchise in the years to come.

"There was that tangible sense that we have some players that have a chance to really impact us this year and in coming years and make us a lot better," recalled farm director Ben Crockett.

Right-hander Matt Barnes, the team's top pick, began his pro career in 2012 with a somewhat conservative assignment in Single-A Greenville, where the Red Sox hoped he'd acclimate to a professional starting pitcher's five-day routine in relatively comfortable fashion before moving up at some point to High-A Salem. Barnes made clear that his initial stop would not be a long one.

In his pro debut, the six-foot-four right-hander sent a succession of blistering fastballs past the bats of his hapless opponents, striking out nine Lakewood BlueClaws in five scoreless innings. It was the first of four consecutive scoreless outings, and by the end of April, Barnes had perhaps the gaudiest statistics of any pitcher in the minors: a 0.34 ERA, 42 strikeouts, and 4 walks in 26⅔ innings.

Greenville manager Carlos Febles thought Barnes had the

best stuff of any pitcher in the South Atlantic League and compared his mound presence to that of Justin Verlander.

By the end of the month, Barnes earned a promotion to High-A Salem. In his Carolina League debut, though the right-hander immediately impressed his new pitching coach with his fastball command and mid- to upper-90s velocity, Kevin Walker had an initial reservation.

"He's going to need to start throwing his breaking ball more," thought Walker.

Barnes struck out twelve, walked one, and allowed one run over six innings in the outing.

"Well," reconsidered Walker, "maybe not."

Yet despite his dominance, Barnes wasn't even the most impressive player in the Red Sox draft class of 2011. That distinction went to Jackie Bradley Jr.

"Jackie was the first one," Billy McMillon, then Salem's manager, recalled. "Anyone who saw him play, going back even to college, defensively, he was going to be a very special player. He was probably one of the more dominant hitters in that league. He was hitting the ball all over the place, hitting home runs, running the bases. The smart money was, barring injuries, he was going to get to the big leagues and impact a club."

Growing up in Prince George, Virginia, on the outskirts of Richmond, Bradley's initial position had actually been catcher before he graduated to the Little League prestige positions, shortstop and pitcher. But Bradley's eighth-grade coach, Donnie Brittingham, recognized a different possibility.

Bradley's team was about to play against a juggernaut, on a field that lacked an outfield fence. Bradley's arm was unrivaled, and Brittingham knew that his young pitcher was a terrific all-around athlete as well. The coach looked at the endless expanse of outfield grass and envisioned his team getting blown off the field. Then he had a thought: Could Bradley play center? The answer was immediate and dazzling.

"He ran down everything. Nothing—*nothing*—got past him," Brittingham recalled.

Bradley immediately fell in love with the nuances of the position. He'd spend hours at the field after his own practice sitting quietly with Brittingham and watching other teams going through their paces. He'd watch players take batting practice, mapping the interrelationship of pitch location, swing path, and where a ball eventually would be hit on the field.

Then, when it was Bradley's time to practice again, he'd apply what he'd seen by "power shagging." Rather than assume a typical posture of chasing after balls hit by teammates at half speed, Bradley chose to replicate game conditions during batting practice in order to hone the efficiency of each of his defensive movements on the field.

Though Bradley's initial exposure to center field had come on a field without boundaries, he became fascinated by the idiosyncrasies of how a field's perimeters influenced the game—how to time his approach to a fence to give himself the best chance to extend his reach beyond it, for instance.

"I always know my surroundings," Bradley said, with a suggestion that the trait had been honed not because of baseball but instead from an upbringing near Richmond, a city that frequently featured one of the highest per capita murder rates in the country during his childhood.

"I wasn't in a horrible part of town, but close enough," said Bradley. "Just having the intuition [to avoid danger] definitely helps."

While Bradley learned to be cautious as he played with kids in his neighborhood, on a ball field he could channel his spatial awareness in more thrilling directions. While much of that refinement occurred when imagining defensive possibilities that few would dare to consider, the young center fielder was similarly interested in refining the details of his offensive game. One summer, he and Brittingham devised a plan not to swing until he saw two strikes in an at-bat in order to force the young player to develop a two-strike approach. Another season, he focused on doing nothing but hitting the ball to the opposite field. Bradley moved around the batting order in an effort to emphasize different forms of situational hitting. In high school, he'd take full rounds of batting practice against nothing but curveballs in an effort to become a better hitter against breaking balls.

"He was a blank slate, taking in everything," said Brittingham.

But among high school prospects, pure tools and physical gifts—enormously strong power hitters, fast runners, six-foot-four giants unleashing mid-nineties fastballs with hammer curveballs—garner notice. Bradley, though a refined player whose feel for the game was far more advanced than that of most of his peers, didn't check enough boxes. He was just five-foot-ten and physically unimposing. It was difficult to imagine him hitting for much power. As a high schooler, he wasn't even invited to the most prominent showcase events and went undrafted as a senior.

But he was an unusually skilled ballplayer, positioning him to excel immediately in college at the University of South Carolina. He hit .349/.430/.537 with 11 homers as a freshman while showing an ability to smash liners from left-center to right-center field, an approach that looked like it would translate to strong averages in the big leagues. As Red Sox area scout Quincy Boyd watched Bradley as a freshman, he was left shaking his head.

"How'd we miss on this guy?" Boyd wondered not just of the Sox but of the scouting community while watching Bradley thrive against elite competition in the best college conference (the SEC) in the country. "You noticed him right away in his freshman year."

Bradley led USC to a College World Series title as a sophomore, hitting .368/.473/.587 with 13 homers while playing extraordinary defense. With a succession of game-changing hits and defensive plays in the most meaningful games of the college season, he was named Most Outstanding Player in the 2010 College World Series.

Boyd diligently wrote follow reports (reports scouts file leading into the spring of a player's draft eligibility, which give a sense of how high a priority the organization should place on scouting a player in the spring) on Bradley during his sophomore year, and other members of the Red Sox organization did the same while watching him play for Team USA during the summer that followed his sophomore-season championship. But as Bradley asserted himself as one of the best college position players in his draft class, the Red Sox questioned whether they should bother focusing the time of Boyd and their crosscheckers in 2011 on such a well-known college talent.

"We were just like, 'Is there any way he gets to this pick?'" recalled Mike Rikard, the Red Sox' national crosschecker in the 2011 draft. "Jackie Bradley was fifth coming into the year after seeing him in the summer. He was a guy we thought we had no chance to take."

That skepticism softened once the 2011 season got under way. Instead of Bradley continuing his consistent college excellence as a junior, his performance took an abrupt downturn.

Many baseball scouts believe in "draftitis," in which a highly touted amateur player struggles in the year of his draft eligibility while trying to play to his reputation. If indeed such a syndrome is real, Bradley is certain that he suffered from it in early 2011, a campaign in which he hit just .247/.346/.432 with 6 homers.

"I was trying to solidify that I was a top player in all of college baseball," said Bradley. "I just think that overconfidence can also be detrimental, as well, because you feel like you can hit everything, you start swinging at things that you shouldn't be swinging at, instead of just staying true to yourself."

Boyd saw a player who was spinning off the ball in order to try to force power rather than staying balanced and maintaining the gap-to-gap swing that had served him well in his first two college seasons. On top of that, Bradley tore a wrist tendon and required surgery while making a diving catch in late April, wiping out any chance he had of pulling out of his slump and potentially ending his college career.

Because of his struggles as a junior, Bradley's draft status took a hit. Entering the year, Bradley had seemed a lock to go in the top ten or fifteen picks. Now he unexpectedly seemed in play for Boston, whose first pick was No. 19. Indeed, it even seemed possible he might slip as late as their fourth pick, at No. 40.

The team was able to look beyond Bradley's 2011 on-field struggles because of its willingness to take the long view with its evaluation of the center fielder. Boyd, the Sox' area scout to the Carolinas in 2011, recognized the things that were causing the twenty-one-year-old's struggles that year—and recognized that the flaws didn't define the player.

"We noted a lot of things that were different from the summer and previous years," recalled Amiel Sawdaye, the Red Sox' amateur scouting director in 2011. "It takes a really convicted area scout who's seen him for fifty, seventy at-bats over three years to say, 'That's not who he is. Who we're seeing as a junior, the swing is completely different.'"

There were some differing views of Bradley, including skepticism about his makeup from an outside consultant whom the Sox employed at the time. But the years of history—Boyd's look at Bradley in his college program, along with conversations with the player's family, his coaches at South Carolina and in the summer Cape League as well as with Team USA—led the Sox to look beyond any doubts.

Boyd felt strongly: Bradley had a bad junior year, but a work ethic that stood out as exceptional among his college peers on top of an unusual passion for the game would allow him to work his way out of those struggles. He didn't waver despite the outfielder's struggles in 2011.

Bradley still possessed a B1 ceiling and a good probability of reaching it. Boyd believed that Bradley had a chance to be a .300 hitter with average power. His running speed out of the box did not stand out, but thanks to his instincts, Bradley featured what Boyd viewed as plus defense—a 60 on the 20–80 scouting scale—in center. Years later, Boyd rued with hindsight that he should have placed a perfect 80 grade on the outfielder's glove.

The personnel inside the Red Sox draft room in the days building to the draft arrived at a strong consensus: if Bradley remained on the board with their fourth selection in 2011, they'd take him. He was, and they did.

"I was very ecstatic," Boyd recalled. "I said, 'I'm going to get to put my name beside that guy.'"

A couple weeks after the draft, Bradley beat his anticipated rehab clock and was back on the field in time to help his school win a second straight College World Series in 2011. As he recovered from his surgery, Bradley wasn't the same dynamic, two-way force that he'd been in Omaha the previous year, but he was nonetheless a defensive game-changer and massive presence on a championship team—an auspicious way to conclude his college career and, once he signed, a springboard into his professional life.

Though Bradley was "just" the Red Sox' fourth pick, he, more than any of their other picks that year, had a reputation that preceded him. When he arrived in Fort Myers, Florida, that September for instructional league workouts, other young Red Sox players did a double take upon their introduction.

"I was in awe. I watched the College World Series. I walked into my hotel room in instructs and it's Jackie there," recalled Mookie Betts, Bradley's instructional league roommate. "It took me a second to realize that I didn't want to be a fan boy."

Once Bradley entered pro ball, though, he again dazzled on the field in a way that left Betts far from alone. In 2012, with High-A Salem, Bradley hit .359 with a .480 OBP and .526 slugging mark along with 16 steals in 67 games. Yet as much as he excelled at the plate, his defense was the true showstopper.

Evan Lepler, the radio voice of Salem, stood one afternoon next to hitting coach Rich Gedman behind the batting cage during pregame batting practice. Bradley had finished his round of hitting and had moved to center field for his "power shagging" routine. His teammates had cleared out to left and right fields, leaving him the vast swath of center-field grass. Bradley tracked one fly ball after another, sprinting in to make a shoestring catch in one moment, racing toward the wall for a Willie Mays–style over-the-shoulder grab the next.

"I remember saying to Geddy, 'Are you watching this?'" Lepler recalled. "He said, 'It's hard not to.' He wanted to watch his hitters. That was his job. But in center . . ."

Bradley starred in Salem through the first half of the year, yet he wasn't the only noteworthy player there. The simultaneous presence of Bradley, Barnes, first baseman Travis Shaw (a 2011 ninth-rounder who, despite coming into pro ball without publicity, dominated the Carolina League with a .305/.411/.545 line), nineteen-year-old shortstop Xander Bogaerts, twenty-one-year-old catcher Christian Vazquez, right-hander Brandon Workman, and other high-ceiling talents in Salem commanded attention.

Big leaguer Rich Hill went to Salem in the early season on a rehab assignment as he worked his way back from Tommy John surgery. The time made an impression. The Red Sox didn't simply have one or two very good prospects who stood out in the Carolina League. Their entire team seemed to have a chance to make a mark at the highest level.

"At that level, they're very, very dominant," Hill said at the time. "That team really did impress me a lot. A lot of guys, you look at them, and you'll look back in five or ten years and say, 'Wow—look at how many of them got to the big leagues.'"

IN LATE 2012, THE CREW at Salem may have seemed a long way from the big leagues. The potential shape of Cherington's Phase Two and Phase Three seemed better defined at that point given the strong prospect performances of Bradley (who moved up to Double-A Portland in the summer), Bogaerts, Barnes, Vazquez, Blake Swihart, Henry Owens, and others, but it wasn't viewed as mature to the point of likely near-term contributions at the big league level.

Thanks to the Dodgers' intervention, Cherington would have a chance to reshape the big league team—both its roster and culture—in the middle of what he'd identified as the Phase One period. Ownership trusted him to do just that. If anything, the way that he handled the chaos of 2012 increased the team's faith in the GM, despite a lousy on-field product.

Amid the daily disappointment of that big league team, Cherington helped guide the club not only by recognizing its shortcomings but also by defining where the organization's strengths were—in its front office, player development, and scouting personnel. The ability to identify those strengths while also acknowledging the myriad shortcomings of the club in that moment earned the young GM trust.

"As frustrating and disappointing as 2012 was, I'm sure in private moments, [Cherington] lost it or got upset, but he didn't show that to anyone—his colleagues or his friends in the front office," said Sam Kennedy, the team's chief operating officer in 2012. "He really was a calming influence."

There were plenty of meetings over the final weeks of the season to discuss what the team needed to do to move beyond a cover-your-eyes conclusion to the 2012 season that dragged the Red Sox through an unfamiliar terrain of failure. The Sox finished the year with a 69-93 record, a .426 winning percentage that marked the franchise's worst since 1965.

On October 4, the day after the season, Valentine met with Red Sox principal owner John Henry, Werner, Lucchino, and Cherington at Henry's house to make official the obvious: Valentine would not return in 2013. That formality out of the way, Lucchino opened a small black book and wrote at the top, "Lessons learned."

A lengthy, candid conversation among the brain trust ensued. The numerous topics covered included the Red Sox players who did and did not look like potential core contributors moving forward, the need to regain dominance of the strike zone both offensively and as a pitching staff, a desire to avoid the sort of long-term deals that had choked the team's payroll in 2012 and a greater emphasis on signings that would improve the team's depth of talent, the need to avoid trades such as the one for Bailey that had compromised the upper levels of the farm system, and of particular importance given the previous thirteen months, the significance of clubhouse culture and the need to reestablish organizational alignment. Toward that end, it was clear that a strong relationship between the next manager and Cherington would be essential. And the Red Sox thought they knew the best person to help fix what had been a broken 2012 dynamic.

Indeed, they had known the right man for the job even before they hired Valentine. Former Red Sox pitching coach John Farrell had left Boston after the 2010 season to manage the Toronto Blue Jays. But he seemed a perfect fit for the Red Sox after the 2011 campaign, given his strong relationships with team owners, front-office members, and players, particularly the pitchers whom he'd overseen from 2007 to 2010. And even though he was in the middle of his contract to manage Toronto, there seemed a path for Farrell to come to Boston at a time when the team needed a steadying voice.

The Jays had a policy that permitted members of the front office and coaching staff to move laterally to other organizations for any number of reasons—money, geography, and opportunity among them. Farrell was hopeful that he might get a chance to talk with Boston, but on October 25—the same day that Cherington was being introduced as the Red Sox GM—the Blue Jays announced that lateral moves would no longer be permitted. Cherington reached out seeking permission to talk to Farrell anyway. Toronto denied it.

"It became a little bit of a contentious moment," Farrell said.

Yet one year later, after finishing with a 73-89 record, the Blue Jays were no longer so protective of their manager. Less than three weeks after Valentine's firing, the Red Sox were granted permission by the Blue Jays to interview Farrell.

Toronto agreed to release the manager from his contract, though per the terms of their new policy, they wouldn't let Farrell walk without receiving compensation from the Sox. In exchange for letting Farrell leave, Toronto received Mike Aviles—the starting shortstop for the Red Sox for much of 2012.

"Who the hell would ever trade for a manager?" Farrell mused several years later.

Aviles, however, was a small price to pay to settle the surf. The trade for Farrell represented a chance to end all of the chaos of the previous year, something that in turn could allow the Red Sox players to turn their attention back to the field rather than wondering what new toxicity might be sprayed into their midst on any given day.

"John Farrell was a perfect tonic," said Werner. "We knew him. We knew we weren't going to make a mistake of hiring someone based on an interview and saying a couple weeks later, 'What happened?'"

The 2012 season had been a dizzying exercise in nearly unfathomable outcomes brought to life. It would not be the last time that the Red Sox under Cherington fielded a team that significantly defied expectations.

CHAPTER 3

THE BRIDGE YEAR

AFTER THE DUMPSTER FIRE OF 2012, the Red Sox were unusually careful to temper public expectations entering 2013. Cherington spoke in late 2012 not of first-place glory but instead of putting "the best team" on the field the next year, one that would be helmed not by the widely disdained Valentine but instead by a familiar, reassuring figure in Farrell.

The Red Sox plotted a course intended to allow their team to be as competitive as possible—one where playoff aspirations seemed at least credible, if not guaranteed—while giving a growing nucleus of minor league talent time to matriculate toward the big leagues. Cherington's vision for the Next Great Red Sox Team did not come with a publicly promised delivery date.

Certainly, few if any onlookers expected the 2013 team to be worthy of the title. The Red Sox cleared nearly $60 million in payroll space for 2013 with the Dodgers deal, yet after their roster flexibility had been choked by the poor performances of players signed to massive long-term contracts, the team wasn't interested in jumping back into the market for superstars. In other off-seasons, Josh Hamilton, coming off a 43-homer season, might have been a prime target for the Red Sox. This year, he wasn't a consideration; the Angels landed him for a five-year, $125 million deal.

The Sox moved aggressively to add veterans on relatively short-term deals, willingly giving players higher average annual salaries than other teams in order to get them to agree to take fewer years than they might find elsewhere. Instead of going toe-to-toe in bidding wars with the Yankees, Angels, and other big-market teams over players who were coming off peak years, the club focused on players who were more actively being courted by mid- and small-market teams.

The strategy was meant to maintain the team's long-term flexibility in a way that the seven-year commitments to Gonzalez and Crawford had not. The Red Sox signed right fielder Shane Victorino on a three-year deal, role players David Ross and Jonny Gomes as well as starting pitcher Ryan Dempster on two-year contracts, and first baseman Mike Napoli, shortstop Stephen Drew, and reliever Koji Uehara on one-year deals. The team also traded for All-Star closer Joel Hanrahan.

Victorino, Napoli, and Drew all had struggled in 2012 but had shown previous upside that exceeded their walk-year performances. Ross, Gomes, and Uehara all possessed standout traits, albeit in limited roles. Those players offered the team the hope of improvement, and perhaps even playoff contention. The Red Sox' internal calculations showed a team whose likeliest projection on paper was 86 wins—tied for the lowest projected wins total for the team since it started making such preseason calculations—though with the understanding that such projections were subject to considerable variance, with a half-dozen wins in either direction well within the range of potential outcomes. The team believed that it had a roughly 30 percent chance of seeing its wins total creep into the 90s, a mark that would make them contenders in the AL East.

Cherington and the front office treated their internal forecasts with something of a grain of salt, recognizing the possibility of enormous divergence from such assumptions. After all, the actual results in 2011 and 2012 had not been kind to the Red Sox' internal projections.

"So much can happen during the season in a place like Boston to sort of push you away from the projections in either direction," said Cherington. "It's a unique place so if things are going well it might push a group towards achieving at even a higher level than we expected. If things are really not going well, it might be harder for a group to even achieve what could rationally be expected."

The Red Sox never considered stepping back from their commitment to try to win in 2013, but ambitions were measured. Wild-card aspirations seemed realistic, with at least a possibility of competing for the top of the American League East at a time when parity ruled the division, but after the humbling experience of 2012, no one was about to declare the Sox the team to beat.

Before the season, team president and CEO Larry Lucchino touted the possibility that the Red Sox would have a "better, stronger" team in 2013 with the possibility of "outstanding ones" by 2014 or 2015. He described the team's identity as that of "scrappy underdogs." The team's marketing campaign at the start of the season struck an almost apologetic tone: "What's Broken Can Be Fixed."

"It's a slogan," Lucchino said. "But I think this one has the added virtue of being true and transparent, that we know that last year and the final month of the preceding year were the beginning of a very downward trend for this franchise, a historic collapse, a disastrous 2012, that it was no secret that things needed to be repaired, reset, rebuilt, reloaded, reset—whatever 'R' word you want to use—and that acknowledging it was probably an honest way to approach the season."

But perhaps as significantly, the presence of established veterans with solid floors at the big league level permitted the team to build a competitor without sacrificing any of its key assets in the minor leagues. Moreover, the infusion of veterans would allow the burgeoning group of top prospects who'd reached Double-A Portland or Triple-A Pawtucket by the end of 2012—including shortstop Xander Bogaerts, center fielder Jackie Bradley Jr., and catcher Christian Vazquez—to develop at their own pace, without being rushed to the big leagues by major league necessity. The Sox wanted to add enough parts to longtime franchise linchpins David Ortiz, Dustin Pedroia, Jon Lester, and Jacoby Ellsbury to compete while buying time for the future to take shape in the form of a new core.

There was an easy and recognizable way of describing what the Red Sox hoped to accomplish, yet everyone in the organization refused to employ the term publicly: bridge year.

Former Red Sox GM Theo Epstein had introduced the idea of the bridge year prior to the 2010 season. The Sox believed that they had a promising kernel of prospects in the lower levels of their system, but they were green, many of them just a few years out of high school and needing more time to emerge. And so, in an off-season where the Red Sox pursued free agents on short-term deals because they did not have big-league-ready prospects to address needs, Epstein coined a phrase that quickly became maligned.

Epstein explained the bridge year concept as one in which veteran acquisitions (most notably that winter, Adrian Beltre, John Lackey, and Marco Scutaro) would help the team compete for a championship while the franchise's top prospects continued their development in the minors. But the notion became wildly misunderstood, with some members of the media and public characterizing a bridge year as one in which the team was acknowledging that short-term competitiveness would be a casualty while waiting for prospects to arrive. For a team charging the highest ticket prices in the game, with fans who expected them to contend every season, Epstein's phrase was not taken well.

"It wasn't his finest Winston Churchill moment," team chairman Tom Werner said in a radio interview on WEEI.

After the team missed the playoffs in 2010, largely due to injuries, those who spoke of the "bridge year" did so sneeringly.

As a result, team officials refused to describe 2013 publicly with the term, even as several acknowledged privately that it perfectly encapsulated their efforts to compete in the short run while building toward a brighter future. The maligned notion of a bridge year likely deserved to be understood in a very different light, particularly given the extreme alternative for a team with a long-term vision of building around prospects.

"What is the alternative [to a bridge]?" wondered Zack Scott, the team's director of major league operations in 2013. "It's a cliff, no bridge—two peaks and you fall in and die. Isn't that worse?"

Some teams were indeed willingly plummeting, Wile E. Coyote–style, into ravines. Virtually all big league teams wanted to build toward homegrown cores that could sustain long-term success. The Royals, Cubs, and Astros organizations, World Series winners in 2015, 2016, and 2017, rose to the top by losing—a lot. All three racked up a succession of 100-loss seasons, gaining access to top talent through the draft, where losses are rewarded with ever-higher draft picks and an ever-larger pool of money with which to sign top talent.

Those organizations committed themselves to the opposite of a bridge year: a determined willingness to tank and absorb years of losing. The bridge represented a way for an organization to pursue prospect-fueled success in the long run but without the embrace of years as a doormat. The Red Sox, wounded by their horrendous 2012 campaign and unwilling to endure the fan fallout that might attend a year of indifference to competitive success in the big leagues, refused to consider the sanctioned sacrifice of a year or years, and they didn't want the mention of a bridge year in 2013 to suggest otherwise.

Even so, as much as the team might tiptoe around the language it employed lest the present be seen as taking a back seat to the future, in spring training it appeared that such an outcome might be unavoidable. The incoming veterans were praised for their makeup and professionalism, and the environment around the team changed drastically with the return of Farrell, but the newcomers lacked star power. They did little to spark the imagination of the baseball world. The Sox' minor league invitees, on the other hand, were a different story.

Though Xander Bogaerts, suffering from jet lag while adjusting in his return from playing with Team Netherlands in the World Baseball Classic, struggled in his time in big league camp near the end of spring training, there was little question about the twenty-year-old's potential. The drumbeat of anticipation for his big league debut already had started to pound.

Yet the anticipation for Bradley proved even greater as he emerged as the headliner of the entire spring. As much as everyone in baseball pays lip service to the idea that spring training is a terrible time for accurate evaluations of players—in part because pitchers are throwing chiefly fastballs to build arm strength rather than working to a specific game plan—the twenty-two-year-old commanded the spotlight every time he stepped onto the field.

He hit .419 with a .507 on-base percentage and .613 slugging percentage that spring while playing breathtakingly impressive outfield defense. Bradley had never spent a day above Double-A, but suddenly, onlookers were no longer asking whether he would one day belong in the big leagues—they were asking whether he belonged on the Opening Day roster.

The downside, for the Red Sox, might be losing an extra

year of team control over him. Debates over CBA minutiae took place, detailed arguments about whether the Red Sox were better off having Bradley on the big league roster to start the year or if the team should delay the start of his big league service time by nine days, thus eliminating the risk that he'd become a free agent after the 2018 season and would instead be controllable—based on his accrued big league service time—through at least the off-season following the 2019 campaign.

Those remarkably detailed disagreements about the value of the 2013 and 2019 seasons took place with an agreed-upon assumption that Bradley was ready for the big leagues—and perhaps even close to being a star. After all, the game looked easy for Bradley that spring. The game *felt* easy for Bradley that spring. "I just felt comfortable," he said. "You never like to say that as a rookie, but I felt comfortable."

To onlookers, a bridge suddenly started to seem less appealing than a leap of faith into the future. The Red Sox didn't quite leap, but they did at least extend an exploratory toe into the void at the start of the season. Bradley broke camp in the big leagues and was in the lineup on Opening Day, walking three times and making a twisting catch on the warning track in left field in a win over the Yankees in New York.

Yet despite that initial contribution, once scouting reports circulated that his swing had a hole easily exploited by fastballs on his hands, the league proved merciless in attacking him with precisely those offerings. A 3-for-31 drought provided convincing evidence that, as promising as Bradley's future appeared, he would not be one of the few players who successfully take player development shortcuts. Less than three weeks into the season, he was sent to Triple-A Pawtucket.

Bradley's absence seemed in a way fitting. The 2013 Red Sox were defined not by youth but by veterans who quickly gelled both with each other and with Farrell and his new coaching staff, who represented the ideal antidote to the poisoned atmosphere surrounding Valentine. Trust flowed freely from coaches to players, as well as players to coaches, in an environment where coaches were willing to let players find their own voices in the assertion of peer-to-peer leadership and a shared passion for the game.

A cultural change was brought about by a new leader and a different cast of players, including boisterous veterans such as Gomes, Ross, Napoli, Victorino, and Dempster, who had long reputations as clubhouse leaders. The natural rapport between the players intensified through a shared sense of purpose that was identified in the wake of the bombings that took place near the finish line of the Boston Marathon that year. Players committed not just to each other but also to the region where they played, in a fashion that contributed to the unlocking of improvement that surpassed even the most optimistic scenarios of the team's forecasting systems. Players prided themselves on their collective baseball IQ, and a combination of talent, professionalism, attention to detail, and team unity—the latter trait amplified by the team's understanding of a civic mission it could serve in the wake of the bombings in April—propelled the team to unanticipated heights.

In contrast to 2012, when the polarization and infighting that surrounded Valentine seemed to suffocate the players, the atmosphere in 2013 carried the team upward. The Red Sox didn't engage in formal efforts at that time to quantify the dark matter of social dynamics surrounding a team, but they regularly reflected on why two straight years witnessed such a profound juxtaposition of the team's performance relative to expectations.

"The most interesting issue in baseball is team chemistry because there is a way of thinking about it that makes sense," said team senior analyst Bill James. "We have to start making progress towards that eventual goal of understanding why it is that you have years when sixty-five or seventy percent of your team underperforms and you have years where everyone on your team is on the same page and they play great."

The Red Sox spent all but roughly three weeks of the season in first place. Nearly every player signed in the off-season delivered at something close to the high end of his projected performance, evidence in the eyes of players, coaches, and team officials of the impact that the culture of an organization could have at both the individual and collective level. The Red Sox thrived with a shared purpose.

The 2013 bridge proved far sturdier than expected—and as the season progressed, it appeared to be providing safe passage for more than just the organization's big leaguers. Bradley, despite his struggles in the big leagues, looked the part of someone who would soon be ready for an everyday job in the big leagues, perhaps as soon as 2014, over the course of eighty games in Triple-A Pawtucket. Mookie Betts was emerging as one of the most dynamic prospects in baseball. And yet even their outstanding performances were overshadowed by the rise of another great talent.

IN MAY 2009, RED SOX Caribbean scout Mike Lord didn't want to clutter the message when filing his report to VP of international scouting Craig Shipley from a workout in Aruba. Though scouting reports were expected to be exhaustive, offering detailed opinions about a player's present and projected tools as a reflection of the premium placed by the Red Sox organization on the currency of information, in this instance, Lord opted for economy.

"I just said, 'Ship, watch this,'" Lord recounted. "In about two seconds, my phone starts ringing."

Shipley's response, as recalled by Lord?

"'Holy crap. Don't leave the island. I'll be there in a couple days.'"

Lord, a globetrotter whose far-flung coverage responsibilities of the Caribbean and Europe seemed to fit his adventurous personality, hadn't entered the day thinking that he would see a future franchise cornerstone. For that matter, he recognized that there was a good chance that he wouldn't see anyone worth signing.

In 2009, the baseball reputation and infrastructure of Aruba—a tiny Caribbean island renowned for its perpetually postcard-perfect beaches—lagged behind the nearby island of Curacao, to the point where some teams didn't bother to scout there. During a two-day stop in Aruba, Lord approached a workout that he'd organized of about fifteen players on what he remembered as a "horrendous" field—half rock, half sand—with relatively low expectations.

One player, Jair Bogaerts, stood out for his power potential, and Lord identified him as someone in whom the Red Sox should have interest. But as the scout neared the end of the workout, Lord uttered a line that changed the future of the organization: "Who else do we need to see?"

The feedback from players and other members of the local baseball community was unanimous: Xander Bogaerts, Jair's twin brother, was the best talent on the island. He'd skipped the workout because he was bedridden with the chicken pox. Lord, who was getting ready for a flight, talked to Bogaerts's uncle, Glenroy Brown, and expressed some urgency: Was there any way to see Xander play? After some coaxing, Bogaerts's mother, Sandra, agreed, and within about thirty minutes, Xander Bogaerts showed up. Players flocked to him instantly upon his arrival.

"When he got out of the car at the ballpark, everyone lit up. It was like everyone already knew he was something special. He was Benny 'the Jet' Rodriguez of Aruba," recalled Lord. "His personality filled the ballpark."

Though Bogaerts hadn't played for weeks, he showed striking ease as he fielded one bad hop after another on the rough playing surface. He took batting practice, and with Lord videotaping, Bogaerts—thin from his weeks in bed, wielding a beaten-up aluminum bat—no longer looked sick, sending missiles around the field.

Barely warmed up, Bogaerts put on an even more impressive show in the game. With a runner on second, a grounder was hit up the middle. Bogaerts dove to glove it, recognized he didn't have a play at first, and instead made a throw while seated on the ground to the plate to cut down the runner trying to score.

In the bottom of the inning, Bogaerts stepped to the plate with a wind pushing in from left field. He demolished a fastball, driving it through the wind and into a residence beyond left field. The next time at the plate, Bogaerts again cleared the fence, this time hitting a homer to right-center field—the type of swing that would have just about any scout shouting for his team to bust out its checkbook.

The Red Sox weren't the only team to scout Bogaerts—some others with a scouting presence in Aruba had already seen him, and Bogaerts recalled that the Astros had made him an offer. Yet to that point, no one had presented the brothers with anything compelling enough to inspire a commitment.

Lord couldn't believe that such a dazzling talent—who, at sixteen years old, would become eligible to hook on with a team as an international amateur free agent in the signing period that started on July 2—hadn't been locked down by another team. He looked around, hoping that no other scouts had dropped in on his workout. When the scout recognized that no other team's representative had witnessed the jaw-dropping display, he wasn't going to let the Red Sox look past a rare opportunity.

"I knew something special was happening," said Lord. "You go to so many ballparks over the years and nothing really exciting happens. It's just another day of hunting but nothing to take a shot at. So when the day with Xander happened, the first reaction is to recalibrate. Am I overreacting? Was that bat speed really special for a sixteen-year-old kid?"

But as Lord reviewed the video, giving him a chance to grade Bogaerts's tools, and after getting to talk to Bogaerts's uncle about the baseball upbringing that he'd provided to his nephews, the scout was sold.

The footage of Bogaerts spoke for itself; the one-minute highlight reel quickly became almost mythical within the Red Sox front office, in no small part because the often-reserved Shipley bubbled with enthusiasm when encouraging other members of the organization to see it.

The Red Sox recognized the talent, and as Lord and Shipley got to know the Bogaerts brothers and their family, they saw players with not just remarkable talent but exceptional makeup. That makeup, in turn, allowed the Red Sox to agree to something of a leap of faith—even though the twins would be eligible to sign with any team on July 2, the Red Sox would wait, in deference to the preference of the boys' mother, until after the brothers completed their high school educations as sixteen-year-olds and then competed in an international tournament that summer in Bangor, Maine, before signing them.

There was some anxiety that other teams might try to swoop in late to offer the Bogaerts brothers a larger bonus than the ones being offered by the Red Sox—$410,000 for Xander and $180,000 for Jair—and indeed, other teams pursued the twins that summer. But when other teams inquired, the family was clear: the two brothers were signing with the Red Sox.

"There were a lot of teams that became interested once we agreed with the Red Sox," said Bogaerts. "But they had so many years to follow us and didn't do anything."

The twins officially became Red Sox when they signed at Fenway Park on August 23, 2009. And once Xander Bogaerts started his professional career, more and more evaluators came across a player who increasingly looked like a potential star. At a workout in Fort Myers shortly after Bogaerts signed, he turned heads by launching what future farm director Ben Crockett described as "low, line-drive two-irons off the fence in the gaps," something that simply doesn't happen with skinny sixteen-year-olds. Xander Bogaerts stood out, in the eyes of some longtime members of the organization, as the most notable prospect at such a young age since Hanley Ramirez.

The twins were assigned to the team's Dominican academy, the standard point of entry into pro ball for almost all players signed out of Latin America. The academy served a number of purposes—providing dormitory housing for players and instilling a sense of and respect for routine by offering both five-times-a-week English instruction (the Bogaerts twins didn't need to take part, with one team official noting that they probably could have taught the class) and life skills training with an emphasis on preparing players for the possibility of life on their own in the United States. (Topics include, among others, how to order food at a restaurant.)

But, of course, those additional programs were wrapped around the daily baseball schedule. And it was hard not to notice the two Bogaerts brothers—Xander, lean and athletic, Jair, a catcher, more round and powerful—as they navigated the fields together.

"They kind of formed a number ten," Duncan Webb, the team's Latin education coordinator in the fall of 2009, said.

The brothers had a presence, with Xander exhibiting the same charisma and joy on the field that had drawn everyone to him at the workout in Aruba. His ability to communicate in four languages—among them English and Spanish—allowed him to be a bridge builder. Meanwhile, he exuded a natural self-assurance that never crossed into arrogance, a combination that made him a beloved teammate who was highly approachable, while also giving him a positive outlook that created the possibility of a rapid growth trajectory.

"He has the ability to not get totally obsessed over a bad at-bat. A lot of guys, you see it affect them defensively or in their next at-bat," said Webb. "Bogaerts, not to say he doesn't take it seriously, but he'll let it go. As we've seen, guys that can do that make huge leaps in player development because they don't get caught up in the mind games of baseball and failure."

Dating to Lord's workout, some questioned whether Bogaerts could remain at shortstop, or whether he'd eventually outgrow the position and be forced to move to either third base or the outfield. If that happened, the team felt that any size increases would come with power gains that would make him a force, regardless of where he played.

But Bogaerts, who grew up idolizing Hanley Ramirez and Derek Jeter, wanted the best of both worlds. He ran religiously during his winters in Aruba, and while he added thirty pounds of muscle early in his professional career, thereafter, he kept reporting back to the Red Sox at almost identical weights from one year to the next, staying constantly between 210 and 215 pounds. He sought out instructors for extra work at shortstop, determined to improve his mechanics at the position to ensure a future there, and that commitment led to steady improvement.

Yet his defensive gains were less noteworthy than the remarkable offensive profile Xander Bogaerts started to develop as he moved through the minors. He had a terrific performance in the Dominican Summer League in his pro debut of 2010, hitting .314/.396/.423, but it was the next year when he started to progress at a level that suggested potential stardom.

Normally, players go from the Dominican academy in their first pro season to extended spring training followed by a short-season league in the States starting in June for their second season. For the Red Sox, that meant either Fort Myers in the Rookie Level Gulf Coast League, a common entry point to pro ball for American high schoolers, or the Lowell Spinners of the short-season New York–Penn League, typically the first stop for college draftees.

But Bogaerts was so good in extended spring training that year that as player development officials considered his potential assignment in the weeks leading up to June, they arrived at a shared conclusion to push him in atypical fashion. The Sox sent him straight to Single-A Greenville—a full-season affiliate in the South Atlantic League, a level where he was one of the youngest players—in early June. He didn't act his age.

"If he has a bad [at-bat], a young kid like that won't know. But he'll come up to you and say, 'I think I was pulling off.' Then, not only that, but the next AB, he'll make the adjustment," marveled Greenville hitting coach Luis Lopez. "I played ten years in the big leagues and sometimes I didn't know what I was doing. This kid, at eighteen, he has an idea. He won't give away at-bats. At that age, that's outrageous. I've never seen anything like it. And when he swings, it's a totally different sound coming off that bat. It's totally different from anyone else."

In a year where the South Atlantic League featured several future stars—among them Bryce Harper and Manny Machado—Bogaerts performed like a player who, if not yet the equal of those better-known peers, need not feel uncomfortable in their company. He hit .260 with a .324 OBP, .509 slugging mark, and a startling 16 homers in a half-season, including some to the opposite field.

"Not only was he hitting them—they were majestic shots, no-doubters right away," remembered Billy McMillon, his manager in Greenville. McMillon, who spent six years in the big leagues, joked that while watching Bogaerts he felt "jealous. At my best, I never hit balls like that, and he was doing it so effortlessly."

The Red Sox started to view Bogaerts as occupying a select class of prospect, and they gained further conviction about his star potential the following year, when at nineteen, he opened the year in the High-A Carolina League with the Salem Red Sox.

That year, Bogaerts continued on a fast track, standing out as one of the most talented players on the field in both High-A Salem and then, at the end of the season, in Double-A Portland. In 127 games in 2011, he hit .307/.373/.523 with 20 homers, in the process becoming the first Red Sox teenager in nearly half a century at any level to hit 20 home runs. Bogaerts no longer just looked like the best prospect in the Red Sox farm system. He was one of the most appealing minor leaguers in all of baseball, a future franchise cornerstone. In early 2013, *Baseball America* ranked him as the eighth-best prospect in the game.

Yet by the middle of that year, even that favorable assessment seemed too conservative. Bogaerts continued not only to hold his own while getting pushed to face older competition—his performance was actually improving. Strides in his pitch selection allowed him to cut down on his strikeouts while boosting his walk rate, and when he did make contact, there was that sound that kept turning heads.

Even as he showed a high-contact approach, he was impacting the ball for extra bases rather than just spraying the ball despite a swing that was geared more for line drives than to sell out for power. Moreover, while he was prone to make errors in clusters, his defensive clock seemed more reliably attuned to the speed of the game as the year progressed, both at shortstop and in his initial professional exposure to third base.

He opened the year back in Double-A Portland. After initially struggling to get into a rhythm in the arctic "spring" offered by Maine, he rebounded to hit .307/.411/.502, forcing his way to Triple-A Pawtucket—the highest rung of the minor league ladder—by mid-June. The transition proved anything but jarring, with the twenty-year-old posting marks of .284/.369/.453 in the highest level of the minors. He made an undeniable case that his time had come.

By JULY THE RED SOX clearly had asserted themselves as one of the best teams in the league. They amassed victories methodically, never losing more than three straight games at any point in the season. A team that entered the year with modest expectations had recast them. A title was now within their grasp, particularly if the group was supplemented in the right way at the July 31 trade deadline, and the Red Sox had the prospects to make a wide range of deals possible.

The team wanted to upgrade—particularly to reinforce its pitching staff—but even with the Sox in possession of one of the best records in baseball at the time, Cherington proceeded cautiously. He recognized the importance of doing something to upgrade—both to add talent to the roster and to reinforce the message to the clubhouse that the entire organization was invested in the group's success—but he also didn't want to compromise the increasingly bright view of the future in an attempt to increase the team's odds in 2013.

"We were comfortable with the idea that we'll give up good players," said Cherington, "but we don't want to give up anyone that we're going to be burned on or that would unnecessarily impact Phase Three."

That outlook took a number of players out of consideration when teams would inquire about them. Bogaerts, obviously, was off-limits. Bradley and left-handed pitcher Henry Owens likewise appeared too important to the team's future—to Phase Three—to consider dealing. Though not as far along as those other prospects, the Red Sox were sufficiently intrigued by the breakout 2013 season of Mookie Betts in Single-A Greenville that they rebuffed the first inquiries they encountered about the twenty-year-old second baseman.

The Red Sox focused on adding to their rotation, with White Sox starter Jake Peavy, a former Cy Young Award winner, emerging as the most appealing target. Peavy could help stabilize the middle of the rotation and, an added bonus, was under contract through the end of 2014. Yet with Cherington refusing to move any of his most prized prospects with a chance to anchor Phase Three, the two teams struggled to find the right headliner to a trade, even after they found common ground on secondary pieces.

The logjam broke in unexpected fashion on July 30, one day before the trade deadline. Reports surfaced that day that Tigers shortstop Jhonny Peralta, who'd been implicated in a PED scandal involving numerous big leaguers at the Biogenesis clinic in Florida, could face a significant suspension that would leave him unavailable to the Tigers for most of the remainder of the season. The Red Sox had a solution.

In the summer of 2009, the Red Sox had made a concerted decision to become far more aggressive in the international amateur market, and went on a shortstop spending spree. In July, the team signed Jose Vinicio—a 130-pound stick figure of a shortstop out of the Dominican Republic whom the team projected to add size and strength—to a $1.95 million bonus. That expected physical maturation never occurred, and when opposing scouts took note of him, it was sometimes because they became confused by the thought that a bat boy had taken the field. One month after signing Vinicio, the Sox signed Bogaerts. Finally, in September, the team reached a four-year, $8.25 million deal with nineteen-year-old Cuban Jose Iglesias, a defensive wizard with a light bat.

But in 2013, Iglesias—pressed into big league duty at third base when incumbent Will Middlebrooks suffered a tear of the rib from the cartilage—went on an amazing offensive run, hitting over .400 through 39 games in the middle of the year. He cooled drastically in July, but his glove alone made him an appealing insurance option for Detroit. For the Sox, the emergence of Bogaerts—and particularly the growing conviction in the organization that he could stay at shortstop—had made Iglesias expendable. In fact, dealing Iglesias might make it easier for the Red Sox to find playing time for Bogaerts at shortstop and third base down the stretch.

And so the Red Sox, White Sox, and Tigers agreed upon a three-way trade headlined by Peavy going to Boston, Iglesias going to Detroit, and Tigers outfielder Avisail Garcia going to the White Sox, along with Red Sox prospects Frank Montas, J. B. Wendelken, and Cleuluis Rondon.

Less than three weeks after the departure of Iglesias, the Red Sox summoned Bogaerts from Triple-A, almost exactly four years after he'd signed his contract with the team in 2009. The team wanted to limit the chaos surrounding a much-hyped prospect, contributing to the decision to have Bogaerts join the club for an interleague West Coast road trip to San Francisco and Los Angeles. With a flight across the country and a relatively quiet clubhouse, the twenty-year-old could gain comfort among his big league teammates before facing the media crush of a home game.

There was, however, one impediment to his comfort, as Red Sox senior director of minor league operations Raquel Ferreira discovered through a phone call from PawSox manager Gary DiSarcina. Somehow Bogaerts had lost a suitcase—including his dress clothes—on a recent road trip.

"DiSar called and said, 'Ugh, Raquel, you've got to take care of Bogey. . . . He barely has any clothes,'" said Ferreira. "I call Bogey and he said, 'What do I do?'"

Ferreira called another member of the minor league operations team, Mike Regan, to tell him to bring in a suit and dress clothes for Bogaerts prior to the team flight on August 19. (Regan was also on the trip, but the suit he lent to Bogaerts was the only one he had. He somewhat sheepishly flew on the cross-country charter in casual clothes.) Ferreira followed that directive with a text to Dustin Pedroia.

"I said, 'Dustin, I need you to take care of Bogey. He doesn't have anything.' He said, 'I got you, Raquel.' This is how our guys are supposed to do it. I always say you have to pay it forward. This is what you do. I knew somebody had done it for Dustin," said Ferreira, recalling how Manny Ramirez had bought suits for Pedroia in his rookie year. "The next day, Dustin Pedroia sends me a picture. He had had somebody in his room fitting Bogey for suits."

On August 20, 2013, Bogaerts—at 20 years, 323 days, and newly introduced to the world of bespoke suits—became the youngest position player for the Red Sox since 1972. He'd traveled an atypical path to the big leagues, a reflection of the belief that he was an atypical talent.

Yet his opportunity on the biggest stage didn't come immediately. Bogaerts started just twelve of thirty-four games after his call-up, and between irregular playing time and a shifting role—he bounced between short and third, and periodically entered games as a pinch runner or pinch hitter—his early returns were modest.

On September 7, however, Bogaerts vividly illuminated a world of future possibility. On a nationally broadcast Saturday afternoon game in Yankee Stadium, Bogaerts crushed a homer to left-center, the ball not merely sailing over the fence but clearing the Red Sox bullpen, a monumental 443-foot blast.

That remarkable display notwithstanding, the Red Sox— who were cruising to an AL East title and the best record in the big leagues with Stephen Drew at shortstop and Middlebrooks at third—saw Bogaerts as a complementary player for the postseason. Bogaerts did not permit that blueprint to remain in place.

In Game 4 of the Division Series against the Rays, with the Red Sox trailing, 1–0, he entered the game in the top of the seventh inning as a pinch hitter for Stephen Drew against left-hander Jake McGee. He negotiated a one-out walk on a full count, setting in motion a two-run rally that gave the Red Sox the lead. He later walked and scored again to provide the Red Sox with an insurance run in their ALDS-clinching 3–1 win.

Bogaerts returned to the bench for the first four games against the Tigers in the ALCS, but looked entirely in control of the atmosphere in his two plate appearances off the bench—a flyout in which he narrowly missed crushing a pitch from Tigers closer Joaquin Benoit in Game 1, and a double to the opposite field against Benoit in Game 4. With the best-of-seven series tied, 2-2, Bogaerts looked like he had a chance to be a difference-maker in the lineup—even if he didn't necessarily see it that way.

"[Mike] Napoli was next to me and he's like, 'Hey, be ready to play tomorrow.' I'm like, 'What the fuck you talking about? Man, I don't even want to play,'" Bogaerts recounted. "It's a big situation. I'm young and I'm like, 'I don't know what you're talking about. I don't even want to play. I enjoy being on the bench.'

"So walking out of the clubhouse, John [Farrell] stops me, like, 'Hey, Bogey.' And I'm like, 'Shit!' And then he's like, 'Hey, you're playing third base tomorrow.'"

Bogaerts was stunned. He'd never been in the playoffs in the minors, and wasn't sure whether he was prepared for the responsibility that awaited him. After all, his experience of the big leagues to that point had been offered in small doses, in a way that hadn't prepared the infielder for the notion that he'd soon be playing a central role in the most important games of a big league season.

Misgivings notwithstanding, Bogaerts used the heads-up to his advantage, preparing both to start and for Tigers pitcher Anibal Sanchez. At 21 years, 16 days, Bogaerts became the youngest Red Sox player to start a playoff game. The previous holder of that distinction? Babe Ruth. Bogaerts did not shy from the moment, going 1-for-3 with a double that proved a key part of a three-run second inning in an eventual 4–3 win in Game 5.

The next game, facing Max Scherzer—the American League Cy Young winner in 2013 on the strength of a 21-3 record, 2.90 ERA, and 240 strikeouts in 214⅓ innings—Bogaerts was even more impressive. In a tense pitcher's duel, Bogaerts faced Scherzer three times, negotiating a seven-pitch walk in the third inning, drilling a full-count double to center and subsequently scoring the game's first run in the fifth, and finally, with Detroit leading 2–1 in the seventh, coaxing a full-count walk off Scherzer to put runners on first and second with one out to end the Tigers ace's night. (Years later, Scherzer remained adamant that a 2-2 slider that Bogaerts took should have been a called strike three.) Two batters later, Shane Victorino blasted a grand slam that gave the Red Sox a 5–2 victory and sent them to the World Series against the Cardinals.

Bogaerts's performance in the ALCS was viewed as little short of a marvel. Against a Tigers pitching staff that at times overwhelmed his more veteran teammates, Bogaerts reached base in six of nine plate appearances with three walks and three doubles. And in the Game 6 clincher, he'd forced one of the best pitchers in baseball to treat him with extraordinary care, while having the maturity to remain disciplined and accept his walks.

"There's no deer in the headlights," said Farrell. "He's beyond his years. He's got a bright, bright future."

Though Bogaerts had an up-and-down performance in the World Series—a six-game triumph over the Cardinals led by a fantastic performance by the pitching staff and an otherworldly offensive contribution by David Ortiz—the ALCS performance had made an impression on the organization. As one Red Sox evaluator concluded after the season, "They may end up making a statue of this guy."

As THE RED SOX CELEBRATED on the field, there was a sense of disbelief. The Red Sox' time had come long before anyone could have imagined just over a year earlier, when the team enacted its blockbuster deal with the Dodgers.

"We expected the step would be in the right direction. We just didn't know how big a step it would be," said Lucchino. "Ben said he wanted to build the Next Great Red Sox Team. He just built it a little faster than he even thought."

It earned that designation rather than carrying it as a birthright. With hindsight, more than five years later, Bogaerts could look back and understand the unlikeliness of what the 2013 group did.

"Our team was supposed to be last place," Bogaerts reflected, still incredulous. "One hundred percent, man, we had not a good team."

But that team that wasn't expected to be good was instead great. The things that made that team great were unusual and hard to replicate. Members of the team understood that there had been a special alchemy involved in the sense of shared purpose in support of both the team and, in the aftermath of the

Marathon bombings, the city. There was also, as Lucchino put it, "a lesson" in the shared sense of purpose of the front office and owners—dating to the previous year's discussion of "Lessons Learned"—as well as in the sense of unity in the relationship between Farrell and Cherington, as well as Farrell and the players.

Still, there was an awareness that the underpinnings of the 2013 team's remarkable success—an almost perfect succession of free-agent signings that yielded phenomenal impact from a typically inefficient market—would be difficult to impossible to replicate. Serendipity factored prominently in the fact that Victorino, Napoli, and Drew had all rebounded from career nadirs in 2012 to deliver something close to career-peak performances in 2013. As much as the Red Sox delighted in their charmed championship run, the team also recognized that sustainable long-term success depended on a different model, and on the growing integration of young players who would emerge as the team's future stars.

For that reason, the team seemed in many ways more optimistic about its prospects moving forward toward 2014 than it had entering the 2013 campaign. Bogaerts had arrived, and other players looked like they weren't far behind, creating the sense that the team stood at the threshold of a bright future. At a time when the Yankees and Rays farm systems looked comparatively barren, a rival executive surmised that the Red Sox were poised to enjoy preeminence in the American League East for the next half decade. Though more measured in their assessments, the Red Sox acknowledged the glowing horizon.

But privately, while there was reason to feel good about both the state and direction of the organization, Cherington understood that challenges loomed. The reigning champions would have to confront a period of coming transition as they moved from an unexpected championship in Phase One of Cherington's blueprint to the period of integrating young players in Phase Two.

"I remember thinking, 'Okay, we're into this phase now that I thought would be the most challenging of all the phases,'" recalled Cherington. "I don't remember saying that publicly . . . [but] I remember thinking that. That was something internally we were looking at, thinking, 'We're in this period. We're going to have to continue to hit it well in free agency and trades, extend the right players, and hopefully bring along the young players as fast as we can.'"

As he navigated toward 2014, Cherington recognized the emergent menace on the horizon, but no one anticipated the size of the iceberg that the Red Sox were approaching.

CHAPTER 4

LOST IN TRANSITION

Roughly fifty miles separate fenway Park from McCoy Stadium, yet while the drive between Boston and Pawtucket, Rhode Island, typically takes anywhere from an hour to an hour and a half, the distance and time that separates life in the big leagues from that in Triple-A is highly subjective.

There are moments, as when a player is called up for the first time, that the time it takes to travel between the two ballparks simply vanishes, the pounding heartbeat of a soon-debuting rookie making the interstate drive from Rhode Island into Massachusetts little more than a forgotten blur. There are others, when returning from the big leagues to Triple-A, that the transit can feel interminable, a reminder to a player that he has not yet established himself as a big leaguer.

And then there's the twilight zone to which Jackie Bradley Jr. committed himself in 2014. Before and after seventy-four Red Sox games at Fenway Park, Bradley made that drive between Boston and Pawtucket, most of them an awful reminder of his uncomfortable liminal state.

Though he'd made the big league team out of spring training due to an injury on the final day of camp to Shane Victorino, he viewed his existence in the big leagues as tenuous, anticipating that he could be sent back to Triple-A at any time. And so, he and his wife, Erin, kept their apartment lease in Rhode Island.

Though the two of them typically made the commute to Boston together—an hour and fifteen minutes to the park, an hour and a half back on most days—a heavy quiet filled the car during a season in which Bradley looked like one of the best defensive players in all of baseball but also, painfully, like one of its worst hitters. The spring and then summer of hitless nights mounted, in a way that muted conversation between the husband and wife.

"She didn't know what to say," Jackie Bradley Jr. recalled.

Erin was not alone in her loss for words and ideas about how to help her husband, and Jackie was not alone on the 2014 Red Sox in his experience of the sometimes incomprehensible struggles of a prospect's uneasy transition to the big leagues, as promise turned to pain for both the players and their organization.

AFTER THE 2013 CHAMPIONSHIP, a team built around veterans seemed ready to incubate a younger core at the big league level. Xander Bogaerts's performance the previous October created a belief in the possibility of blending youth into a group of wise, bearded elders in a way that would let the Red Sox to enjoy safe passage across the player development ravine while allowing the team to maintain its perennial mission to chase championships.

Such views, fairly widespread among the national media in the spring of 2014, anticipated that the Red Sox were ready to leap from Phase One of Ben Cherington's blueprint, with veterans supplemented through free agency and trades in order to deliver a championship, to Phase Three, a team led by its new core. But that outlook failed to account for the unavoidable realities of

Phase Two, the integration of young players to the big leagues, which typically follows a jagged rather than straight line.

Performance is especially volatile at the beginning of players' big league careers. Cherington and John Farrell—both former farm system directors—knew this well. One reason for the bumpy transition is simple: the level of competition is much tougher. Pitchers throw harder, possess better command, and feature complementary pitches with more movement than nearly anything thrown in the minor leagues. Scouting, meanwhile, turns mild minor league shortcomings into devastating flaws. Hole in your swing? It won't be long before big league pitchers find ways to exploit it. And big league hitters possess far better hand-eye coordination and are stronger than their minor league counterparts—a challenge not just for rookie pitchers but also for young fielders who have to recalibrate their on-field clocks to keep pace with a game speed that vastly exceeds anything they've previously experienced.

Meanwhile, the focus of the game shifts from the subtleties of player development in the minors—the individual progress of a player working to develop his skills—to a different, more binary standard after a promotion to the big leagues: Is a player helping the big league team win or not? Against that backdrop, the expectations for young players, particularly on a team expected to win, are extremely high and can pose a significant culture shock.

Typically, according to Zack Scott, the Red Sox director of major league operations in 2014, the team expected a player's adjustment period to last about 600 plate appearances—a full season of at-bats. And that's just the average; in some cases it might take even longer.

After the 2013 season, the Red Sox had a growing inventory of talent in the upper levels of their minor league system. But while that group gave the organization increasing confidence about what Phase Three might look like, a pair of questions loomed: How much could a defending champion in Boston—where the goal every year is to win—tolerate the uncertainty and transitional tumult born of players graduating into big league roles? And how quickly could the organization help those young players get through a period of adjustment to become stable contributors?

For that off-season, major personnel decisions loomed. The Red Sox had a number of 2013 mainstays who became free agents after their title, with openings confronting the team with decisions about the extent to which they could rely on players with significant upside but without a well-established baseline of performance in the big leagues.

One course of action was clear to the Red Sox. The team wasn't interested in dealing any of its most prized minor league assets in an effort to try to repeat. While the Sox had the breadth and quality of prospects that would have permitted them to entertain trade conversations about virtually any player, the organization still remained committed to the eventual development of a homegrown core.

The team let shortstop Stephen Drew, center fielder Jacoby Ellsbury, and catcher Jarrod Saltalamacchia depart in free agency, mindful that it had near-term alternatives at each position. At short, the team had Bogaerts—a player with lingering defensive questions but who looked like he could be ready to assume a significant place in the Red Sox lineup.

"You knew he was a special player," said Eddie Romero, then the director of international amateur scouting. "Especially after [the postseason], it was like, we may not even know what we have or know how good he could be."

In center, the team had Bradley, who hadn't been able to handle big league pitching in 2013 but who had shown enough in Triple-A to suggest that he might be ready to graduate in

2014, particularly given that his spectacular defense had a chance to offset short-term hitting deficiencies he endured.

And in the upper minors, the team had two catchers—Christian Vazquez in Triple-A and Blake Swihart in Double-A—who ranked among the best prospects at their position in the minors. Neither was viewed as ready to be part of the start of the team's title defense at the outset of the year, but it wasn't far-fetched to imagine one or both being ready by 2015, if not sometime in the middle of 2014. The Red Sox tried to sign free-agent catcher Carlos Ruiz, but when that pursuit failed, the team turned to catcher A. J. Pierzynski, who had the advantage of being signable on a one-year deal—thus leaving the door open for Vazquez or Swihart—but came with considerable questions about his clubhouse fit.

Finally, there was holdover third baseman Will Middlebrooks, who had been a slugging beacon of hope on a miserable Red Sox team in his rookie season of 2012, before his performance plummeted in 2013. Middlebrooks, at 660 big league plate appearances, was just past the sweet spot where performance usually stabilizes, but still the Red Sox weren't sure: Was Middlebrooks an everyday third baseman in the big leagues?

Middlebrooks encapsulated the forecasting challenge faced by the Red Sox. Was he the above-average everyday third baseman he'd looked like in 2012, the below-average one who'd been pushed out of the lineup by Xander Bogaerts in 2013, or something in between? Entering 2014, it was hard to peg where he might fall on that spectrum of possibilities. The same was true of Bradley and Bogaerts, players whose talent was not in question but whose ability to translate it to sustained big league production was.

Given the uncertainty, the Sox tried to build in fallback plans for their young players rather than committing unconditionally to Bogaerts, Bradley, and Middlebrooks. The team's greatest confidence was in Bogaerts, so the Sox dealt for utility infielder Jonathan Herrera as a complement rather than a legitimate challenger for an everyday role. Former All-Star Grady Sizemore was signed either to take the center-field job from Bradley or, if Bradley proved ready to seize an everyday role, to serve as a backup.

For a time, the team thought it had the perfect complement to Middlebrooks at third, nearly reaching an agreement with infielder Justin Turner on a minor league deal in January. But hours before Turner was set to sign with the Sox, the Dodgers—his hometown team—swooped in with a big league offer. In Los Angeles, Turner emerged as a star in 2014, one of the best pure hitters in the majors and a mainstay of the Dodgers lineup for years to come.

"A killer," Cherington later lamented of the Dodgers' eleventh-hour coup.

Without Turner, Middlebrooks would need to be ready. The Sox had a great deal riding on one of the most volatile commodities in the game: talented but unproven young players.

As a farm-director-turned-pitching coach-turned-manager, Farrell experienced something of an internal struggle when it came to evaluating players from the perspective of the short and long term. He didn't blend the perspective of the two positions so much as he experienced them as distinct, depending on whether he wore his uniform or not.

As manager, he tended to view players through a prism of immediacy to determine who might be able to contribute the most to wins in the short term. He was still capable of examining the team as a farm director might, but only by literally changing his surroundings.

"I can't do it in the dugout or this office," Farrell said of the longer view. "I probably have to do that when I'm on my way home or at home, think a little bit more objectively."

In 2013, the Red Sox had forged an unanticipated championship path thanks in no small part to a culture of shared on- and off-field purpose that helped to maximize individual performances and exceed collective expectations. A team that prided itself on its baseball acumen reveled in the ability to manufacture wins by amplifying its talent through high-level execution. The dialogue about finding in-game edges was constant in the clubhouse that season.

The culture changed in 2014, for a reason it often does: money. While the Red Sox had reached extensions with two of the team's identified three long-term pillars—Dustin Pedroia in 2013, David Ortiz in 2014—the effort to extend left-hander Jon Lester, a homegrown player entering his thirteenth season in the Red Sox organization and his ninth in the big leagues, went badly awry.

During the off-season following 2013, Lester discussed repeatedly and openly his desire to stay in Boston, and suggested he'd take a discount to do so. A sense prevailed that Lester could anchor the pitching staff for years to come, much as Pedroia and Ortiz could do so for the position players.

That optimism quickly faded. The Red Sox made an opening offer to the left-hander of four years and $70 million—well below what the market suggested an ace should consider for a long-term deal. It was meant to be an initial salvo, much as had been the case when the Red Sox and Pedroia negotiated back and forth on what ended up being an eight-year, $110 million extension the previous summer.

But it was so far below market standards—in a spring where a less-decorated starter, Homer Bailey, had been given a six-year, $105 million extension from the Reds—that it became a terminus rather than a starting point in negotiations.

"We blew that signing in spring training," Red Sox principal owner John Henry later lamented.

The consequences extended beyond just Lester. The closeness of the players, which had worked so much toward a common goal of winning in 2013, now seemed to work against it. Resentment, particularly among members of the pitching staff, toward the organization became a common sentiment.

Lester's stature inside the clubhouse was as enormous as his six-foot-four, 240-pound frame. He commanded immense respect not just for his eight seasons of excellent performances but for his considerable toughness born not just of a baseball upbringing in Boston but also of his status as a cancer survivor.

Disbelief spread that the team would slight a player who was not only an unquestioned front-of-the-rotation presence—a dominant October force who'd played a key role in the 2013 title—but who seemingly represented everything the team would want in a player in the Boston baseball crucible.

"They were a pretty tight group, really tight group. It's one of the reasons why we won in '13. I wasn't privy to those [extension] conversations, but I think it's fair to say that it brought some dissension amongst the team," said Dana LeVangie, who in 2014 was in his twenty-fourth season in the Red Sox organization and his second as bullpen coach. "I thought there was some bitterness throughout [2014] that was disappointing. Those were some of the factors that I felt like they weren't all in for the team, in it to the end."

And there were other problems brewing. Pierzynski, a longtime lightning rod, became a pariah. Many players came to avoid his corner of the clubhouse, retreating from the cutting sarcasm that some found funny while others found brutal. Some in the organization, however, believed that the way that Pierzynski was placed on an island reflected not as badly on him as it did on his teammates, who so clearly had each other's backs the previous year. The championship environment of 2013 was proving impossible to replicate the following year.

In 2013, young players who'd been called up—particularly

Bogaerts and Brandon Workman, a pitcher who became a bull-pen mainstay through the October run to a championship—arrived to a welcoming atmosphere. Older players greeted younger teammates by trying to guide them on and off the field in a way that would allow them to contribute. In 2014, the winds changed direction.

"In 2013 almost one hundred percent of mental energy was, or closer to one hundred percent, was focused on what do we need to do to win tonight. In 2014, the truth is probably it was less than that," said Cherington. "Any young player coming into that environment sees that, starts to ask, 'Why? How do I fit in here? These aren't the things I was associating with the team last year.'"

Opening Day revealed a youth movement under way. Bogaerts started at shortstop. Middlebrooks was penciled in at third. Bradley had lost the center-field job to Sizemore but made the team as a reserve when Victorino—a Gold Glover and offensive sparkplug in 2013—suffered a hamstring injury during the team's final spring training game. In the season opener against the Orioles, Bradley entered late as a pinch runner, then came to the plate with two outs in the top of the ninth inning for his first plate appearance of the 2014 season. He struck out.

"Jackie was maybe forced into a situation where he was maybe there a little bit early," said bench coach Torey Lovullo.

Even so, his reserve role quickly shifted. Though Sizemore had an electrifying spring that harked back to his days as one of the preeminent five-tool players in the game, the performance proved a mirage. His range—and indeed, the overall range of the Red Sox outfield—was taking a huge hit with Victorino on the sidelines and Ellsbury lost to free agency. There was an obvious in-house fix. Less than two weeks into the season, Bradley—understood as a potential Gold Glover, and already viewed by the Red Sox as a better defensive player than even the well-regarded Ellsbury—became the starter in center field.

On the surface, it seemed like the opportunity of a lifetime. Instead, it set the stage for what Bradley described as "probably the worst year of my life of baseball."

Even as playing time came his way steadily, Bradley understood that he hadn't been in the team's plans to open the year until Victorino's eleventh-hour injury. Thus the decision to keep the apartment near the team's Triple-A affiliate, and the long, desolate drives before and after games.

The commute offered frequent opportunities to reflect on the on- and off-field difficulties of the year. Among the most poignant: On April 21, two days after Bradley turned twenty-four, his grandmother, Martha Brown—a constant presence in his upbringing in Virginia, and someone who'd encouraged his dreams of being a big leaguer from his earliest childhood—passed away.

The impact of her loss was enormous, and felt for the entire season. Bradley would etch her initials ("MB") along with those of his best childhood friend, Matt Saye ("MS"), who'd died in a single-car accident three years earlier, into the dirt when approaching home plate, a reminder to maintain perspective and to remember that there were more important things in life than baseball. Still, the recognition of that truth also served as acknowledgment of another—that loss and grief could not be set aside easily.

Yet Bradley rarely brought up the extent to which his grandmother's death affected him to anyone in the Red Sox clubhouse, aside from strength and conditioning coach Mike Roose. He did not want to be seen by members of the club as an excuse maker.

"I had a whole season to sit there and dwell on that," said Bradley. "That hurt."

The field provided infrequent refuge. Though Bradley patrolled center field at what some felt was the highest level they'd ever seen by a Red Sox player, his offense was abysmal. Bradley's batting average fell below .250 on April 16 and never again surpassed it, and indeed kept tumbling to a .198 mark with a major-league-worst .531 OPS. Not long after the passing of his grandmother, Bradley would be tested again. One day in April, he got his hair braided on a day when he was scheduled to take early batting practice. The appointment went long, Bradley got ensnarled in traffic, and he missed the early session of work with his coaches. Though Bradley had alerted his hitting coaches and apologized for the misstep, the team's veterans did not take kindly to the idea that a youthful mistake had compromised the behind-the-scenes commitment that many felt Bradley needed in order to catch up to his competition.

On some teams, a mistake like this would have represented a teachable moment and an opportunity for some good-natured ribbing. But that year, in that clubhouse, the response was different.

The young players were being held to a high account. The defending champions desperately wanted their teammates to transition from their growing pains to maturity, and at times made that clear in blunt fashion.

"They just didn't understand," said Pedroia. "They were excited to be at that level and they were wanting just to perform well, instead of trying to win. That takes time."

The 2014 Red Sox featured a roster of veterans who believed, quite reasonably, that baseball wisdom—the awareness of how to play the game the right way, and to do the right things to prepare for games and thus to perform in them—had played a critical role in securing a championship. The experienced holdovers wanted their new, young teammates to come to the big leagues as developed players, not to experience the big leagues as another developmental level.

"Coming off being world champs, you're expected to win

the following year, and you have these young guys trying to perform up to a big league level and learning, making mistakes that most veteran guys weren't making the year before. Jackie Bradley is going to make more mistakes than Jacoby Ellsbury," said catcher David Ross. "We had players in there who took other guys' roles, who didn't perform, and didn't fit in as much with that group and how we went about our business. There was just a lot of missing pieces from the uniqueness of what we had the year before."

Of course, it wasn't just Bradley and other young players who struggled. In fact, nearly every returning lineup member suffered a significant production decline from 2013 to 2014, whether due to simple regression from the peak performances of the title run or to injury. By mid-April, Victorino, Pedroia, and Napoli were either sidelined or diminished by a variety of ailments. Daniel Nava, a rags-to-riches success story in 2013, endured a considerable drop-off that resulted in his demotion to the minors.

Each individual player's struggles seemed to have an amplifying effect on those around him. A lineup characterized by top-to-bottom strength that made the whole greater than the proverbial sum of its parts in 2013 endured the opposite effect in 2014. Naturally, some veterans on the team started hunting around for scapegoats.

"When you're losing, everybody picks at every little thing a rookie does, and it's not good," said Raquel Ferreira. "There wasn't anybody around that could pick these younger guys up because when you're losing, all you're focused on is, 'We suck, we're losing.' And so it wasn't the healthiest environment, I think, for our new guys to be brought into."

And there were many rookies to pick apart. Pedroia recalled with gratitude how, in 2007, he was the lone rookie being asked to contribute to a team of established performers who were expected and ready to win. The second baseman performed poorly in the first six weeks of that season, hitting well below .200. But the team had the elite veterans around him to withstand his early season struggles, and teammates like Mike Lowell, Alex Cora, and Manny Ramirez were generous with their time and advice as he adjusted to the big leagues. By the middle of that year, Pedroia was raking; he would go on to win Rookie of the Year.

In 2014, with so many young players trying to make a potentially overwhelming transition, the task was completely different. The Sox didn't have the luxury of that gradual progression. After letting so much of the 2013 team walk in free agency, they needed Bradley, Bogaerts, and Middlebrooks to excel in a crash course where mistakes couldn't merely be shrugged off as part of player development.

Skepticism mushroomed in some corners of the Red Sox clubhouse about Bradley in particular, as his numbers continued their decline. Was he coachable? Was he committed enough to baseball? Was he tough enough to handle Boston? And for Cherington, the biggest question of them all: Did this guy belong in the team's plans for Phase Three?

"Jackie was a tough one. He struggled so much that you said, 'Maybe he's not going to be,'" said Zack Scott. "How long do you wait? Do you pull the plug?"

Bogaerts did not raise such questions—at least not early in the season. His 2013 postseason served as a springboard into the start of the regular season, with the twenty-one-year-old shortstop posting solid numbers through the initial months of the season. Entering 2014, he had been anointed the number two prospect in the game by *Baseball America*, and he looked every bit the part.

Yet while Bogaerts was hitting early, his defense at shortstop lagged behind his offense. His range and fluidity were limited by the fact that he was adjusting to a much faster pace of the game than what he'd faced in the minors. One Red Sox coach told another that the team would never win a World Series with Bogaerts at shortstop.

Of course, the team had already won a World Series with Bogaerts at third base, where Middlebrooks was now trying to play through injuries and struggling mightily. His average fell below .200 in mid-May before he landed on the disabled list with a broken finger—the latest in a succession of injuries that saw a rapid two-year erosion from potential franchise building block in 2012 to someone whose place in Boston had become very uncertain by 2014.

On May 20, days after Middlebrooks landed on the DL, the Red Sox felt they needed to do something to prevent the season from slipping away. Even amid a four-game losing streak, at 20-23, the team believed it still had time to salvage contention in a tightly packed AL East in which the Sox were 3½ games behind the first-place Orioles. The team re-signed shortstop Stephen Drew, who'd remained stuck to that point of the season in a free agent twilight zone, in an effort to upgrade their offense and defense.

But doing so would require Bogaerts to move off shortstop—a traumatic notion for the twenty-one-year-old, who—with the exception of the brief move off the position in late 2013—not only had always played the position but had built his baseball identity around doing so. He wore the number 2 in homage to legendary shortstop Derek Jeter. All the days of running on the beaches of Aruba, all the tireless off-season workouts, all the extra time spent with Red Sox infield instructors in the minor leagues had been done to ensure a future at the most glamorous infield position and to defy the many expectations of an eventual move to third base.

Cherington and other members of the Red Sox insisted that they continued to view Bogaerts as their shortstop of the future, and that they wanted to take advantage of an in-season opportunity to upgrade that didn't require them to trade any of their most valued assets. They tried to communicate that outlook to Bogaerts. But in the moment, it was hard for the rookie to take such claims at face value.

Though Drew would need time preparing in the minors to face big league competition, on the night of his signing, a shaken Bogaerts made a pair of errors at shortstop in a 7–4 Red Sox loss, the team's fifth of what eventually ran to nine straight defeats. He heard boos from the crowd in response to his defensive miscues. The moment crushed Bogaerts and led him to question the organization's view of him and his future.

"What am I supposed to think?" Bogaerts wondered in the clubhouse following that game. "How will I know that if we're twenty-and-thirty next year and I'm playing shortstop, they won't do this again?"

Bogaerts tried to explain what the decision felt like, poking a finger in the chest of his converser to indicate the air being pushed out of his lungs.

"I spent so much time working there and for what?" he wondered. "If I move now, how am I supposed to get better so that I can stay there?"

For the first time in his professional life, Bogaerts faced doubt—and he couldn't compartmentalize it. Within weeks he went from a startlingly mature player who seemed capable of building on the experiences of the previous October to someone who suddenly felt out of place and out of sorts in the big leagues. His production spiraled starting in early June, and over a period of almost three months into late August, he was one of the worst hitters in baseball, posting just a .147 average with a .405 OPS over 63 games.

His nadir arrived on July 26 against the Rays—the same team against whom he'd announced his arrival on the postseason stage in 2013. With runners on the corners, Bogaerts stepped into the box to face Rays reliever Grant Balfour. On 2-2, he took a 93-mph fastball over the outer third of the plate for a called third strike—his second of three punchouts that night. Distraught, he stood frozen for a moment, then placed his helmet, bat, and batting gloves on the ground, anticipating that a bat boy would return his equipment to the dugout as he made his way to *third base*—ugh—during the inning change.

But there was a problem: Bogaerts's strikeout represented the second out of the inning, and not, as he thought, the third. He had to make the embarrassing return to the batter's box to pick up his gear before a walk of shame back to the dugout.

"Terrible," Bogaerts said after the game. "That can't happen."

The lack of situational awareness—at a time in the game where contact might have allowed the team to score at least one run in an eventual 3–0 Red Sox loss to the Rays—amplified the sense on the part of the veterans that the team's young players weren't ready to win at that level.

"He had raised that expectation so high that when he was struggling, we were like, 'What is this?'" reflected Lovullo. "He was having a tough time dealing with that. I could see the frustration written all over his face—him and Jackie."

Bogaerts and Bradley both would have benefited during that time from the help of a mental skills coach—an area in which the Red Sox had been relatively early adopters of a formalized program. Starting in 2004, the team employed longtime big league pitcher Bob Tewksbury to develop the first mental skills program in the Red Sox organization. Over a decade, he won the trust of Red Sox minor leaguers as he helped them to develop techniques and mental routines to pursue success and manage adversity. Many players remained close to him even after they graduated to the big leagues.

But after the 2013 season, Tewksbury left the organization to take a job with the MLB Players Association, hoping to broaden the pool of players he could help. The Red Sox did not immediately move to replace the longtime presence given how delicate such a position could be. The fit had to be precise for both the players and the manager; better, the organization concluded, not to have anyone than to rush to hire the wrong replacement. And so in 2014 they didn't have a mental skills coach available to help big leaguers cope with their struggles.

It's impossible to say how much of an impact such a person might have had in 2014, but by the middle of the season, it became increasingly apparent that the team's young players—particularly Bogaerts and Bradley—were confronted with failure to an extent that they'd never before experienced it, and that they didn't have a clear sense of how to overcome it.

By late June, the Red Sox' hopes for the season were deeply imperiled. The brash ambition to repeat as champions had given way to a growing sense of dread. As the All-Star break approached, they were running out of time. And so Cherington and the front office decided to attempt something of a Hail Mary. It was time to hail Mookie.

CHAPTER 5

MOOKIE

THE NUMBERS DIDN'T MAKE SENSE—AT least to members of the Red Sox organization. But there was a part of Mookie Betts that wasn't surprised, that viewed his woeful start to the 2013 season not as evidence of the whims of the baseball gods but instead as a devastating indictment of his ability and future in the sport.

Despite the fact that his uncle, Terry Shumpert, had been a big leaguer, and that Betts had made himself at home in professional ballparks since grade school, the Tennessee native grew up with an omnipresent kernel of skepticism about his talents. Often that self-doubt propelled his improvement. But at the start of his second full professional season, the willingness to question his own talent—amplified by the horrendous numbers he'd amassed at an early stage of the season—clouded his future.

On May 2, 2013, Betts was submerged in a month-long rut with Single-A Greenville, a .145 batting average and .603 OPS that offered cause for curiosity if not outright alarm. Some Red Sox officials wondered whether the twenty-year-old might need to be sent back to extended spring training and to repeat at the same level—short-season Lowell—where he'd spent his first full professional season in 2012.

His coaches at Greenville were more sanguine. The young second baseman, they said, was hitting rockets—it was just that these rockets kept finding their way into opponents' gloves. Indeed, by many metrics, he was having great at-bats; he had nearly twice as many walks as strikeouts. Still, future big leaguers didn't tend to hit .145 in Single-A. Betts couldn't look beyond the anemic batting average.

Most players who sign big league contracts out of high school do so in anticipation of a long big league career ahead. Not Betts. When he decided to sign with the Red Sox as a fifth-round pick in 2011, walking away from his commitment to play baseball for the University of Tennessee, his goals were rather more modest. He figured he'd play for five years in the minors, a requirement to collect the entirety of his $750,000 bonus, and then go to college, where he might dabble in his other great love, basketball. Now, struggling at Greenville, Betts felt his baseball career approaching a crossroads.

"I was actually getting ready to say, 'I'm just gonna go ahead and call it a day. It was fun, these last couple years have been cool, but I'll take a different route in life and probably go play basketball somewhere,'" Betts recalled.

He lined up opportunities to play college hoops—a possibility he discussed with Division 1 Lipscomb University and Division 2 Trevecca Nazarene, both in his home state of Tennessee—with the idea that he'd enroll in college after he wrapped up the 2013 season in Greenville. He'd accepted that it might be time to move on with his life, that baseball might not be his calling.

"It's getting into a month and things should be turning around a little more by that time," said Betts. "But they weren't."

THAT BETTS WAS IN THE Red Sox system at all pointed to one scout's power to shape the course of an organization.

By 2010, area scout Danny Watkins had more than a quarter century invested in the game, with seventeen years as a college coach and another eight as a scout, including six with the Red Sox. He'd developed a bit of a legendary reputation in the team's scouting department.

Watkins possessed a Bear Grylls–style doggedness, most evident during the annual SEC tournament in Hoover Met Stadium in Birmingham, Alabama. There Watkins was perennially the only person with the special mix of tenacity and insanity required to weather the scorching sun, 90-degree temperatures, and swamplike humidity from the shade-free second row of the scouts section for the entire days-long tournament.

Most of the rest of the year, Watkins treated six- or eight-hour drives between Tennessee, Alabama, and Mississippi as if they were routine trips to the grocery store. Yet while his car—littered with dip cups and empty two-liter bottles of Mountain Dew, part of a breakfast of champions—represented a comfort zone for the scout, other members of the Red Sox organization found his driving skills so terrifying that they'd long since agreed: better to rent a car and drive separately to a game rather than ride shotgun with the scout.

That said, his evaluations were heralded not just for their precision but also for the colorful vernacular he used to describe players. He'd describe admiringly a player who had "shit in his neck" (toughness), or one who had a "greasy" fastball (deception that made it hard to hit).

While Watkins had a one-of-a-kind scouting style, he nonetheless understood the broader realities of his profession. Players more often broke the hearts of scouts than lived up to the imaginings of what they might become.

"I've got a lot of body bags," admitted Watkins. "I wish you could see my lists over the years. There are so many misses."

Even so, Watkins understood that a scout is like a basketball sharpshooter—the misses can't deter a willingness to take another shot. And in June 2010, Watkins saw a shot worth taking at an event featuring 100 to 125 Tennessee high school underclassmen. There his eyes kept being drawn to the skinny five-foot-eight shortstop who "just kind of flowed through the game" with an athleticism rarely seen.

It's easy for scouts to look past undersized high school players—something that helps to explain why Dustin Pedroia, for instance, went undrafted before he played for Arizona State. The failure rate of high school players is so high that teams are reluctant to invest hundreds of thousands or even millions of dollars in a player who lacks physical resemblance to a typical big leaguer.

But as Watkins watched teenagers navigate a typical work-out, Betts just kept commanding his attention. Betts's offensive tools were special, his athleticism elite. At shortstop he showed both an explosive first step and outstanding anticipation that translated to significant range as well as unusual body control. On one grounder hit behind the bag at second base, Betts ranged far to his left, stretched to grab the ball, and flipped it behind his back to get a force-out at second.

"I knew right then that, okay, this is a guy, let's start to dig a little deeper," said Watkins.

The more Watkins dug, the more intrigued he became. It turned out Betts was the nephew of a former big leaguer, Terry Shumpert. In fact, one of the central aspects of Betts's baseball upbringing had been shaped indirectly by an opportunity the Red Sox had declined to provide to Shumpert.

After the 2003 season, Shumpert, then thirty-seven, had a premonition about the Red Sox, for whom he'd played in 1995. He believed that in 2004 the team would win its first World Series in eighty-six years. He wanted to be a part of that life-changing event and reached out to Jerry Dipoto, a former teammate who was working in the Red Sox front office, in hopes of hooking on with Boston.

Shumpert signed a minor league deal with the Sox, hoping to win a bench job in spring training. But he suffered a hamstring injury that took him out of the running for a season-opening spot in Boston and, instead of cracking the Opening Day roster, was offered a role in Triple-A Pawtucket. As he prepared for what he expected to be his last professional season, Shumpert turned down that offer in order to play for the Pirates' Nashville-based Triple-A team, the Sounds, close to his family—including eleven-year-old nephew Mookie Betts.

Though Shumpert's premonition came true, he never got his ring with the Sox. But the year nonetheless proved rewarding for the chance it gave him to spend time with his family, particularly the energetic nephew who invariably sought out adults to humor his athletic interests.

"It'd be, 'Oh, here comes Mookie again. Terry, deal with him,'" said Shumpert. "I used to crack up. He was always coming around, talking noise, 'I'll do this, I'll do that,' and I'd just laugh at him."

Through his uncle, Betts received a remarkable apprenticeship throughout 2004. He'd head from school to Herschel Greer Stadium, the home of the Nashville Sounds, where he could hit, shag fly balls, and take grounders with his uncle—and see what it was like to play baseball for a living.

Certainly, those unique experiences played into the comfort Betts showed on the field by the time he'd reached high school. And the fact that he had not only a relative who'd been a big leaguer but experiences around the professional game added to the intrigue for Watkins.

As Watkins scouted the high schooler in the summer following that initial workout, the diminutive Betts had little power but otherwise excelled at the plate. He had good balance, didn't chase pitches out of the strike zone, didn't swing and miss at pitches in it, and had the timing and hand-eye coordination to make solid contact and shoot the ball into gaps. Watkins wanted to know more.

Then he attended one of Betts's high school basketball games. Betts, a point guard, was again one of the smallest players on the court. But he had great court vision and a feel for the pace of the game. And it was clear that his teammates looked to him as a leader. Then, in the third quarter, an otherwise measured performance became jaw-dropping when Betts took a pass on the left wing, juked right, then drove hard to the basket along the left baseline.

As Betts elevated, Watkins anticipated a layup. Instead, the eighteen-year-old threw down a dunk. Watkins turned to Mike Morrison, Betts's baseball coach.

"I had probably a look of amazement," said Watkins. "He had a look of, 'Yeah, I see that every day.'"

Watkins sought reasons to keep watching Betts play that spring. He wasn't typically in the habit of attending high school practices, but one day he headed over to Overton High School in Nashville to see Betts in just such a setting. When Betts's team was rained out, Watkins stayed to watch the young shortstop hit inside.

"I just liked watching him," said Watkins. "If that's a gut feel, I guess that's a gut feel. I had a feeling that this guy was going to be pretty good, but more than anything else, I just enjoyed watching the kid do things. In this business, we're wrong so much, but once you get a gut feel on a guy, you can't be afraid to follow it."

Watkins was convinced that Betts had considerable upside that, to that point, was untapped—precisely the sort of profile of player that the Red Sox were targeting in the 2011 draft. He already looked so natural on the field that with added physical strength and further skill refinement, Watkins saw a potential impact player—a B2 with an unusually solid likelihood of reaching that ceiling for a high schooler.

That spring, he watched Betts, now a senior, play four games (on top of the practice, the indoor hitting session, and the basketball game). Because of his conviction, the Red Sox placed Betts on their spring follow list and sent in three other evaluators—a national and regional crosschecker as well as a special assignment scout—to get additional looks at Betts during his senior spring.

Another relatively new component of the Red Sox' scouting efforts raised further intrigue about Betts's potential. Neuro-Scouting, a Cambridge-based start-up founded by Drs. Wes Clapp and Brian Miller near the science and technology hub of Kendall Square, had worked with the Red Sox since 2008 to develop video-game-like computer exercises to assess players' hand-eye coordination, and later to develop games meant to improve pitch recognition.

But in 2011, the partnership expanded. NeuroScouting developed software that was installed on scouts' iPads for potential draftees to use. The performances offered the potential to quantify how quickly a player could recognize, for instance, the direction of the seams on an image of a baseball.

"A ball popped up [and you'd] tap the space bar as fast as you could. If the seams were one way, you tapped it. If it was the other way, you weren't supposed to tap it. I was getting some of them wrong," said Betts. "I wasn't getting frustrated, but I was like, 'Dang, this is hard.'"

If it was hard for Betts, it was vastly more difficult for almost everyone else in the country whom the Sox tested. Betts's scores ranked among the best that the Sox had encountered. The activity offered statistical insight into how quickly a hitter might be able to recognize and react to pitches. The program's potential was huge. For decades, teams had struggled to accurately gauge the pitch-recognition skills of high school hitters, who normally face pitching that is nothing like what exists in the big leagues. NeuroScouting hoped their software could show teams which high schoolers might be wired to one day adapt.

But the Red Sox still didn't know exactly what Betts's strong scores meant. The program was still in its infancy, and there wasn't enough data to define a correlation between performance in the simulation and in-game professional success. But Betts performed so well that members of the organization took notice. Some even viewed his future success, or lack thereof, as a sort of referendum on the value of this form of scouting.

"If this guy turns out to be a prospect," one front-office member reputedly said in reference to Betts, "we'll know this shit works."

Still, the NeuroScouting data at the time was only a small piece of the equation with Betts. More significant were the reports that kept getting filed from Tennessee from Watkins and the other scouts who made the trip to see the player.

"Everyone came out saying, 'We've got to get this guy,'" recalled Amiel Sawdaye, the Red Sox' amateur scouting director in 2011.

With that shared belief, however, came a curiosity: Why weren't other organizations on Betts? The Padres and Royals both showed interest in him as a high schooler, but few other teams were doing so, and none matched the attention committed by the Sox. Ultimately, Watkins and the Sox didn't concern themselves nearly as much with the question of why other teams weren't scouting Betts heavily as with the fact that the lack of industry interest might create a tremendous opportunity.

As the Red Sox lined up their board heading into 2011, the conversation wasn't whether the team should try to land Betts but instead how high the team needed to pick him in order to ensure that another team didn't beat them to the punch.

His athleticism, speed, and bat (the Red Sox gave solid 60 grades for his projected hit tool on the 20–80 scouting scale) all represented strong attributes, even with below-average power projections. There wasn't a single standout trait that was so impressive that it would vault him into the team's upper handful of picks, but the Red Sox saw a player with so many things working in his favor that they didn't want to miss a chance to bring him into their system—particularly given Theo Epstein's mandate to chase high-ceiling players who might not be as widely available in future years.

The team viewed Betts as someone who, on talent alone, would be a reasonable third- or even a second-round selection. But given the light interest elsewhere, they strategized that they could wait a little deeper into the draft to pick him. Watkins would have to sweat it out.

"Every time it's your pick, you're thinking, 'Will we get another chance at him if we don't take him here?'" Watkins remembered.

He started to get antsy in the fourth round, but by the fifth, he was convinced: the Red Sox wouldn't get another shot if they didn't take him. The team didn't test that theory. They grabbed Betts in the fifth round with the 172nd selection in the draft, thrilled to get a player with such considerable promise at that spot. Yet after his late decision to sign for $750,000, his first impressions in the organization hardly suggested a potential star in the making.

ELEVEN DAYS AFTER BETTS SIGNED with the Sox, he made his pro debut on August 26, 2011, in the final game of the season for the Rookie Level Gulf Coast League Red Sox in Fort Myers. Betts went 2-for-4 with a pair of singles, drove in a run, and stole a base—a solid offensive debut. That performance had nothing to do with why he got called into the principal's office after the game.

Betts made three errors, and did not suffer them well. The first was a straight fielding error on the first play of his professional career in the top of the first inning. Not a big deal. But in the fourth inning, Betts fielded a ground ball and threw to first, where his throw—not a bad one—tipped off the glove of Zach Kapstein, who was still relatively new to first base. Betts looked into the dugout, where manager George Lombard, Red Sox field coordinator David Howard, and catching coordinator Chad Epperson were standing. He raised his arms in befuddlement.

"Mookie's looking in, like, 'Why is that guy not catching the ball?'" remembered Lombard.

Two batters later, with runners on first and second, Betts gloved a ball going up the middle to his left and made a back-handed flip to second to try to get the force-out. The only problem: the second baseman wasn't covering the bag. Betts was charged with his third error. He chastised his double-play partner—an unacceptable way of treating a teammate.

"We said, 'Okay, let's nip this in the bud,'" Lombard recalled. "We called him over and said, 'You don't want to show up anybody.' [Betts] said, 'But the throw was right there!' We said, 'Okay, we'll talk about this later.'"

After the game, Lombard brought Betts into his office. The goal wasn't to punish Betts or to yell at him but instead to teach, to let Betts know what the expectations were for a professional and a teammate. Lombard made clear: his role was to be a teacher, to help Betts understand the right way of doing things so that he would be able to improve and help others along the way.

The eighteen-year-old needed to know that he was being held to a professional standard, but perhaps more important, needed to hold himself to such account. Evaluators—inside and outside the Red Sox organization—were always watching him.

How he acted would shape perception, and potentially form misperceptions, about him, in a way that could affect anything from decisions about future promotions to trade interest. "That was our first encounter of Mookie," Lombard remembered in 2018. "To this day, every time I see him, we joke around about that day."

Two years later, when Lombard was a roving base-running and outfield instructor in the Red Sox organization in 2013, he had a chance to appreciate how much Betts had taken those lessons to heart. Betts flew out, narrowly missing the sort of flush contact that would have resulted in an extra-base hit; frustrated, he jogged to first. After the game, unprompted, Betts sought out Lombard to apologize for the lack of complete effort.

If Betts grew as a person and a professional between that 2011 debut and the 2013 base-running incident, he still hadn't done much on the field to distinguish himself. When he roomed with Jackie Bradley Jr. during the instructional league after the two were drafted in 2011, the college star was struck by the fact that his younger teammate possessed "zero confidence in himself." Bradley was twenty-one; he had already struggled against the highest levels of college baseball and then come back to conquer them. Betts was eighteen, living away from home for the first time, and radiated self-doubt.

"It was unbelievable," remembered Bradley. "You would think he was going to quit the next day. That's how much confidence he had in himself. 'Man, I just don't know. Baseball might not be it for me. I'm going to go play some basketball.'"

In 2012, in short-season Lowell, Betts clustered six throwing errors in thirteen games at shortstop. Through those struggles, in a sign of how the early lessons from Lombard had taken hold, Betts made a favorable impression on Spinners manager Bruce Crabbe through his commitment to use those mistakes as learning opportunities.

"He would come to me, ask me, talk to me, and we'd work on it," said Crabbe. "He knew he was making mistakes. He wanted to learn how not to make them."

The fact that Betts, still a teenager, showed a thirst for instruction—perhaps the product of his omnipresent humility about his abilities—encouraged Crabbe's vision of the player Betts might grow into. Still, one had to squint pretty hard to see it.

The Sox slid Betts over from short to second on a full-time basis when the team's 2012 first-round draft pick, Deven Marrero, joined Betts with the Spinners. Offensively, there were intriguing elements of what Betts did in Lowell, particularly the fact that he showed an elite feel for the strike zone while walking more times (32) than he struck out (30), and he swiped 20 bases in 71 games. But he hit a modest .267 with absolutely no power.

"I remember watching Mookie hit a baseball when he could barely get it out of the infield," recalled Blake Swihart. "I was like, 'Dude, can you hit a home run?'"

At the time, the answer was no. Betts failed to hit a single home run and had just nine extra-base hits in almost 300 plate appearances in Lowell. When *Baseball America* published its much-referenced annual Prospect Handbook after the 2012 season, it listed the top thirty prospects in the Red Sox system. Betts didn't make the cut; he was No. 31.

"I have pretty vivid memories of seeing Mookie in Lowell—not being blown away," recalled Duncan Webb, the Red Sox' assistant farm director at the time. "You see those guys a lot—undersized, extremely athletic. The hit percentage on those guys is so small."

Betts knew it. He emerged from that season convinced of the need to improve. As a multi-sport high school athlete, he'd focused his time and attention on practices and games, with minimal time in the weight room. But after his season in Lowell, he understood that to make the most of his professional baseball career, he'd need to get stronger.

"I had nothing coming out of the bat," said Betts. "That was definitely my thought: I needed to get into the gym and at least get it to the fence."

Back in Nashville that offseason, Betts was getting a haircut and mentioned this goal to his barber. His barber knew a guy. Deon Giddens had played football for Tennessee State, then played professionally for the Buffalo Bills' practice squad and in the Arena Football League. Now he trained athletes—mostly football players and boxers—in Nashville. The introduction made, Betts went to Giddens's facility.

Giddens had never heard of Betts, and the guy who walked into the gym that first day didn't exactly look like a professional athlete. Giddens recalled, "I started grabbing his arms when I first saw him, like, 'Man, what do you play again?' I was like, 'You sure? You play pro baseball?'"

Betts entered Giddens's gym at 155 pounds. By the end of the offseason of workouts, he'd added fifteen to twenty pounds of muscle. But then he arrived at Greenville, descended into his torturous slump, and none of it seemed to matter anyway.

On MAY 2, BETTS WENT 0-for-4 with a pair of strikeouts as his average sank to .145. Something had to change. Enter U L Washington.

Washington spent eleven years in the big leagues before Betts was born, having become a somewhat iconic player despite a modest performance history due to the omnipresent toothpick in his mouth on the field. By 2013, he had nearly a quarter century of coaching experience, including eleven seasons in the Red Sox minor league system. The bespectacled fifty-nine-year-old offered feedback that tended to be unvarnished, in a way that some players struggled to accept. At one point, Betts was one of them.

"Initially we butted heads," said Betts. "He had his viewpoint on things and I had my viewpoint on things. It ended up being one of the best things that ever happened to me, I think, once we pushed that to the side. . . . Once we figured it out, that was my guy, man. For everything—infield, hitting—everything I needed or wanted to know, he had answers for me."

By May, Greenville manager Carlos Febles recognized in Washington and Betts a relationship that was "like a father and son." Staffers who went through Greenville were struck by how much the gruff Washington cared about Betts and was invested in his development, particularly valuable given that Betts was a bottomless well of questions about how to get better.

Betts was kept out of the lineup on May 3—one day before a scheduled off day on May 4—to have a chance to catch his breath and work with Washington in the batting cage. The hitting coach had been watching Betts's mechanics carefully over the previous few weeks. The young second baseman had an exaggerated timing mechanism, a leg lift so dramatic that it almost mimicked a pitcher's. If Betts could diminish his pre-swing motion and instead gently stride toward the pitcher in order to maintain his balance, he could more easily be on time to the ball and start driving pitches with his newly developed strength.

Betts, ever eager to apply the advice he received from a trusted source of counsel like Washington and unusually capable of implementing it thanks to extraordinary body control, achieved an almost immediate transformation. May 7, Betts went 2-for-2 with three walks. On May 8, he went 2-for-5 with a homer, double, and three walks in a doubleheader. On May 10, he had four hits with two doubles and a homer. Starting with his return to the lineup after the cage session with Washington, Betts went on a nineteen-game hitting streak in which he hit .441 with a .511 OBP and .770 slugging mark.

"He became a beast overnight," recalled Febles.

Betts suddenly could drive the ball in a way that he'd never been able to before. The pitch recognition that allowed him to draw a ton of walks could also be applied to attack pitches and demolish them. He'd gone from a player without a distinctive profile to one who was routinely the best on the field, a standout hitter who was growing into at least gap power while also maintaining the explosiveness to steal bases and play brilliant defense at second.

Yet around the clubhouse, one wouldn't have noticed that anything had changed. Betts remained as unassuming as he'd been while struggling, asking questions about pitching, about hitting, about offensive approach of anyone with knowledge to share. At one point, Alex Hassan—who'd advanced to Triple-A Pawtucket in the Red Sox system but was playing for Greenville in May and June of 2013 on a rehab assignment while recovering from a broken foot—couldn't help but take some amusement in Betts's curiosity.

"He had literally no idea [how good he was], but that made him special," remembered Hassan. "I was happy to offer him what I knew, but I knew, even at that time, this guy is so much better of a baseball player than I am."

Betts moved up to High-A Salem in July, where he was perhaps even more impressive than he was in Greenville given the more advanced state of competition. On the way to posting a .341 average, .414 OBP, and .551 slugging mark with 7 homers in 51 games at a level where he was among the youngest in the league, Betts started to command attention outside the Red Sox organization.

In late July, the Brewers were shopping reliever Francisco Rodriguez. The Red Sox—who'd spent most of 2013 in first place in the AL East—were looking to upgrade their pitching. Milwaukee GM Doug Melvin asked if the Red Sox would consider a Betts-for-Rodriguez deal—the first time that Sox GM Ben Cherington could recall a team asking about Betts. Cherington declined—the first of many asks about Betts he'd turn away. The Sox weren't ready to say definitively that Betts had All-Star potential, and they already had an entrenched star, Dustin Pedroia, at Betts's natural position, second base, but they'd seen enough to know that they didn't want to part with him before seeing what he might become.

Betts reached base in each of Salem's final thirty games of the regular season, hitting .418 with a 1.151 OPS, then served as a tone setter as Salem swept all five of its playoff games to win a Carolina League championship.

Late in the year, farm director Ben Crockett was trying to make sense of Betts's trajectory, and to reconcile his modest 2012 season with a dominant 2013 campaign. He asked longtime Sox catcher Jason Varitek for his thoughts, and took note of the conviction evident in the answer.

"He said, 'This guy is going to be a major league All-Star. No doubt,'" recounted Crockett.

For Betts, 2013 represented a breathtaking breakthrough. He hit .314/.417/.506 with 15 homers, 55 extra-base hits, and 38 steals, while showing Gold Glove–caliber defensive potential at second. At twenty years old, he represented one of the best five-tool prospects in the minors. He had a now-obvious chance to be part of a Phase Three championship foundation in Boston.

Less obvious was how soon Betts would be thrown into the big leagues, and how overwhelming he'd find it there.

•   •   •

MOOKIE BETTS MADE THE PROSPECT handbook in 2014. He was now No. 7 in the Red Sox system, No. 75 in all of the minors. Still, he wasn't expected to be in the big leagues that year.

Early in Cherington's tenure as farm director, the Red Sox had introduced an almost-annual January Rookie Development Program in Boston. The one- to two-week program was meant to ease the transition of players to the big leagues. The organization identified players who were viewed as likely to reach the big leagues in the next twelve to eighteen months. In most years, a group of eight to twelve players came to Boston to take part in daily workouts (involving both baseball activities and strength and conditioning sessions), gain familiarity with Fenway Park, and meet members of the Red Sox coaching staff.

In 2014, five members of the draft class of 2011—first-rounders Matt Barnes, Blake Swihart, and Henry Owens, fourth-rounder Noe Ramirez, and ninth-rounder Travis Shaw—were among the ten players invited to take part. Betts wasn't. But when Double-A Portland opened its 2014 season, the Red Sox got their first signal that the snub may have been a mistake.

The Portland team featured a remarkable depth of high-ceiling, standout prospects, what seemed a forming embarrassment of riches in the Red Sox farm system. The team featured Owens, who started the All-Star Futures Game for the U.S. team that July. Swihart likewise stood out behind the plate, a player whose athleticism, offensive potential, and leadership would earn him the designation as the consensus top catching prospect in the minors by the end of 2014. Left-hander Brian Johnson, first baseman Travis Shaw, and shortstop Deven Marrero likewise looked like solid future big leaguers.

It was an exceptional team—and the continuation of years in which the Red Sox featured a minor league team in their system not just with an isolated prospect but with a wave of them. The

Sea Dogs went 88-54, the best record in the history of the franchise, earning recognition from *Baseball America* as the Minor League Team of the Year. The team's manager, Billy McMillon, enjoyed pushing the group with an eye toward a bigger future prize.

"We're trying to get you to have major league value, and major league value for us means being able to play October baseball," McMillon told his players. "We're trying to mold kids so that when it's the eighteenth inning of Game Three of the World Series, playing on the West Coast, we're able to perform."

From the first day of 2014, Portland performed. If there had been any questions about whether Betts's 2013 breakout was an illusion, they were dispelled that first game. Facing Reading left-hander Jesse Biddle, at the time considered one of the better left-handed pitching prospects in the game, Betts worked a full count before blasting a homer to left-center field. That was his first hit in a 4-for-4 game.

In Portland, Betts burst from his modest profile to become one of the most hyped prospects in the minors. He opened the year by reaching base in 35 consecutive games—running his on-base streak to 66 straight games dating to the previous year in High-A Salem, 71 straight including the previous year's playoffs. He'd become a celebrity prospect, the diligent chronicling of his daily deeds on WEEI.com (disclaimer: I was the chronicler) introducing the hashtagged phenomenon of #featsofmookie.

Yet with the Red Sox struggling and Betts occupying a position—second base—occupied by Dustin Pedroia, whose contract extension with the Red Sox ran through 2021, speculation swirled that the twenty-one-year-old might become a trade candidate. Nothing could have been further from the truth.

The Red Sox, who'd kept Betts out of trade discussions in 2013 while waiting to see what they had, now knew: Betts looked like a potential A2—a perennial All-Star, and a moldable one at that, someone whose athleticism should allow him to move to a position other than second base.

The question was which position. Though Betts was drafted as a second baseman, he had also played short and center field in high school, and in fact suggested that he was most comfortable in the outfield. Mindful of Pedroia's ownership of second, Betts made a point every day with Portland of spending a round of batting practice in the outfield, trying to simulate game conditions in case the Sox elected to move him there. Still, given that he remained a second baseman in early May, Betts wasn't necessarily anticipating a quick rise to the big leagues.

"I'm only a hundred miles away [from Fenway], but it feels like a thousand," Betts said. "I may be close to [Boston], but it doesn't mean that I'm close to playing for them."

Yet at Fenway, outfield production was fast becoming a problem. Victorino was still dealing with injuries. Sizemore, after a hot start, had tapered off. Bradley and Daniel Nava, another 2013 Icarus whose wings melted in 2014, were offering little offensive production. It was time to move Betts into the left lane of player development.

On May 17, he went 0-for-4—the first time since the previous August 1 that he'd failed to reach base at least once in a minor league game. The next day marked the first of the rest of his baseball life, as Betts, who was hitting an amazing .383 with a .452 OBP, .593 slugging percentage, 6 homers, and 18 stolen bases in 37 games, started in center field.

Shumpert was there with Betts at the time. If Betts had any uncertainty about what the exposure to the outfield meant, his uncle cleared it for him: the Red Sox were trying to create a channel that Betts could travel to reach the big leagues.

"Now we go," Betts recalled thinking at the time.

By early June he was in Triple-A Pawtucket. Red Sox players and coaches were aware of the twenty-one-year-old's electrify-

ing performance in the minors, the daily stories of his remarkable feats, and were antsy for his arrival in the big leagues. In
Triple-A, Betts quickly gave further validation to those sentiments.

In his second game for the PawSox, he stepped to the plate
against the Durham Bulls (the top minor league affiliate of the
Tampa Bay Rays) in the top of the eleventh inning in a contest
tied, 7–7. In the scouts' section behind the plate, where Red
Sox coordinators George Lombard and David Howard sat, chat-
ter increased. One scout of another team said that Betts would
go deep. Another scoffed that Betts had no shot at clearing the
fences. Betts almost immediately blasted a pitch over Durham's
Blue Monster, a thirty-two-foot-high, Fenway-like wall in left
field.

From then on, the scouts doubted Betts at their own peril.
In Triple-A, he hit .346 with a .417 OBP, .503 slugging mark,
and 5 homers in 45 games. By late June, in the span of roughly
thirteen months, Betts had gone from a player considering the
end of his baseball career to one on the cusp of the big leagues
who'd been the best player on the field on most nights at four
different levels of the minors.

As he made a virtually seamless transition to center field and
then right, he'd fulfilled all the on-field prerequisites. On June
27, Betts and his fiancée were headed out for pizza following a
PawSox game when he received a call from Kevin Boles. Something had happened, the Pawtucket manager said. Betts needed
to return to McCoy Stadium.

"It kind of scared me, honestly," said Betts.

It shouldn't have. Boles simply wanted to deliver the news
face-to-face: Betts was getting called up to New York. He made
his big league debut on Sunday night in a nationally televised
game against the Yankees and went 1-for-3 with his first hit (a

single) and a walk. Yet Betts would soon be challenged in ways that no one had expected.

During his ascent through the minors, Betts had emerged as one of the most popular players in the system, connecting easily with players at every level. He frequently organized activities and meals with teammates. In the majors, where deference to veterans was expected, Betts didn't feel like he could do the same. Attempts to create bridges were at times rebuffed by teammates with an implied suggestion that Betts should respect his place and the nature of seniority. Betts, in conversations with Farrell and Cherington, expressed confusion.

The older players on the Red Sox such as Jon Lester and John Lackey weren't necessarily malicious so much as they were repeating the lessons they'd been taught, in the same way that they'd encountered them. That said, as more and more players were getting called up in 2014 and further altering the personality of the previous year's champions, the tone of the veterans hardened, the tough love became ever tougher.

"We had the old-boy crew," said bullpen coach Dana LeVangie. "They expected that [the young players] were going to go through the same shit that they did."

The managers and coaches—many with backgrounds of coaching in the minors—didn't particularly care for it, but it was difficult to ask the players who'd been so good at minimizing their own mistakes the previous year to become suddenly forgiving of them the next.

Then, during Betts's first homestand as a member of the Red Sox, he had a close friend from Nashville in town. Before a game, he invited him into the clubhouse. For Betts, who'd grown up attached to his uncle's hip inside the culture of professional baseball, the idea of a friend being in the clubhouse before the game seemed relatively harmless—even if Betts understood that it was inappropriate for his friend to be drinking a beer as game time neared. But to the Red Sox veterans, it was a significant transgression for a young player, a point made clear to him in harsh terms.

As Betts would later explain, it was an innocent mistake. "I didn't know those type of rules. From what I knew, the clubhouse is like your home." But other players saw it differently and let Betts know it.

Betts's sense of being an outsider was further heightened just before the All-Star break. Before a game in Houston, he showed up to the clubhouse hours before most of his teammates to take early batting practice. With time to kill, Betts stretched out to take a nap on a couch. Again, the team's veterans jumped on him, and Betts got called into Farrell's office to be advised on some of the unwritten rules of which he was running afoul. (Hindsight suggests Betts was a pioneer: a couple of years later, the Red Sox installed a sleep room at Fenway, and encouraged players to nap before games if so inclined.)

Raquel Ferreira, perhaps the most trusted voice for young players in the organization, reached out to Betts. She ticked off a handful of transgressions.

"He said, 'Raquel, what am I doing right?'" Ferreira remembered. "I had to explain to him, 'This team is losing. When you're losing, things become magnified to a degree that you have no control over. We want you to be comfortable. Just don't act comfortable, because there's a difference.'

"But with that 2014 team, they took things to another level, scrutinizing every little thing that some guys did, where all it takes is someone to pull you aside and say, 'Hey, don't do that.'"

Both Bogaerts and Bradley largely believed the veterans had good intentions, but Betts couldn't fathom why teammates would treat each other in the fashion he experienced. His struggle was reflected on the field. He got sent back down to Triple-A once in July and again after a brief call-up in early August.

For most, a demotion from the big leagues to the minors feels like a descent into purgatory. Nothing could have been further from how Betts felt after being sent down for the second time. He arrived in the PawSox clubhouse, dropped his bag with dramatic flair, and pronounced, "I'm back."

"It was almost a sigh of relief," said Betts. "I could go back to Triple-A with all my boys and I could have fun. Play the game, have fun, I'm playing every day, I can laugh and joke and all those type of things."

He felt at home again.

To CHERINGTON AND OTHERS IN the front office and player development system who knew Betts, his turbulent transition to the big leagues suggested that something had gone awry. A tension had formed between the culture created by the 2013 holdovers and the new wave of players graduating to the big leagues. The younger players came across as polite, humble, and unassuming, a contrast to the brashness of the 2013 group or the prior standout wave of Red Sox prospects (headlined by Dustin Pedroia, Jonathan Papelbon, and Hanley Ramirez) that had come through the minors.

Moreover, there was a cautiousness about them not just at the field but also away from it, perhaps a reflection of the changing possibilities and perils of celebrity in an age of social media and changing technology. ("Thank God," one Red Sox veteran once recalled of his early career shenanigans, "I came up before there were camera phones.")

It was noteworthy that Pedroia, Papelbon, and Jacoby Ellsbury had arrived in the big leagues after playing for elite college programs, teaching environments that had refined their fundamentals so that they didn't have as much to learn in pro ball. Betts and Bogaerts were arriving in the big leagues at ages when that previous wave had still been in the cocoon of school.

The new group was "very, very different—not just personality-wise, but I think in their approach to the game, too," said Ferreira. "The other group was crazy. These guys, a little more mellow, reserved, laid-back."

Members of the organization recognized an unanticipated issue, and had to address it to avoid oil-and-water cultural divides. First, they had the Triple-A staff offer clearer outlines of the behavioral expectations that awaited players transitioning from the minors to the big leagues. "Down below, they heard it from a stern voice that, 'We need to fix this. We need to do this right. When these guys get up here, there's no more fun and games,'" recounted LeVangie.

But while there were lessons to be learned, the catastrophic 2014 season—which ended with a 71-91 record—remained disquieting. The Red Sox had put their young players in an unfair position—insufficiently welcomed and supported, easily scapegoated for the struggles of their team, held to unrealistic expectations given their experience levels and the lack of production from the veterans around them.

The Red Sox were left to answer a lot of questions. Had they erred in their evaluations of their young players? Or did the problem instead rest with the big league culture? At a time when the farm system appeared to be loaded with impact prospects, some team officials endured an existential crisis.

"I do remember our farm system being very highly rated, but, 'Okay, what's that worth?'" said Duncan Webb, the 2014 assistant farm director. "As a group, we were collectively asking ourselves, 'Who cares? We've got this great farm system but we can't help them make the transition to the big leagues.'"

Cherington wasn't wavering on what he saw as the value of his team's prospect inventory. For the most part, he remained convinced of the talent of all of his young players even through their struggles, and simply felt that it was up to the team to do a better job of putting them in a position to succeed. As the Red Sox spun out of contention, he did question how he'd constructed the roster, and with July 31 approaching, he had decisions to make.

The Red Sox were slipping out of contention and had several potentially attractive trade chips in upcoming free agents Jon Lester, Andrew Miller, and Jake Peavy. Plus, there was John Lackey, who was under contract through 2015 but had made clear to the team that he, too, wanted out.

Typically, cellar dwellers will deal veterans for prospects who are either in the minors or in the earliest stages of their big league careers. But Cherington didn't follow script.

For one thing, he knew other teams were placing an increasingly enormous value on their own young potential standouts, even in the minors. Clubs interested in the Red Sox' stable of rental players simply weren't willing to discuss parting with six or more years of control over premium prospects in exchange for players who would provide just a few months of help. Second, Cherington had designs on competing in 2015.

Peavy was dealt on July 26 for a couple of young relievers (most notably Heath Hembree)—a traditional trade of a rental player. But on the morning of the July 31 trade deadline, Cherington traded Lester and another pending free agent, outfielder Jonny Gomes, to the A's for former All-Star slugger Yoenis Cespedes, who would be eligible for free agency after the 2015 season. Lackey was dealt to St. Louis for Allen Craig, an All-Star first baseman in 2013 whose production in 2014 had fallen apart due to a foot injury, as well as pitcher Joe Kelly, who'd pitched against the Sox in the 2013 World Series.

Though Miller was dealt to the Orioles for a very promising minor leaguer, left-hander Eduardo Rodriguez, the trade deadline showed a Red Sox team focused on adding players who had already gone through the transition to the big leagues and were, theoretically, in their prime seasons of their mid- to late twenties.

The return "was certainly influenced by the phases we were in and the knowledge that this isn't going to be a three-year reset," said Cherington. "We need to win in 2015. That did influence the targets, for sure."

That quest continued over the rest of 2014, as the Red Sox signed twenty-seven-year-old Rusney Castillo, who'd defected from Cuba, to a seven-year, $72.5 million deal on the assumption that he'd be ready to be a starting outfielder in the big leagues by 2015.

The Red Sox had been overreliant on young players who weren't ready for the considerable responsibility with which they'd been entrusted—and who, frankly, shouldn't have been given so much responsibility—through much of 2014. The team was focusing its capital to correct those missteps.

At the same time, the team was resisting the urge to overreact to the struggles of its young players by trading them.

"I don't believe 2014 was a referendum on young players," Cherington said late that year. "It was a lesson learned and we can take things from it. We just underperformed across the board. And now we're trying to build a winning team and one that can hopefully sustain a level over time, and young players are going to be a part of that."

BETTS RETURNED TO THE BIG leagues for good on August 18. He would put on a show for the next month and a half, hitting .304 with a .391 OBP, .857 OPS, four homers, and six steals in the final 39 games. Bogaerts hit .320 and smashed four homers in his final 25 games of the season. Castillo made a strong ten-game cameo at the end of the year, hitting .333 with a pair of homers.

Middlebrooks struggled to the end of the season and ultimately the Red Sox decided that he wasn't the player they'd once hoped he would be. He was dealt in the off-season to the Padres for backup catcher Ryan Hanigan.

Bradley likewise never emerged from his pronounced offensive difficulties in 2014. Indeed, he got sent down to Triple-A Pawtucket for a time in August, so lost in an offensive wilderness that Tim Hyers was summoned back from a scheduled stretch at home to try to help him fix his swing.

The disappointment and even embarrassment of a demotion can crush players. Some believe that they must make fundamental alterations to who they are in order to move on from failure—a potentially dangerous proposition. In Triple-A in the Red Sox organization, Bradley encountered voices that helped him to avoid that trap.

In 2013, Kevin Boles had managed Bradley on his ascent to Portland. As Bradley's manager in Triple-A Pawtucket in 2014 and 2015, Boles could remind the outfielder who he'd been and who he could be.

"You can't be a frontrunner in player development," Boles said.

Boles expressed disbelief at the suggestions that Bradley was uncoachable and remained steadfast in his faith in the player. At one point, when it seemed as if Bradley was lost in an organizational shuffle with the acquisitions of Cespedes and Castillo, the PawSox manager pulled Bradley aside during batting practice at McCoy Stadium.

"I know what a player looks like, and I know you're an All-Star-caliber player, I know you're going to win Gold Gloves," Boles told him. "Whatever it takes, whatever we've got to do, just understand, whether it's in this uniform or another, don't ever forget what you're going to be, and don't listen to the noise."

Unquestionably, some members of the organization had become skeptical of the outfielder's potential to thrive in Boston. But Bradley had enough backers—people who believed the suggestions of his lack of coachability were unfounded, and who recognized his defense as so remarkable that he still had a good chance to be a valuable big leaguer even with a modest offensive profile—that the Sox never considered dumping him for a complementary piece.

"Ben's patience with players was off the charts. He knew what he had. And he was going to live and die by it," said LeVangie. "Thank God for that."

Despite the many challenges of 2014, the Red Sox continued to prize the young talent in their system. Their view of the value of such players was undiminished. In fact, within months of the Red Sox' second last-place finish in three years, the team offered a sign that it placed as high a premium on elite young talent as any organization in baseball.

CHAPTER 6

MONCADA AND THE DRIVE

Two numbers announced the arrival of Yoan Moncada in Greenville, South Carolina, when he made the most anticipated prospect debut in Red Sox history on May 18, 2015.

The first was 24, the uniform number he was to wear for the Greenville Drive. For the first time in their franchise history, the Drive—the South Atlantic League, Single-A affiliate of the Red Sox since 2006—produced and sold T-shirts with a prospect's name and uniform number, hoping to capitalize on the fascination with an international sensation.

Drive management wasn't alone in its recognition of a potential watershed opportunity. Major League Baseball sent two authenticators to Greenville to collect mementos, including a signed jersey from Moncada's first official minor league game. Such attention—and marketing dreams—had been reserved previously for the first professional games of No. 1 overall picks, like Stephen Strasburg and Bryce Harper, or for standout prospects just before their big league call-ups (Carlos Correa and Kris Bryant).

Never before had a teenager signed as an international amateur received this sort of attention. But then, none had ever had a path to professional baseball quite like Moncada's. Nor, for that matter, had there ever been a number that hovered over a prospect's debut quite like the second one that followed Moncada to Greenville: sixty-three million.

In the more than fifty-year history of the amateur draft that baseball had introduced in 1965—a system that rewards the worst team in baseball with the top pick the following season—the Red Sox have never had one of the top two selections in the first round. At times, team officials had tossed around the question of how much enormously talented players at the top of the draft, such as Strasburg or Harper, might fetch if they were free agents rather than subject to a process that entrusted a player's rights to a single team. Strasburg got a $7.5 million bonus as part of a four-year, $15.1 million deal when he was drafted by the Nationals; Harper got a $6.25 million bonus as part of a five-year, $9.9 million deal. If all thirty teams could bid, would a player who had never participated in a single professional game command $30 million, $50 million, or perhaps even more?

In Moncada, the team essentially had a chance to answer that question.

"Opportunities like this seldom come to you," said Ben Cherington. "There's a scarcity thing that's there, that's in play, on top of the raw evaluation."

The Red Sox had come to understand the scarcity of a talent like Moncada over the course of five years and through in-person looks at him at more than twenty international games. Latin America crosschecker Todd Claus was the first member of the organization to write a report—a brief one, as it were, a single line on an Excel spreadsheet—on Moncada as a fifteen-year-old whose physicality and explosive tools stood out in a sixteen-and-under tournament in Mexico in 2010.

The Sox had seen him develop for years in international tournaments and through the grainy video feeds of Cuba's Serie Nacional, in which he'd played in 2012–13 and 2013–14. They'd further gotten a glimpse of him at a showcase for all thirty teams organized by his agent, David Hastings, on a hastily sculpted field in November 2014 in Guatemala.

"I went down a week ahead of time and the grass was, like, up to here," Hastings said, holding his hand at knee height.

Finally, on January 16, 2015, Moncada took part in a work-out at the Red Sox spring training facility in Fort Myers, with an armada of front-office members and scouts watching as the switch-hitter took live batting practice against five pitchers who displayed a wide range of throwing styles—righties and lefties, hard throwers and junkballers.

After seeing Moncada take roughly thirty at-bats, the team arrived at the belief, collectively, that he projected to have a plus bat, good for at least a 60 grade on the 20–80 scouting scale. It wasn't outlandish to envision him hitting .280 to .300 with an excellent on-base percentage, given his apparently discerning eye at the plate. His left-handed swing was particularly promising, commonly drawing comparisons to that of Mariners second baseman Robinson Cano—a player whom Moncada so revered that he not only wore Cano's number 24 but also named his son Robinson in homage.

Moncada showed power; his incredible strength gave him the obvious potential to clear fences. And he had the attributes of an average to above-average defensive player, with potentially elite speed. At the least, he looked like an above-average every-day big leaguer—a B1 on the Red Sox scouting scale. If all of his skills came together at the same time, he had a chance to emerge as a five-tool superstar.

That combination was almost never available to the Red Sox—or, for that matter, to other teams—in amateur circles. Over and over, the native of Cuba was described as a linebacker in a baseball uniform, a six-foot-two, 225-pound force whose power did not compromise his running ability.

"He lights you up, for sure," said one scout.

The curiosity about him extended beyond his skill and physique. Moncada had gone through legal channels to file the paperwork and visa application necessary to seek official permission to leave the country in 2014—a startling contrast to the many players who'd endured harrowing defectors' tales, some of which had included smuggling and kidnapping. That Moncada had managed to avoid such lengths was a subject of fascination in baseball circles—though such curiosity about his journey out of Cuba was dwarfed by speculation about what he might be able to do on a Major League Baseball field.

He represented the kind of dynamic, spectacular athlete who is almost invariably fitted with shoulder pads in the States. Even if Moncada had pursued a baseball career as a teenager attending a U.S. high school, his combination of baseball skill, strength, and athleticism would have made him a candidate for the top pick in some MLB drafts. The Red Sox, who never had the chance to pick at the top, recognized a rare opportunity, and a player worthy of a whopper of a check.

The Sox weren't alone. While some teams had reservations about Moncada, particularly after seeing him get carved up in private workouts by left-handed pitchers with diverse pitch mixes, there was nonetheless considerable interest in his services. A player who had made four dollars a month playing baseball in Cuba was certain to receive a signing bonus that would blow past all precedents.

"It will be a fucking massive acquisition cost," said one National League evaluator at the time. "We're all going to be like, 'You've got to be shitting me,' when we see what the final number is."

Zack Scott, the Red Sox director of major league operations, synthesized the projections of the different evaluators who'd seen Moncada—the baseline expectations, ceiling, and most likely performance level—to create a probabilistic model of the player's future performance that could, in turn, serve as the basis for a financial valuation. What was the likelihood that he'd be a B1 or an A2? How likely, based on the team's internal assessments, was it that he'd be just a C1 or, God forbid, a bust? The likelihood of each scenario would have to be weighted in coming to a final number.

The Red Sox made an initial bid of a $25 million signing bonus, but mindful of the considerable interest of other teams— particularly the Yankees and Padres—and believing other teams would go north of their initial bid, they eventually bumped it up to $31.5 million. Yet even that wasn't the full extent of the Red Sox' liability. They had already spent beyond their permitted international amateur bonus pool of $1.88 million in 2014–15 by signing a class headlined by pitcher Anderson Espinoza ($1.8 million) and Christopher Acosta ($1.5 million) at the start of that bonus period. And even if they hadn't, Moncada's bonus would push them well beyond that mark—with the consequence that under the terms of baseball's Collective Bargaining Agreement, the team would also have to pay a 100 percent tax to Major League Baseball on any further money they spent that spring—a massive disincentive, and indeed a potentially prohibitive one for teams without the incredible reserves of the Red Sox. (At least one team involved in the bidding for Moncada was capped by the possibility of having to write MLB a check for more than $25 million to pay the penalty.)

At the same time, the CBA created some motivation for the team to damn the torpedoes and keep spending. Because the Sox had already spent past their suggested bonus pool limits during the 2014-15 signing period, they'd be unable to sign any players to bonuses in excess of $300,000 in the next two international signing periods of 2015–16 and 2016–17. That restriction would keep the Sox away from the elite international teenagers in the next two years. Moncada might represent their last shot at a true standout international prospect for a while.

(In 2015–16, the Red Sox signed some of the most highly regarded international amateur prospects out of Venezuela for $300,000. In mid-2016, Major League Baseball determined that the Red Sox had engaged in "package" deals, in which the team signed multiple players who worked with the same trainer for the maximum allowable bonus of $300,000, and let the trainers redistribute bonus payments from lesser prospects to the best ones in an attempt to circumvent their spending limits. Once MLB made that determination, it made the players who'd signed via package deals free agents while banning the Red Sox from signing any international amateurs during the 2016–17 international signing period. Though MLB penalized the Sox, the practice of package deals was considered relatively commonplace in the industry, with one international scouting veteran from another team rolling his eyes at the thought that, in the relatively lawless international amateur scouting realm, the Sox had their driver's license suspended for going 60 in a 55.)

The opportunity to add a teenager with such extraordinary physical gifts, a player to whom the Red Sox otherwise wouldn't have access, and a chance to take one last hellacious swing for the fences in the international amateur market was compelling. To the Red Sox, $63 million—the $31.5 million bonus and $31.5 million penalty paid to MLB—represented a worthwhile risk.

Even at that incredible sum, the team wasn't sure that it would land him. But on February 23, 2015, while eating lunch with his parents in Jupiter, Florida, Red Sox international scouting director Eddie Romero received a phone call from David Hastings.

"I was pessimistic. I thought we had a great offer. [But] I knew there were other teams involved in it," said Romero. "[Hastings called and] was like, 'Hey, we've got a deal.' . . . I was floored."

Romero stepped outside to confirm what he'd just heard: the Red Sox had won the bidding for Moncada. A flurry of phone calls followed. Romero called Cherington, who had to reach out to principal owner John Henry—a task made somewhat more difficult by the fact that Henry, the principal owner of Fenway Sports Group (the parent company that owned the Red Sox, Liverpool Football Club, and Roush Fenway Racing, among other interests), had been preoccupied while attending Daytona 500 weekend. It took forty-five minutes of triangulating calls, but finally, Romero returned to lunch with his parents.

"I remember my mom being like, 'So did you get Moncada?'" recalled Romero. "My family went crazy [at the news]. That was funny. My mom was the first one [to know]. I think had we not gotten him she would've started criticizing me right there."

It wasn't *that* hard to understand why the Red Sox would make such an outlay. After all, a year earlier, when the team had explored the trade market for left-hander Jon Lester, they found a dearth of suitors willing to part with top prospects. Players like Julio Urias and Corey Seager of the Dodgers and Tyler Glasnow of the Pirates were off the table, even though Lester was a perennial All-Star. If Moncada became a top prospect, his value would justify and likely exceed what the Red Sox were willing to spend. Talent, not money, was baseball's most valuable currency.

Still, the sum inspired some sticker shock, even inside the organization.

"Honestly, my initial reaction was, 'Holy shit,'" said Claus, who explained that he wasn't stunned so much by the magnitude of the sum as by what it said about the team's commitment to spare no expense in building its prospect base.

That incredible dollar figure for a teenager struck some as preposterous. Certainly, all expectations about Moncada were framed by that record-setting sum, one that made the switch-hitter famous in the baseball world—and to a degree, outside it—even among those who had never seen him play. The Red Sox had placed a dollar figure on the true worth of a prospect, with a sum that still had many shaking their heads as he prepared for his minor league debut.

ACROSS THE FIELD FROM MONCADA in Greenville on May 18 was a man with a unique perspective on Moncada-mania. Glenn Hubbard, the bench coach of the Lexington Legends, the Royals' Single-A affiliate, couldn't help but be amused by the pomp surrounding the debut.

Twenty-five years earlier, Hubbard had been a Braves minor league coach in the Rookie-Level Gulf Coast League when Atlanta's top draft pick—and the first overall selection in 1990—made his debut. There was, Hubbard noted wryly, no one on site to authenticate memorabilia from Chipper Jones's first professional game.

Then again, Jones signed with the Braves for $275,000—less than one-half of a percent of what the Red Sox had invested in Moncada between his bonus and the MLB penalty. Moreover, Jones began his eventual Hall of Fame professional career in relative obscurity, long before the Internet made it possible for prospect hounds to find a player's box scores the day after the game, let alone to watch a video feed of his game in real time from just about any corner of the world. No one cared, or in all likelihood even knew, that Jones hit a meager .229 with a .592 OPS as an eighteen-year-old in his first professional summer in the Braves organization. Moncada, Hubbard recognized, was walking into circumstances impossibly different from those that greeted Jones at the inception of his stellar career.

"Could he become a Cano? Who's to know?" said Hubbard.

"But you'll never live up to it. He'll never live up to thirty million dollars, whatever he does. . . . It's hard to live up to all the hype."

The Red Sox were mindful of that notion, and so they wanted to take their time to allow the Cuban sensation to acclimate to professional baseball life before thrusting him into a spotlight by assigning him to an affiliate. Whereas the Padres had discussed with Moncada a path to the big leagues in his 2015 pro debut, both the Red Sox and David and Jo Hastings—newbies to the agent game (David Hastings was a CPA, Jo Hastings the owner of Habana Café, a wonderful Cuban restaurant in St. Petersburg whose appeal had brought them in contact with the expat Cuban baseball community) who had taken on the role not just of Moncada's agents but also as surrogate parents for a player who was trying to acclimate to a new culture—believed that there was no rush.

It made more sense to build a solid foundation at the bottom of the minor league ladder than to accelerate toward the top of it, particularly given that Moncada was not merely adapting to a new professional routine but a new life in which he seemed eager for any stability he could get. When Moncada got his bonus and could buy a place of his own, he chose to live down the street from the Hastingses in St. Petersburg rather than moving to Miami. Even with a place of his own, he often chose to crash in a loft above the Hastingses' garage, in a room where the logos of the Red Sox were on the blanket and towels.

One insight into the startling novelty of what Moncada was encountering came in spring training, shortly after he signed.

"I remember seeing a giant trash bag—one of the giant outdoor trash bags—of Twinkies. I asked somebody, 'What's with the Twinkies?'" recalled J. T. Watkins, a catcher in the Red Sox system at the time.

The entire, enormous bag of Twinkies belonged to the

sculpted Moncada, who had swooned when first introduced to the dessert by a teammate that spring.

"We all have our vices," said Watkins. "Twinkies aren't so bad. It could be worse."

Still, the Red Sox recognized that even something as small as Twinkies underscored the need to educate Moncada not just in their routines but also in nutrition and other aspects of his professional life. He had a lot to learn, and the team didn't want everything to fall on him in a crash course.

Cherington, Crockett, and several minor league coordinators took part in a conference call to establish a blueprint for Moncada's career. Once Moncada reached High-A Salem and especially Double-A Portland, they felt, the temptation to rush him through the system to help at the big league level, and potentially to shortcut some aspects of his player development, might be considerable.

A stay of more than two months in extended spring training in Fort Myers—where games took place in the obscurity of back fields often visited by no more than a dozen onlookers, most of them friends or family of the players—followed by an assignment to Single-A Greenville thus represented the best chance to give Moncada a professional foundation. No full-season level in the minor leagues is more focused on establishing the significance of routines than A-ball, as became evident starting at 3 P.M. on May 18, when Moncada joined his fellow Drive teammates in the extensive pregame work that Greenville manager Darren Fenster and his coaching staff emphasized.

"This level is such a huge part of their development. It's the foundation of what they're going to do," said Fenster. "For the majority of kids, it's their first full season. For the guys who were in the [Gulf Coast League], it's their first time playing the games under lights in front of crowds. They're going to remember this. This is the base of everything that gets built."

For Moncada and other players in Single-A, Greenville represented a place not just to play but also for the introduction of norms—how to act like a professional on and off the field, being at the right place at the right time, the kind of work to do in preparation for games, and even off-field considerations such as regular English classes. (In this regard, in particular, Moncada would follow a different development path, as players from Latin America who come through the Dominican academy have regular English classes from a much earlier age.)

The idea that work habits and routine mattered more than in-game results initially proved jarring to Moncada in a way that it did not to other players who had already spent months or years more in the Red Sox farm system. In his first days in Greenville, for instance, he would wonder what he'd done wrong when hitting coach Nelson Paulino—"Pepe," who in 2015 was entering his eighteenth year as a Red Sox minor league coach—asked him to meet for early batting practice, a setting in which the instructor could provide the player with additional one-on-one attention.

"Moncada went to him and said, 'Why am I in trouble? Why don't you like me?'" recounted Tim Hyers, the Red Sox minor league hitting coordinator in 2015. "[Moncada] almost felt like it was punishment that he was out there doing early work. He didn't understand that it's what we do out here and we valued his development. Development is having daily routines and sticking to it."

That message likely was easier for the Red Sox to deliver in Greenville than any other affiliate level. Undoubtedly, Moncada's reputation—and awareness of his historic bonus figure—would precede him in every city where the Drive played in the South Atlantic League.

But in Greenville, he wouldn't be isolated. The Drive roster featured a startling depth of talent among players who were close in age to Moncada, who turned twenty in his second week with Greenville, to the point where it was fair to wonder whether he was even the best prospect on the team.

Moncada initially underwhelmed in games. He went 0-for-3 with a walk in his debut, reaching on an error and committing one of his own when he tried to rush a throw and lifted his glove too soon while trying to field a grounder, thus letting it sneak past him. The next night, he committed two more errors and was hitless in his first four at-bats with a pair of strikeouts before he dribbled an infield hit down the third-base line—with the ball immediately being removed from the game for authentication and future auction.

Yet while Moncada didn't necessarily put together a prospect highlight reel in his initial two games, several of his teammates did.

Third baseman Rafael Devers, a cherubic eighteen-year-old whose braces were frequently displayed by the smile that seemed constantly affixed to him whenever he stood on a field, proved a show-stealer in Moncada's first game. Twice he lofted what appeared as routine fly balls to center off the bat. Both times those balls kept traveling deeper and deeper, clanging off the fence roughly four hundred feet from the plate for doubles. Those hits would have signaled middle-of-the-order power for a player in his mid-twenties; for an eighteen-year-old, such shows of strength were eye-opening.

Devers shared time at third base with Michael Chavis, the Red Sox' top pick in the 2014 draft. Chavis—a five-foot-eleven fire hydrant of a power hitter—had delighted as an amateur in taking aim during batting practice at cars passing on a road behind the left-field fence of his high school. It was only natural that in Greenville, the right-handed hitter was similarly tempted to target an apartment building in left-center.

His approach was crude. In 2015, Chavis's solution to struggles in his first full professional season seemed to be to swing harder in hopes of clearing the fences by an ever-larger margin, often with the result that he'd strike out. But when he did connect, it wasn't hard to imagine how his power might translate one day to Fenway Park. Moncada's debut offered an opportunity to engage in such day dreams, as Chavis (serving as designated hitter) threatened the apartment residents with a long homer to left-center in his 1-for-4 day.

Shortstop Javier Guerra, a native of Panama who'd signed with the Red Sox, often anchored the Greenville infield. He was one of the signature additions of Romero's first full international signing class in the summer of 2012.

Guerra exhibited an uncommon earnestness about every aspect of his development, whether in English classes or on the field. His minor league managers made a point of trying, often unsuccessfully, to get him to smile, yet they had enormous appreciation for his skill and determination. In the Gulf Coast League in 2014, manager Tom Kotchman once informed the entire team that he could imagine no better lineup than one that was composed of nine Guerras. (The declaration was greeted with bewildered silence from other players, who wondered why they would not make the cut.) The shortstop's sense of purpose had allowed him to make significant strides in each of his professional seasons since signing. By 2015, the nineteen-year-old displayed not only defensive skills that were amplified by a tremendous baseball IQ but also emergent offensive abilities that permitted reveries about an above-average everyday shortstop.

After sitting out Moncada's debut—a product of the prospect

crowd in Greenville's infield—Guerra collected two hits and stole home in his new teammate's second game.

"He might have the highest ceiling of the group, because in addition to physical tools, he has instincts that are incredibly hard to teach," said Fenster.

Guerra and Moncada were slated to share time with middle infielder Mauricio Dubon, who had entered the system as a virtual unknown in the 26th round of the 2013 draft ("He was my backup guy on the left side of the infield," Fenster recalled of his time as Dubon's manager in the Gulf Coast League in 2013) but who had quickly forced the team to view him as something more than roster filler.

Prior to his junior year of high school, Dubon left Honduras—a country with almost no baseball infrastructure—to play summer ball while living with a host family in Sacramento. It was a jarring choice for a kid whose mother in his home country had never even permitted him to sleep over at a friend's house.

"That she let me go to another country was kind of surprising," Dubon said. "It was hard, but I knew what I wanted. If that was what it was going to take, I was going to do it."

Dubon had attended a bilingual school in Honduras, which gave him a foundation with which to connect quickly with others in the States, both in school and after he was drafted. By the time he was in Greenville, the charismatic twenty-year-old was not only bilingual but bicultural—an incredibly valuable clubhouse presence who was treated, at times, as an extension of the coaching staff (Dubon took it upon himself to translate for teammates when they spoke to reporters, for instance).

The Red Sox had Dubon room with Moncada in 2015, and in 2016 he roomed with Devers in High-A Salem. He showed tremendous leadership and was seen as an asset in helping the development of other players, even as the skinny middle infielder began to gain strength and emerge as an impressive prospect in his own right.

In Moncada's second game, Dubon—who showed the athleticism and arm to play short or second, the speed and instincts to steal bases, and strong bat-to-ball skills that suggested a hitter who would be able to hit for average in the big leagues—hammered a ball to the warning track in left-center for a double. That growing ability not just to spray singles over the infield but to occasionally drive the ball suddenly had Dubon commanding attention as a potential big leaguer, possibly even a middle infield regular.

"Those two middle infielders, Guerra and Dubon, you watched them turn double plays and do stuff that was like, 'Wow, it's like watching the Cuban national team in the middle infield,'" observed Jason Varitek, the longtime Red Sox catcher who by 2015 was a member of the front office.

And there was more. Right-hander Michael Kopech, who'd been selected shortly after Chavis in the first round of the 2014 draft, was likened by one scout to a Greek god—presumably Zeus, armed with a quiver of thunderbolts.

Kopech, who had grown up in East Texas idolizing Nolan Ryan and Randy Johnson, fulfilled a teleological quest by crossing the 100-mph threshold for the first time in his life in early 2015. He regularly overpowered opponents solely on the strength of one of the most explosive fastballs in the minors.

Brian Bannister, then a pro scout who would later in the year be named the team's director of pitching analysis, saw in the pitch data reports on Kopech a fastball whose combination of velocity (mid-90s to triple digits), spin rate (2600–2700 RPM), and spin direction (Kopech had "true spin" on the transverse axis, giving his fastball what hitters experienced as an explosive ride as it whooshed across the plate) most closely resembled superstar Justin Verlander. No one knew if Kopech would develop the complementary arsenal to emerge as a starter or if he'd be a late-innings reliever, but it required little imagination to recognize a pitcher whose four-seam fastball alone gave him a chance to dominate opposing hitters.

And even beyond that celebrated group, there were other, less-heralded players who, like Dubon, were offering glimpses of talent that exceeded their modest amateur profiles. While pitcher Jalen Beeks, a short left-hander without a clear plus pitch in his repertoire whom the Sox selected in the 12th round of the 2014 draft out of Arkansas, was overshadowed on the roster, he didn't let that fact diminish his own big league ambitions.

"We're the most loaded minor league affiliate in all the minor leagues, but it's really cool, because they're all really talented," observed Beeks, who turned twenty-two during the season. "Everybody has their own path to the bigs. I try to stay in my little lane, let everything happen around me. I'm not going to throw one hundred like a lot of these guys are. Kopech throwing gas, I can't compete with raw talent like that. I've just got to pitch my game and hopefully it gets me where I want to go."

On a team as deep in prospects as Greenville, it would have been easy for Beeks to slip through the developmental cracks. But the opposite happened, with Drive pitching coach Walter Miranda working with the left-hander to start a process that saw Beeks overhauling every pitch he'd thrown in college all the way through the minors.

That sort of attention represented a hallmark of a player development system under Cherington, one that didn't take a stars-and-scrubs approach to advancing players through the minors. It wasn't hard for Fenster—a player who had embarked upon a professional career as a 12th-round selection after his senior year at Rutgers, and who'd advanced as high as Double-A in the Royals system before blowing out his knee in a big league spring training game in 2005—to commit to such an egalitarian approach.

"In terms of my ability to look at a guy in A-ball and say this guy is a surefire big leaguer and this guy surefire isn't, I'm not comfortable doing that," said Fenster. "If we just say in A-ball, with these guys so young, these are your future big leaguers and these are the guys we don't care about, we may miss out on a handful of guys in this group. . . . My job is not only to help prospects. It's to help everyone in uniform."

Still, while that approach created the possibility of long-term payoff through skills development of Beeks and others, in 2015 it was hard to look beyond the Drive players whose present tools screamed of future big league impact—particularly given that Moncada was not the last dazzling prospect who would join that affiliate group that year.

By mid-August, outfielder Andrew Benintendi—the Red Sox' first-round pick with the No. 7 overall selection out of the University of Arkansas in 2015—had demolished the New York–Penn League (a common entry point to pro ball for an advanced college prospect), hitting .290 with a .408 on-base percentage, .540 slugging mark, seven homers, and seven steals in 35 games.

He received a promotion on August 16 to full-season Greenville, a development track that the Red Sox employed only rarely for their most advanced players in their first professional seasons. He continued to pound opposing pitchers in the South Atlantic League, hitting .351/.430/.581 with more walks (10) than strikeouts (9) while clubbing four homers—including a tremendous at-bat that concluded with a walk-off homer on a 2-2 pitch against a 95-mph fastball on September 3—in nineteen games.

"Picture [Dustin] Pedroia playing center field with more speed and better overall instincts," one scout gushed upon seeing Benintendi with Greenville that August. "Him and Betts hitting one-two in the order in 2017 will be the best one-two combo in baseball."

And in the final days of the season, right-hander Anderson Espinoza—a starting pitcher who worked at 94–100 mph, spun nasty curveballs, and choked diving changeups—became the first seventeen-year-old Red Sox prospect to make a start at a full-season level in nearly forty years. The Venezuela native's pitch mix, small frame (five foot eleven), flexible fingers that permitted him to produce remarkable spin on his pitches, intelligence, and self-confidence reminded some onlookers of a teenage Pedro Martinez.

Martinez himself was among those who bought into the similarities.

"I firmly believe that he's going to do everything that I did in the big leagues if he's healthy, God willing," said Martinez. "This kid, he has no ceiling."

The same could be said about Moncada. After his initial struggles with the acclimation to Greenville, where he hit .200 with a .287 OBP and .289 slugging mark in his first 25 games, a chance to step back and decompress during the South Atlantic League All-Star break in late June permitted Moncada to secure his footing, in part thanks to an on-field redefinition.

Moncada's favorite aspect of the game in Cuba had been running, in part because of the connection it built between him and his father. His dad would take him to the beach and have him walk in the water while wearing boots that went over his ankles. While wearing the wet footwear, Moncada would then run a series of sprints in the sand—building the powerful stride that represented a signature trait.

Moncada's father, sensing his son's struggles in their roughly twice-a-week phone conversations, offered his son reassurance: Relax. Be yourself. Moncada had an idea of how to do just that.

After the All-Star break, Fenster moved Moncada up from the sixth spot in the batting order to the leadoff spot, where he'd spent most of his career in Cuba. The lineup move carried an implied message to Moncada that he was free to be the player he'd always been—and particularly the same game-changing force on the bases.

The dazzling tools started to show up in dazzling performance. In the remaining 56 six games of the season, he hit .310 with a .415 OBP, .500 slugging mark, 7 homers, and perhaps most astonishingly, stole 45 bases.

"It's been something that I don't even believe," Moncada beamed through a translator at the end of that season. "If I had done my best in the beginning, I would have gotten one hundred, easily."

With on-field performance came comfort off it. Moncada started to connect more easily with other members of the team and organization, who comfortably kidded him about his audacious style. A picture of 1980s celebrity Mr. T was taped in Moncada's locker after he'd run afoul of the organization's "no mohawks" policy. Moncada, who'd entered the Red Sox organization under unique circumstances that were almost sure to prove isolating, no longer felt like a player who occupied a bubble removed from the rest of his teammates. Even though Dubon was promoted to High-A Salem after the All-Star break and Kopech was suspended in July for testing positive for a banned stimulant—one that the right-hander insisted he did not knowingly take—any glimpse of the Greenville team for even a couple of days at any point in 2015 offered grounds for belief that the Red Sox had a bright future.

Members of the Red Sox weren't the only ones who felt that way. Greenville attracted droves of both agents—looking to add new clients who might one day be major league stars—

and scouts of opposing teams who were looking for players who might one day be pried from the Red Sox in trades that might transform their own organizations.

"Looking at that list on one team, that's going to be one of the most heavily scouted teams in the minor leagues because of its depth and quality. When you can go to one spot and see all those guys under one roof, it doesn't matter whether you think they'll move them or not; that's a place where you're going to want to spend some time," observed longtime scout Tom Mooney, who covered the Sox system for the Brewers for several years, including 2015. "There are affiliates you're going [to] and you're trying to find two or three guys to like. . . . It's so much more fun to scout when you've got five, six, seven guys. You might go two or three years and not see another club like that."

One evaluator after another made a point of seeing that Greenville group—yet there was one notable omission from the group that visited Fluor Field.

On August 13, 2015, with the Red Sox two weeks beyond the trade deadline, GM Ben Cherington was finally scheduled to travel to Greenville to see the group that had a chance to change the organization's fortunes—a roster in which the Red Sox had invested more than $70 million, more than some big league payrolls.

Yet on a layover in Charlotte, Cherington received a shocking call: during surgery to repair a hernia on August 10, manager John Farrell had been diagnosed with an aggressive but treatable form of non-Hodgkin's lymphoma that would require an almost immediate start of a chemotherapy regimen. Cherington returned immediately to Boston. He wouldn't have another chance to see the prized prospect group he'd assembled.

CHAPTER 7

CHANGE AT THE TOP

A SHOCK WAVE RAN THROUGH FENWAY Park at 9:39 P.M. on August 18, 2015. In the late innings of a 9–1 victory over Cleveland, the Red Sox issued a startling announcement via press release—a matter of such urgency that the team felt it could not wait until the next day or even the end of the game to make it:

**DAVE DOMBROWSKI TO JOIN RED SOX IMMEDIATELY
AS PRESIDENT OF BASEBALL OPERATIONS**

**Distinguished and Experienced Baseball Executive to Be
Responsible for All Baseball Matters**

Embedded in the same release was the note that Ben Cherington had "declined the opportunity to continue as General Manager."

In a way, Dombrowski was the antithesis of the Red Sox' roster building under Cherington. Just two weeks after he'd been fired at the conclusion of an impressive fourteen-year run as the Tigers architect, the Red Sox owners made sure they were first in line to hire a veteran front-office star—in many ways, the same aggressive approach that had characterized Dombrowski himself over the course of more than twenty-seven years as a GM and team president.

After the Red Sox' repeatedly poor returns on deals for big league players over the span of roughly twenty months, Dombrowski's appeal seemed obvious for the needs of the organization at that moment. He was a fearless dealmaker, with a long track record of successful blockbusters, perhaps most dramatically in trades that landed Hall of Fame talents such as Miguel Cabrera and Max Scherzer and helped turn the Tigers from a laughingstock franchise into a two-time American League pennant winner and five-time division champion under his watch.

Yet as impressive as his résumé was—"distinguished and experienced," to be sure—his entry to the Red Sox organization was startling both for its suddenness and for what it might represent. After thirteen seasons of general philosophical continuity under Theo Epstein and Cherington, the hiring of Dombrowski—whose fourteen-year tenure with the Tigers had been characterized chiefly by the willingness to trade prospects rather than build around them—signaled a potentially dramatic shift.

The Red Sox were less than two years removed from a World Series title, a marker of success in Phase One of Cherington's long-term blueprint. The team seemed to be moving closer to a brighter future—Phase Three—built around the young wave of players who had either entered the system during Cherington's watch or developed under it.

But Boston is a market that neither permits satisfaction with past glories nor suffers well the wait for better days ahead at the expense of *now*—particularly when faced with immediate circumstances that are not merely disappointing but embarrassing. The Red Sox sat in last place in the American League East in mid-August 2015, at risk of last-place conclusions to consecu-

At the Red Sox' spring training and extended spring training facility in Fort Myers, a signpost reminds players of the distance from the facility to the different affiliates in the organization. *(Alex Speier)*

ABOVE: Jair and Xander Bogaerts at Fenway Park on the day that they signed with the Red Sox as sixteen-year-olds in August 2009. *(Jair Bogaerts)*

RIGHT: Rafael Devers at the time of his signing with the Red Sox in the summer of 2013. *(Eddie Romero)*

Yoan Moncada at JetBlue Park on February 25, 2015, days after reaching an agreement to sign with the Red Sox for $31.5 million. *(Stan Grossfeld/ Boston Globe)*

LEFT: In 2011, eighteen-year-old Xander Bogaerts hit sixteen homers in 72 games with Single-A Greenville. *(Greenville Drive)*

ABOVE: Jackie Bradley Jr. made his pro debut with the Lowell Spinners in August 2011. *(John Corneau/Lowell Spinners)*

LEFT: As a nineteen-year-old, Mookie Betts didn't hit any homers and amassed just nine extra-base hits in 71 games with the Spinners. *(John Corneau/Lowell Spinners)*

Greenville Drive players, including Rafael Devers (second from left),
Mauricio Dubon (third from left), and Javier Guerra (far right), congregate
in the dugout on May 19, 2015, prior to Yoan Moncada's debut. *(Alex Speier)*

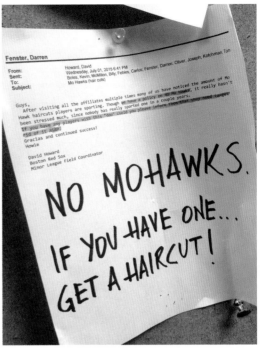

Yoan Moncada in the Greenville dugout prior to his second game with the Drive in May 2015. *(Alex Speier)*

Inside the Greenville clubhouse, a directive sent by field coordinator David Howard to affiliates offers a reminder of the rules governing coiffure. *(Alex Speier)*

Andrew Benintendi, remnants of shaving cream still on his face and shirt in celebration of his walkoff homer, walks to the clubhouse of Fluor Field in Single-A Greenville. *(Alex Speier)*

The minor league journey of Andrew Benintendi: from Fluor Field of the Class A Greenville Drive (top) to Double-A Portland (middle), then to the 2016 All-Star Futures Game at Petco Park (bottom), a showcase for the best minor league talent. *(Alex Speier)*

LEFT: In high school, Betts was named Tennessee state boys bowler of the year. In Single-A Greenville, he did a photo shoot at a bowling alley. *(Greenville Drive)*

ABOVE: Jackie Bradley Jr. in Triple-A Pawtucket in April 2013, a level to which he was assigned following his big league debut at the start of that season. *(Kelly O'Connor)*

LEFT: Xander Bogaerts at McCoy Stadium after his promotion to Pawtucket in June 2013. *(Kelly O'Connor)*

Mookie Betts warms up in Double-A Portland prior to a game in April 2014. *(Kelly O'Connor)*

After being taken with the No. 7 overall pick in the 2015 draft, Andrew Benintendi made his pro debut with the Spinners. *(John Corneau/Lowell Spinners)*

Rafael Devers hit .400 with a pair of homers during his nine-game stint in Pawtucket before getting called up to the big leagues in 2017. *(Kelly O'Connor)*

ABOVE: Rafael Devers (center) and Yoan Moncada (right) emerge from the World team dugout at the All-Star Futures Game in Miami in 2017.
(Alex Speier)

RIGHT: Pitcher Michael Kopech and infielder Mauricio Dubon (not pictured) joined fellow 2015 Greenville Drive teammates Devers and Moncada at the 2017 Futures Game.
(Alex Speier)

Welcome to the bigs: Christian Vazquez emerges from the dugout prior to his Red Sox debut on July 9, 2014. *(Jim Davis/Boston Globe)*

ABOVE: Xander Bogaerts announced his arrival in the 2013 playoffs. Here, he watches a double off of Tigers starter Max Scherzer in Game 6 of the 2013 ALDS. *(John Tlumacki/Boston Globe)*

RIGHT: David Ortiz, mentor to the Sox' young core before his retirement, celebrates a win with Bogaerts. *(Jim Davis/Boston Globe)*

Dave Dombrowski and John Farrell by the batting cage prior to Game 3 of the 2016 American League Division Series. *(Barry Chin/Boston Globe)*

Jackie Bradley Jr. (left), Andrew Benintendi (middle), and Mookie Betts (right) convened after Red Sox victories in 2016 and 2017 with their "Win, Dance, Repeat" celebration in the outfield. *(Barry Chin/Boston Globe)*

The exceptional outfield defense provided by Mookie Betts, Jackie Bradley Jr., and Andrew Benintendi emerged as one of the Red Sox' most consistent and significant advantages. Betts and Bradley are Gold Glovers, while Benintendi produced one of the Sox' most dramatic defensive moments ever with his diving catch that saved Game 4 of the 2018 ALCS (right). *(top: John Tlumacki/Boston Globe; middle: Jim Davis/Boston Globe; bottom: Barry Chin/Boston Globe)*

Alex Cora's "Win Wall" became so crowded during the 2018 season that eventually photos had to be added to additional walls in his corner office in the Red Sox clubhouse. *(Stan Grossfeld/Boston Globe)*

Alex Cora (back to camera) and Mookie Betts had plenty of reasons to celebrate throughout 2018. Here they embrace after the Red Sox clinched a World Series berth by dispatching the Astros in the ALCS. *(Barry Chin/Boston Globe)*

Champions: Christian Vazquez jumps into the arms of Chris Sale after the final out of the World Series. *(Barry Chin/Boston Globe)*

A crowded, champagne-soaked visitor's clubhouse at Dodger Stadium served as the setting for the Red Sox celebration after the team won the World Series. *(Stan Grossfeld/Boston Globe)*

Trophy in hand, Alex Cora and the Red Sox made the flight back across the country after winning the World Series. *(Stan Grossfeld/Boston Globe)*

tive seasons for the first time since the earliest days of the Great Depression.

"We really, really needed to crawl out from a hole," said chairman Tom Werner. "We'd finished last three out of four years. That was not acceptable."

PATIENCE REPRESENTS PERHAPS THE FOUNDATIONAL virtue of the creation and development of a championship-caliber home-grown core. Players do not arrive at their peak performance levels on a schedule, nor can they rush through their acclimation to the big leagues—the equivalent, in many ways, of puberty—simply because a team feels like it is time to win. A built-in tension between short-term and long-term success is at some point inevitable, a fact reflected in the fallow periods endured by many of the World Series winners of the 2010s.

The San Francisco Giants emerged as a powerhouse starting in 2010 and won three championships in five seasons. Yet their success under Brian Sabean, their general manager from 1997 to 2014, derived in no small part from the four-year stretch from 2005 through 2008 in which they finished with losing records, thus permitting them access to early first-round picks in 2006 (Tim Lincecum with the No. 10 pick), 2007 (Madison Bumgarner, No. 10), and 2008 (Buster Posey, No. 5).

San Francisco did a remarkable job of nailing their selections in each of those three years, identifying players whose impact vastly exceeded that of most if not all of the players taken in front of them. But that four-year stretch of losing had been essential for acquiring the draft capital.

The Royals averaged 96 losses from 2004 to 2012, perennially picking near the top of the draft under Dayton Moore (hired as their GM in the middle of the 2006 season), before accumulating a critical mass of talented young players that finally broke through with a winning record in 2013. That group reached the World Series in 2014 and won it the next year, Moore's tenth.

The Cubs hired Theo Epstein in the fall of 2011 with the long view in mind. He oversaw a couple of the worst seasons in Cubs history in 2012 and 2013 while accumulating elite young players via the draft, international signings, and trades. The Cubs made the playoffs in 2015 and ultimately brought the franchise its first championship in more than a century in 2016, Epstein's fifth at the helm.

The Astros endured three straight seasons of losing at least 106 games from 2011 through 2013, becoming the first big league team ever to reach such sustained depths, as well as the first to have the No. 1 overall draft pick three straight years. They lost another 92 games in 2014 before emerging as a budding contender in 2015. Now stocked with a flourishing core of standout young talents, complemented with a tremendous mix of veterans, they won the World Series in 2017. That championship served as the validation of a long-range vision overseen by Jeff Luhnow, who was hired as the team's GM after the 2011 season.

That sort of willingness to accept losing year after year after year in exchange for a payoff down the road was never a consideration in Boston. In a region with immense passion for baseball, a home ballpark that played at something close to capacity on a near nightly basis, and a sizable TV market share, the effort to lay a long-term foundation did not come with a tolerance for compromising the on-field product. Rebuilds were to be measured in months, not years. Cherington understood that his job description required him to thread the needle of short-term and long-term success.

"In Boston, you know that the results do matter," said Cherington, "and there isn't a long time to get there."

But it's hard to cheat the timetable of developing a winner, even for a team with resources. The Red Sox had managed to do so in the championship bridge year of 2013, getting top return on an extraordinary number of midlevel free agents, but the collective crash of those veterans in 2014 underscored how remarkable—and unlikely—it had been to leverage free-agent dollars into victories.

In fact, the relationship between payroll spending and on-field success was becoming ever more tenuous. In early 2014, Martin Kleinbard, a graduate student at Columbia University, authored "Can't Buy Me Love: Why Money Is Not Baseball's Most Valuable Currency," a paper he presented at the MIT Sloan Sports Analytics Conference. In it, he found that whereas payroll spending once had been almost perfectly correlated with and a primary driver of team success, the relationship between the two had wilted. In the twenty-first century, winning had a lot less to do with spending than with the presence of young, dominant players who had not yet reached free agency.

During the 2014 season, Brian MacPherson of the *Providence Journal* conducted a similar analysis. Based on an examination of ten years of Opening Day payrolls and win totals, he highlighted the increasing inefficiency of money in trying to build a winning team.

"Less correlation exists this year between the standings and the payroll rankings of teams than between the standings and alphabetical order of teams' home cities," MacPherson wrote in 2014.

Red Sox owners, Ben Cherington, and everyone else associated with the team's decision making understood the shift in the industry. There had been a time when financial might translated to obvious on-field advantages, but increasingly, teams had come to recognize that young big-league-ready talent was a more valuable form of currency.

"Resources," said Sam Kennedy, who took over as team president during the 2015 season, "don't necessarily equal winning."

All the same, recognition of the diminishing value of payroll advantages didn't alter the expectations for what the Red Sox were supposed to achieve on an annual basis. The Red Sox had contended for a postseason spot for nearly every day of the ownership group's first ten seasons in Boston from 2002–11. Even with the palliative of a championship between two horrendous seasons, the Red Sox weren't about to accept last-place finishes in 2012 and 2014 as evidence of a new normal under changing market conditions. Entering 2015, there was a sense among members of the front office that winning could not wait.

"We can't put a last-place team on the field," said assistant GM Brian O'Halloran. "We felt like in this market, with these resources, this is unacceptable."

CHERINGTON FELT SIMILARLY DURING AND after the 2014 season—the second sell-off of veterans he'd overseen in his three seasons as general manager. His moves at the 2014 trade deadline spoke to that feeling, as the Red Sox didn't simply trade veterans for prospects who might help a few years down the road, but instead focused their deals around players who were seen as potential contributors to a winning team in 2015.

There was an unspoken unease in the organization. Cherington felt that the need to win had gone from "sort of an expectation to more of a clear directive: 2015 cannot go like this."

Even with the in-season moves for Cespedes, Craig, Castillo, and Kelly, the Red Sox entered that winter with numerous shortcomings that the team had to work aggressively to address. After placing too much weight on the shoulders of the young players, Cherington thought that he needed to provide more established lineup contributors. He needed to find a way to win while pushing through the latter part of Phase Two, at a time when Phase Three—anchored by Betts, whose season-ending performance in 2014 had created considerable optimism about his potential for 2015, as well as Bogaerts—seemed almost within reach. The Red Sox didn't merely want to upgrade the roster. The team wanted to hit the sweet spot of finding good players in their primes—long viewed as the late twenties to early thirties—while minimizing the commitments to players into their mid-thirties. The failed negotiations with Lester had reflected that preference. As much as the team liked and admired Lester, in December 2014, the organization's leaders felt what one source characterized as almost a sense of relief that he'd gone elsewhere.

By contrast, the Red Sox were willing to set or at least match the market on a pair of free agents whose age and positional profile arguably made them higher-probability gambles moving forward. On November 24, the Red Sox stunned the baseball world by reaching agreement with twenty-eight-year-old Pablo Sandoval on a five-year, $95 million deal and with soon-to-be-thirty-one-year-old Hanley Ramirez on a four-year, $88 million contract—a pair of signings meant to help the team's offense recover from its pitiful 2014 output of 3.91 runs per game (11th in the American League).

"Those two major signings, that was clearly in response to that [sense that], 'Hey, it's time for us to win again,'" said manager John Farrell.

Yet there were concerns with both. Sandoval's offensive numbers had declined for three straight years, a development that, in conjunction with well-publicized weight problems throughout his career in San Francisco, led some to believe that he might have started an early decline phase in his career. Even so, the fact that the Giants—the team that knew Sandoval the best—had been willing to offer him roughly the same deal in length and size as the Red Sox offered some measure of reassurance that the investment wasn't outlandish.

Ramirez, meanwhile, had played mostly shortstop throughout his career, but was no longer suited to that position, having slowed while adding size and strength as a middle-of-the-order hitter over his career. Third base—where Ramirez had played rather unhappily for a time in 2012—seemed a natural new destination, but the Sox had signed Sandoval to play there.

When the Red Sox asked Ramirez whether he'd play left, he expressed openness to the suggestion if it meant returning to the organization with whom he'd started his professional career—and getting a contract unlike any other that was being offered to him. Still, there was uncertainty in a midcareer position shift—and in the veteran's long history of creating headaches for managers and front offices.

Despite any concerns, however, the Red Sox barreled ahead with deals for both because they were interested in the idea of paying for years that were as close as possible to a player's peak. They didn't reach out to older alternatives who likewise were available on the open market and would have come at lesser expense, such as corner outfielder Nelson Cruz—a thirty-four-year-old who'd led the majors with forty homers in 2014 and whom David Ortiz had long heralded as an ideal target.

"You want to be investing in players' primes," Cherington reflected years later. "The problem with going too far with that is you really limit the player pool. There aren't too many guys that are available to invest in that happen to be at the right ages."

While offensive upgrades featured a choice by the Red Sox about the type of free agent well from which they wanted to draw water, the team faced a broader array of possibilities when it came to the necessary reconstruction of its rotation.

Before the trade deadline in 2014, the team gutted its starting pitching staff, parting with Lester, John Lackey, Jake Peavy, and Felix Doubront. The team acquired one replacement for 2015—Joe Kelly—but needed as many as three more options during the off-season.

When Lester went to Chicago in free agency, the Red Sox' stockpile of elite young talent gave the team latitude to explore any number of trade candidates, with one name seeming particularly obvious as a possible front-of-the-rotation left-hander to succeed Lester: Cole Hamels.

The Phillies, for whom Hamels had been World Series MVP in 2008, were inching closer to the sort of teardown-rebuild that the Red Sox wanted to avoid. Philadelphia's aging veteran core had endured back-to-back 73-win seasons in 2013 and 2014, and with more years of losing in front of the team, Hamels—in the middle of a six-year, $144 million deal that ran through the 2018 season—seemed less valuable to Philadelphia as a pitcher than as a trade asset. The two teams exchanged ideas for months, starting at the 2014 trade deadline.

"I think '15 was probably the year where we really had to look ourselves in the eye and say, 'Should we trade any of these guys?'" said Amiel Sawdaye, the Red Sox' amateur scouting director in 2015. "Cole Hamels at the time was a tough decision. We didn't know which way we were going to go."

But the conversations between Cherington and Phillies counterpart Ruben Amaro never truly gained traction. While the Red Sox saw Hamels as a potentially valuable addition— even as they had reservations about how he might adapt to the American League East—Amaro sought a deal headlined by the best young players in the Red Sox system.

At the time, the Red Sox viewed Betts and Bogaerts as essentially untouchable, with catcher Blake Swihart enjoying nearly the same status. Amaro and Cherington discussed plenty of names, but with Jackie Bradley Jr., Swihart, Henry Owens, and others viewed by Philadelphia as secondary pieces, the sides never got particularly close to a deal, despite months of conversations that kept the idea floating in the rumor mill.

"I think Mookie was the one guy that I loved the most, we

loved the most, and [Cherington] was going to be pretty stringent about not moving," said Amaro. "He was right."

(Two years later, in the off-season of 2016-17, Amaro joined the Red Sox as a first-base coach. In January 2017, he met several Red Sox players for the first time while at the team's Winter Weekend event. "Bogey, Swihart, Mookie, [Christian] Vazquez were like, 'Were you really trying to get us?'" Amaro recalled. "And I said, 'You're damn right. I asked about you, you, you, you, and you.'")

Hamels hadn't represented the only opportunity Cherington had that off-season to exchange young position players who were still working to establish themselves in the big leagues for more proven veteran talent. But he wasn't dealing Betts or Bogaerts, and Bradley's value was depressed after his poor big league showing in 2014, and so inquiries about him—with the assumption that he represented a fourth outfielder—typically came with an offer of a middle reliever in return.

There was a need to win, but also a shared desire by the front office and owners to find a way to do so while protecting the future.

"There was lots of discussion after '13 about how to continue to sustain success. It would have been, looking back, perhaps easy to follow up '13 in '14 and '15 by moving Mookie or Xander or Jackie," said Sam Kennedy. "We held on and it was a difficult period. Those were hard years, but we did have the confidence in the evaluators and people who were making the decisions to ferociously protect them to try to get them through to that next great Red Sox team."

Cherington and the Red Sox were not ready to give up on the idea of who Bradley—or Betts, or Bogaerts—might become, even if there was a growing acknowledgment of the potential professional risk involved in remaining committed to the team's forming prospect group.

"Ben had a plan. He made some missteps, and was the first one to say that, but keeping this young core together was the primary part of his plan," said Zack Scott. "He'd joke about it. He'd joke about all these articles that he never trades his prospects. He'd say, 'The next GM is going to really enjoy these guys.'"

RATHER THAN GIVING UP ON the young players, Cherington and the front office took an introspective approach to try to determine if there was more that they could have done to support the young players during their transition to the big leagues. In early 2015, Red Sox officials convened at a resort in Puerto Rico for a retreat that became known in team circles as "the Summit."

The primary impetus for the gathering was the introduction of the team's new Behavioral Health Program. Cherington long had wanted to integrate mental skills and support as well as access to psychological services into every level of the organization, from players' entry into pro ball to the big leagues, so that seeking the counsel of such coaches felt natural rather than an option of last resort.

The Red Sox always had been relatively forward-thinking about sports psychology. They'd hired former big league All-Star pitcher Bob Tewksbury, who'd gotten a master's degree in sports psychology and counseling after retiring, to work with their minor leaguers roughly a decade earlier.

Yet through 2013, the Red Sox typically had just one sports psychology coach for the entire farm system, sometimes with an additional mental skills coach at the major league level. And in 2014, when Tewksbury—who'd started working increasingly with the big league team by 2013—left the organization for a year to work with the MLB Players Association, the team lacked a designated source of counsel to help players work through their frustrations and insecurities at the big league level. The organization's one remaining mental skills coach, Laz Gutierrez, was spread thin covering the entire minor league system.

The Behavioral Health Program—"Ben's baby," in the words of Raquel Ferreira—was formed to ensure that this critical aspect of player development wasn't left short-staffed again. Moreover, the Red Sox wanted to take an even more comprehensive approach to the needs of their players, and to have such programs feel like a standard part of their professional lives, starting from the moment they signed with the Red Sox.

Under the supervision of Dr. Richard Ginsburg, the team planned to feature three mental skills coaches, with Tewksbury returning to the organization to work with players in the big leagues and Triple-A, Gutierrez working with players in Double-A, High-A, and Single-A, and a new hire, Justin Su'a, coming to the Red Sox to work with players in short-season levels. The team gathering in Puerto Rico served to introduce those new roles, and to explain more broadly how the program would be integrated into the team's structure at every level.

Yet while the meeting outlined the mental skills support infrastructure that would become available, the Summit also offered an opportunity for the organization to digest lessons from the previous year. Many of those surrounded efforts to graduate young players from the minors to the big leagues in 2014. The organization discussed the need to treat the big leagues as a level where player development continued.

The just-arrived and still-coming waves of young players would require support in their integration to the big leagues that was distinct from that typically conferred upon established veterans, and it was up to front-office members and coaches— ideally, in conjunction with established players—to provide it moving forward.

But while the Red Sox had a clear vision of what they wanted to become, the 2015 season would soon prove a challenge to Cherington's vision.

IF 2013 REPRESENTED A BEST-CASE scenario for an incoming free agent class, 2015 was its opposite. The cobbled-together rotation of holdover Clay Buchholz and newcomers Rick Porcello, Justin Masterson, Wade Miley, and Kelly confronted skepticism about whether it featured a front-of-the-rotation presence with an awkward attempt at a fashion statement. Each day in spring training, the scheduled starter sported an undershirt that proclaimed, "I'm the Ace," while his four colleagues wore deferential "He's the Ace" shirts.

The sartorial suggestion convinced no one—particularly when the catcher expected to anchor the group, Christian Vazquez, tore his ulnar collateral ligament in spring training, necessitating season-ending Tommy John surgery. The group forged a 5.54 ERA through the team's first twenty-eight games, which served as a prelude to the firing of pitching coach Juan Nieves four weeks into the season.

Even the usually upbeat David Ortiz seemed defeated. "Our pitching at the beginning of the season didn't give us any chance," he said.

Ramirez and Sandoval, the big ticket acquisitions, were atrocious. The Red Sox had been optimistic that Ramirez would find a move to left field relatively straightforward, but the experiment turned into a fiasco. Ramirez was simply awful in the outfield, frequently turning routine fly balls into hits. For a time, the team could stomach his defensive deficiencies when it appeared that he'd be able to offset them by delivering a middle-of-the-order offensive performance (Ramirez put on a spectacular power-hitting display in April) and eventually improving in the field.

But he showed little desire to work on his outfield defense after the start of the season, particularly after he suffered a left shoulder injury while crashing into a wall at Fenway while trying to make a catch in early May, an injury that not only made him even more sheepish defensively but that also hindered his swing.

He became not only a yearlong liability with the glove but also the subject of resentment from the coaching staff due to what seemed like indifference to his team's well-being. Cherington considered intervening—something he might have been in position to do, given that he'd overseen Ramirez's progression through the Red Sox farm system more than a decade earlier. But based in part on his experience of 2012, he didn't want to undermine the authority of his manager, John Farrell, or the coaching staff by creating a direct line between GM and player.

Ramirez had come to Boston with good intentions, willing to play a new position, but as he struggled mightily in the outfield, and with designated hitter occupied by a still-elite Ortiz, Ramirez tiptoed for the rest of the year around his awkward fit for the club. Meanwhile, a cloud seemed to hover over Sandoval as his performance fell well below the expectations of the team, the fans, and himself. His woeful defense, a major drop-off from his performance in San Francisco, concentrated even more attention and scrutiny on his career-long weight issues. Additionally, he proved so overmatched while batting right-handed against left-handed pitching that he abandoned switch-hitting midyear.

Both players were not merely disappointments in their first free-agent season but liabilities. Of the 211 position players who received at least 400 plate appearances, Sandoval ranked 203rd in the calculations of wins above replacement by Baseball-Reference.com, having been 0.9 wins *worse* than a replacement-level player. Ramirez ranked 208th, 1.3 wins below replacement level.

"Proof of the theory," Tom Werner later lamented, "[that] you're better off building from your core."

Yet those two were only the most visible examples of the team's poor signings. Rusney Castillo, who in the middle of the 2014 season signed a seven-year, $72.5 million deal, proved overmatched in a month-long exposure to the big leagues in May and June and was sent back down to Triple-A.

There he joined Allen Craig, who'd been demoted after hitting .139 with a .432 OPS in 65 games with the Red Sox after they acquired him for John Lackey in 2014—the worst average and OPS in franchise history by a nonpitcher. For that duo, the Red Sox ended up paying nearly $100 million in salary for players who, while in the employment of the organization, spent virtually all of their time in the minors.

Meanwhile, the production of two of the last holdovers who'd been signed prior to the 2013 season, Mike Napoli and Shane Victorino, cratered. The result was a high-priced failure of a team. Despite a payroll of just under $200 million (as calculated for luxury tax purposes) that ranked as the fourth highest in the big leagues, the team dropped below .500 on May 3 and never returned above that modest threshold of respectability.

There was a silver lining in the form of Betts and Bogaerts, who by the middle of the season looked like emerging stars as twenty-two-year-olds—arguably the most impressive tandem of players the Red Sox had seen at such a young age since Ted Williams and Bobby Doerr jointly set out on their Hall of Fame careers in the late 1930s and early 1940s. Their performances gave hope to the team's long-term outlook, promising glimpses of Phase Three.

But the succession of poor outcomes in free agent moves—and the inarguable reality of last place—forced the Red Sox to reconsider what they'd done, and why so many of their decisions had gone awry.

IN EARLY JUNE OF THAT year, with the Red Sox baseball operations department elbows deep in preparations for the 2015 draft, principal owner John Henry held a rare in-season media session. The Red Sox were 22-29, in possession of the second-worst record in the American League. Yet despite their record, Henry expressed confidence in his leadership.

"The general manager is going to be the general manager of this club for a very long time," Henry said on June 2. "I have nothing but respect for him and the job that he does. I think we've been on the same wavelength, so you have to blame ownership as much as you can blame the general manager."

That sense of shared responsibility permeated conversations between Henry and Cherington at a time when team leadership atop the masthead was undergoing change. A long-planned transition by CEO/president Larry Lucchino to an emeritus role was in progress, and his replacement as president, Sam Kennedy, wasn't made public until August.

With an in-progress shift of day-to-day operational control of the team, Henry and Cherington worked closely together, rather than through an intermediary such as Lucchino, to take stock of the baseball operations department.

"It was the most engagement I'd ever had with him," said Cherington. "He was very interested in learning more about what was going on."

The two shared an understanding that the team needed to find a way to improve the organization's decision making after so many poor transactions, and confronted the question broadly in search of answers. Was it driven by personnel, was it bad luck, had the organization been too slow to adapt to certain drivers of change in the game? Was the team too reliant on analytics, or was the team's analytics structure inadequate at the time, or both?

(The Red Sox, who'd been ahead of the analytics curve a decade earlier, had seen competitors zoom past them; amid an explosion of data from the introduction of Statcast in 2015, the Red Sox still had just three full-time analysts—Zack Scott, Tom Tippett, and Greg Rybarczyk—who often were tasked with additional responsibilities.)

Henry did more than talk with Cherington. He also accompanied the Red Sox on a greater-than-usual number of road trips, and met with other members of the baseball operations department.

Cherington wasn't territorial or defensive about the undertaking. He told Henry that he was open to anything that would help make the Red Sox better—including a structure that would feature a president of baseball operations above Cherington, or a baseball operations department without Cherington.

"I didn't want that elephant in the room to get in the way of a constructive conversation," Cherington said of the acknowledgment that anything, including his replacement, was fair game for discussion. "I think that helped us have a lot of constructive dialogue over the course of the summer. [Henry] understood I really just wanted what's best for the Red Sox."

The advantages and disadvantages of installing someone above Cherington were discussed, as were potential candidates who might oversee Cherington and the rest of the baseball operations department. Among those discussed as possibilities to install above Cherington—should the Red Sox decide to pursue such a structure—were Cleveland president Mark Shapiro and GM Chris Antonetti, Pirates GM Neal Huntington, and Athletics GM Billy Beane.

But on August 4, a speculative candidate pool was changed by the sudden introduction of a front-office free agent. Dave

Dombrowski, who'd been the Tigers president, CEO, and GM for fourteen years, was fired days after a trade deadline selloff of stars David Price and Yoenis Cespedes. Immediately Henry wanted to see if there was a fit.

By 2015, DOMBROWSKI HAD NEARLY forty years of experience in the game and roughly a quarter century as a general manager or head of a baseball operation. His had been less a job than what he'd envisioned as a calling.

In college, Dombrowski wrote his thesis on the history of the position to which he aspired. "The General Manager: The Man in the Middle" in many ways laid out Dombrowski's vision for the job he'd hold for most of his adult life, in part through a contact he made while working on the project. He'd reached out to a number of general managers, and White Sox GM Roland Hemond was among those who replied.

Not only did Hemond meet with Dombrowski for a face-to-face interview, but he eventually helped the recent college graduate to get his first job offer in the Chicago front office in 1978. While the White Sox featured a larger-than-usual front office at that time—eight full-time scouts and thirty front-office employees—the organization remained small enough that it was possible for an entry-level employee to get to know, and work with, everyone.

Already, based on the work he'd done for his thesis, the aspiring GM recognized that the most significant skill for someone in that position was great talent evaluation. And so, during a game, he tugged at Hemond's elbow.

"How do you learn about this game? How do you learn to evaluate players?" Dombrowski asked Hemond.

Hemond told Dombrowski to look around in the stands. How many people were truly paying attention? At least three-quarters, Hemond estimated, weren't focused on the game. It was the job of a front-office decision maker to be in the minority group.

"You watch the game," Hemond told Dombrowski. "You never miss a pitch."

Hemond further sharpened Dombrowski's skills as an evaluator by constantly seeking his feedback about players, particularly their trade value. A GM, Hemond told Dombrowski, always needed to know the value of players—both his own and those on other teams—so that he could be decisive when considering a trade.

The education took place both in the office and on the road with baseball lifers. Dombrowski accompanied longtime scouts like Walt Widmayer and Fred Shaffer on two- and three-week jaunts covering big league teams; he rode on minor league buses with White Sox affiliates; he got an education in pitching from longtime player, manager, GM, and scout Paul Richards—an influential proponent of power pitching; and he made international trips throughout the Caribbean with Angel Vazquez, the White Sox scout in Latin America.

He was welcomed into the conversations of scouts, often talking late into the night over drinks about deliveries and mechanics, player flaws that were and were not fixable.

"Phenomenal conversation," Dombrowski remembered wistfully. "I was blessed with having a mentor like Roland who said, 'You need to do this. This is how you're going to learn about the game.'"

That was Dombrowski's entry point into the game: watching the game, learning from scouts, constantly examining every player he saw to define his trade value. Decades later, that foundation remained at the core of how he did his job. Dombrowski still kept score, still never missed a pitch, still viewed the foundation of his job as watching the game.

(While such a stance might sound intuitive, it is not. Cherington, for instance, once acknowledged that because of his endless array of organizational responsibilities as Red Sox GM, "I didn't feel like I could watch a lot of baseball. Even when I was watching baseball, I didn't feel like I was watching baseball.")

Dombrowski trusted his instincts in a way that shaped his view of how an organization should run. The Red Sox had believed in what Cherington described as a "flat hierarchy" without silos, one in which front-office members were encouraged to cross-pollinate between departments to bring multidimensional perspective to conversations. Dombrowski, by contrast, believed in more rigid lines and more clearly defined perimeters for each department, all assembled with a clear reporting structure that featured one unquestioned decision maker at the top: Dombrowski. He believed in soliciting feedback—often directly from scouts, rather than using a go-between such as a director of a department—and could be swayed in his evaluations of players, but Dombrowski wasn't a believer in decision making by consensus if a collective view was different than his own.

"As the person who's going to make the final decision, you have to believe in it yourself," said Dombrowski.

He forged a track record and reputation for decisiveness, in a way that made him a popular call recipient when it came time to make deals. Other GMs knew that Dombrowski wasn't going to waste their time if they reached out to discuss a potential swap— he'd get to the endgame quickly, and wouldn't always sweat the third or fourth players (or sometimes both) in deals in the way many other GMs did.

Henry knew those traits well. Before he'd become the principal owner of the Red Sox in 2002, Henry had owned the Florida Marlins for three years. Before he agreed to purchase the team in late 1998, however, he sought reassurance: He didn't want to do the deal unless Dombrowski, the architect of the

Marlins' 1997 World Series winners—who, at the orders of his former boss, Wayne Huizenga, had just gone through the unenviable task of stripping that championship club for parts in one of the most gruesome selloffs in baseball history—would agree to stay with the Marlins. The two were together for three years before Henry gave Dombrowski permission to pursue the job of Tigers president at a time when the Florida owner was trying to buy another franchise—initially the Angels, then eventually the Red Sox.

The Marlins were just one part of Dombrowski's far-ranging résumé. He'd overseen low-revenue teams with limited budgets (the Marlins and Expos) as well as teams with more robust payrolls (the 1997 Marlins and the Tigers). Across a variety of circumstances, he had a consistently strong transactional track record.

At a time when the Red Sox were stuck in a cycle of poor moves while building their big league roster, Dombrowski's track record—and his history of working well with Henry—carried considerable appeal. Henry reached out to Dombrowski on August 5, the day after he'd been fired.

"Dave Dombrowski is an architect of team-building the right way," Henry explained of the appeal of reaching out to Dombrowski. "For almost three decades now, he's earned the respect of everyone in the game."

A meeting with Dombrowski, Henry, Werner, Kennedy, and Mike Gordon (the second-largest stakeholder in the Red Sox and the president of Fenway Sports Group) was set for August 13, during a meeting of MLB owners in Chicago. Cherington was not told of the meeting.

There was recognition at that time on the part of the owners that the team was readying to enter a new phase. With the flourishing farm system yielding players who had started to produce at the big league level, even though the Red Sox were amid their second straight last-place season, the team saw itself as moving from a period of accumulating raw materials—hoarding, cultivating, and developing prospects—to one of asset management, with choices to make about who to keep and who to trade, as well as identifying the right veterans with whom to surround an emerging young core.

Dombrowski's track record and experiences suggested to the team owners that he was the right person to oversee the next stage of what awaited the organization, and to leverage the considerable resources of the Red Sox in a way that produced on-field success.

"Dave was the perfect guy," said Werner.

For Dombrowski, meanwhile, the Red Sox represented as desirable a next destination as one could find, given the team's emerging talent base at the big league level, its financial resources, as well as its farm system strength.

"There aren't very many opportunities like this that exist," said Dombrowski.

The Red Sox wanted to move forward with Dombrowski as their president of baseball operations. On August 15, Henry met with Cherington in the GM's office to let him know that the team planned to pursue Dombrowski.

In itself, the idea that the period of self-examination would yield an altered baseball operations structure didn't come as a shock to Cherington. He'd been prepared for a number of possible changes to his role, including the chance that at some point, the team's owners would decide to move forward without him.

"Look," he would say in hindsight, "it's a grown-up business. When you invest what we've invested in the team and the results are the results, the GM of the Red Sox maybe isn't ever fully responsible, but certainly is fully accountable."

Still, Cherington felt blindsided by the pursuit of Dombrowski at that moment, and indeed by the idea that the Red

Sox had reached a definitive determination to install a president of baseball operations without his ongoing input.

Throughout the summer, Cherington had felt as if he and Henry were collaborators in trying to get the Red Sox back onto firm footing. But the after-the-fact revelation of the meeting with Dombrowski struck Cherington as running counter to that spirit of collaboration, particularly given that the Red Sox GM had come away from conversations with Henry earlier in August (after Dombrowski's firing in Detroit) with an understanding that the team had no immediate plans to add a president of baseball operations.

Indeed, during the eight days between Dombrowski's firing in Detroit and his meeting with Red Sox owners in Chicago, Cherington and Henry had agreed that the team should hire Jerry Dipoto—who'd resigned as Angels GM earlier that season—as a consultant to evaluate the organization's prospects as well as its pitching infrastructure. Before they proceeded with the hire, Cherington asked for clarification so that Dipoto wouldn't find himself in an awkward position in a changing organization.

"I asked again about his vision for the front-office structure . . . if there was something going on that I didn't know about or some major change," Cherington recalled. "At that time, [Henry] said no."

Dipoto's hiring became official on August 12—one day before the owners met with Dombrowski, three days before Cherington said he found out about the pursuit of the former Tigers boss.

On August 18, the owners reached agreement with Dombrowski on a deal that would make him president of baseball operations through 2020, a role in which he would have ultimate authority on baseball decisions. Based on the conversations that had taken place that summer, Henry and the team owners thought it possible that Cherington would stay and work under the newly installed president of baseball operations, maintaining his GM title albeit in a different role.

"The way it was described to me, I really thought the possibility existed [that Cherington would stay]," said Dombrowski. "I was really hopeful that he would."

But Henry and Werner also recognized that hiring Dombrowski created "a substantial risk" that Cherington would leave.

If the team wanted Cherington to stay, it failed to communicate that sense to him effectively. He perceived the pursuit and hiring of Dombrowski as faits accomplis, rather than ideas about which his input was valued. Though he recognized that the team's owners had the right to proceed in whatever fashion they saw fit in order to pull the organization out of its funk, Cherington received an underlying message that his participation in the process of pulling the Red Sox out of their tailspin was no longer considered essential or even valuable.

"I wasn't part of that conversation in a way I felt I could be sort of all-in and helping it work. That's really what it came down to," said Cherington. "The public narrative was that it was sort of my choice. I didn't really feel like there was a choice. For a combination of reasons it was just very clear that [leaving the organization] was the only thing [to do]."

Shortly after the press conference at which Dombrowski was introduced as the new Red Sox head of baseball operations, Cherington met the media to discuss his own departure from the organization. Cherington, hired as an area scout in 1999, was the longest-tenured member of the baseball operations department. Many members of the organization responded to his departure with shock and heartbreak.

Though they recognized the appeal of Dombrowski, some nonetheless felt that Cherington had been pushed aside too hastily—particularly given the possibility that deals that looked bad in 2015, such as that for Porcello, might look far better with the benefit of more time.

The team recognized that it was entering a new phase, with its owners feeling that the coming roster additions and subtractions were best overseen by someone who could manage their resources and assets in a different way than Cherington. But while the Red Sox had slogged through two undeniably painful years, there was a sense that sustained success might be nearing. The players who'd been assembled, developed, and protected by Cherington—despite the considerable pressures to win—had a chance to reward that faith, and soon.

"The shame of it," John Henry said in a largely empty Fenway concourse after the conclusion of the two press conferences, "is that Ben won't be here to see it."

CHAPTER 8

PRICE IS RIGHT

FEW PEOPLE AROUND THE RED SOX had a framework with which to comprehend the chaos of mid-August 2015. Certainly, none of the young players who were still creating their big league identities had any idea what to make of the fact that, in the span of a few days, they had seen both the only manager and general manager for whom they'd played leaving those roles.

Bench coach turned interim manager Torey Lovullo felt their uncertainty. Indeed, he shared it. When Farrell addressed the team to tell them that he was stepping aside for the duration of the season to undergo chemotherapy, Lovullo stood by his side but could offer no words. In the days that followed, he could barely mention his friend's cancer diagnosis without tears welling in his eyes. He refused to take up residence in the Red Sox manager's office out of deference to Farrell, whom he'd known dating to their time as teammates with the Angels in 1993. Lovullo was tiptoeing through the situation delicately.

But when the team made the mid-game announcement of Dombrowski's hiring and Cherington's departure from the organization, Lovullo recognized that the players needed reassurance from someone else in uniform. After team president Sam Kennedy broke the news of the baseball operations change to players after their 9–1 win over Cleveland on August 18, Lovullo addressed them as well. The team was in a confused and emotional state. Lovullo sought to direct those sentiments toward something productive. On the team level, the players remained representatives of the Red Sox, and were expected to play to win every day—to play relentless, winning baseball. On an individual level, the players were expected to conduct themselves professionally, to be good teammates, and to play with an understanding that they were constantly being evaluated to determine if they'd be part of the organization's future.

"We weren't going to play American Legion–style baseball," said Lovullo.

The team was amid a drastic roster reshaping. In late July, the Red Sox had traded Shane Victorino to the Angels; on August 7, Mike Napoli had been shipped off to the Rangers. With those two trades, every key veteran who'd been acquired for the 2013 season and who'd become a critical part of a unique clubhouse culture—Napoli, Victorino, Jonny Gomes, David Ross, Jake Peavy, Ryan Dempster, and Stephen Drew—was gone. So were Jon Lester and John Lackey.

Until the final dissolution of that group, a major piece of the team's identity had been inextricably bound to the 2013 veteran core. Now a new identity could finally take shape. David Ortiz remained the clubhouse elder (Mookie Betts often referred to his teammate not by his famous "Big Papi" moniker but instead with the even more affectionate appellation of "Large Father"), and Pedroia, too, remained as a leader. But beyond them, Lovullo's words made clear, there was an opportunity for an emerging generation of players to redefine who the Red Sox were.

When Mookie Betts had been demoted for the final time in

August 2014, relieved for his return to Triple-A after his rocky first exposure to the big leagues, he and Blake Swihart had spent long hours in the clubhouse talking about their vision for the future. Both players, as they rose through the minors, had been regarded as leaders to whom teammates gravitated—not because of the rigid enforcement of traditions or mores, but because they brought out the best in teammates who thrived when the game was fun. When the two 2011 draftees made it to the big leagues for good, they wanted to bring that atmosphere with them. They didn't want to mimic Betts's first experience with the veterans in Boston when *they* were those veterans.

"We always said as we were coming up, when we do get to the big leagues, we want to be the guys that the young guys look up to and feel like you can talk to," said Swihart, who'd been rushed to the big leagues that May due to a rash of catcher injuries but who, by August, looked like part of the future core.

By the beginning of the 2015 season, Betts already had begun to seek out a new role in the clubhouse. He organized team dinners during spring training and on road trips that included players like Ortiz and Pedroia in an effort to bridge the youngster-veteran gap that he'd encountered the previous year. Now, with Ortiz and Pedroia among the only veterans left, he could play an even larger role in setting the team's direction.

The younger players on the roster already knew each other well. With so many members of the 2011 draft class together in the big leagues—position players Betts, Bradley, Swihart, and Travis Shaw, along with pitchers Matt Barnes, Henry Owens, and Noe Ramirez—newcomers to the big leagues felt at ease among their friends. Off the field, they hung out constantly. They'd cook meals or go out together. The big leagues became an exercise in familiarity—more akin, Betts thought, to their rampage through the Eastern League in 2014 than to his uncomfortable rookie season.

Lovullo, too, was fresh blood; though just three years younger than Farrell, he related to his young players in a different way than they'd experienced. Farrell had earned his stripes as director of player development for the Cleveland Indians, overseeing their farm system. Lovullo, meanwhile, had also worked for the Indians, but as a minor league manager. He had spent nine years ascending the minor league ladder, from Columbus, Georgia (Class A), to Zebulon, North Carolina (High Class A), to Akron, Ohio (Double A), and finally to Buffalo, to manage the Bisons, the Indians' Triple-A affiliate, before moving to the Red Sox to manage the PawSox in 2010.

Farrell's player development role, in a way, had been that of the principal—an administrator. Lovullo, by contrast, had traveled the same minor league journey as his players—first during his own playing career and more recently as a manager. He had years of hands-on teaching experience working with players who were still developing.

The interim Red Sox manager—a social psychology major in college who exhibited a remarkable natural curiosity about virtually anyone with whom he came in contact—made the players feel at ease. He cared about their lives off the field and developed individual relationships with them in a way that built trust and kept them at ease when there was a mistake on the field that required correction.

It was, even in Farrell's view, a departure from his own managerial mien at that time. The mounting losses over two years had weighed on Farrell in a way that he came to recognize during his treatments as perhaps counterproductive for his players.

"Maybe there were things that I was responsible for. Maybe I had given off a different vibe. Maybe I was wearing the expectations, the pressure to win that was felt by players," said Farrell. "I certainly can't deny that."

Several players felt greater freedom to perform and find their way under Lovullo than they did under Farrell. An early-inning struggle didn't prompt an immediate call to the bullpen. A mistake on the field was greeted by a quick conversation in the dugout about what had happened and how to fix it—usually framed by a smile and an acknowledgment that the game isn't easy, and that mistakes are a part of growth. The goal of such conversations was not to make a player feel bad but to help him improve. A couple of bad games by a young player didn't mean that he'd sit.

Amid that changing atmosphere, the young core flourished. Betts hit .342 with a .953 OPS down the stretch under Lovullo. Bogaerts seemed like he got a couple of hits every night. Bradley, who'd hit just .193 with a .556 OPS in his first 191 career games, emerged as a force over his final 47 games of the season, after Lovullo took over. He hit .283 with 8 homers and a .936 OPS to conclude the season. A player who looked in 2014 like he might not hit enough to be a fourth outfielder instead looked like an All-Star. Swihart likewise hit .330 with a .909 OPS under Lovullo, and looked like he had a chance to hit his way to future All-Star status behind the plate. Shaw—usually an afterthought in the prospect evaluations of the team—started blasting homers at a surprising pace, going deep 11 times in his final 48 games.

"Torey," said Bradley, "was very special to us."

"You've got a guy that's able to relate to the younger guys," agreed Betts. "The way he communicated, the way he made us all feel comfortable, he believed in us and you could definitely see it. And that made us believe in ourselves."

If there was one night down the stretch that embodied this emerging sense of possibility, it was September 25, when the Red Sox shut out the Orioles, 7–0, at Fenway Park. A number of elements made the game memorable. On a two-run double, Bogaerts slid across the plate safely a fraction of a second behind

Dustin Pedroia, with both players eluding the catcher's tag in a fashion reminiscent of an iconic moment in the movie *Major League*. Rich Hill, who earlier that summer had been pitching for an independent league team, threw a complete game shutout—an amazing reversal of fortune that served as a metaphor for the Red Sox' own worst-to-first aspirations. And his shutout was preserved by an extraordinary game-ending catch from Mookie Betts, who leaped at the bullpen fence in right to pull back a potential home run. After the turmoil under Farrell, Lovullo's young group was finally having fun; the interim manager compared them to "a bunch of sixteen-year-olds running on the beach playing Frisbee." It no longer seemed like they were searching for their place.

The Red Sox finished 2015 with 78 wins and 84 losses, good for last place in the AL East. The last time the franchise had posted back-to-back last-place finishes, Herbert Hoover was president. In a baseball town like Boston, this ordinarily would have been cause for outrage—and yet, the prevailing sense at the end of the 2015 season was not one of deficiency but instead of coalescing promise. The perceived chaos of the transition of mid-August had given way to confidence about the team's direction moving forward.

On the last day of the regular season, Dombrowski announced that Farrell would return as manager in 2016—a decision made palatable when Lovullo agreed to return as his bench coach, and not to pursue any managerial vacancies that off-season, giving the team an insurance policy in case the physical demands of managing proved too onerous for Farrell. It meant also that the man who played an integral role in unlocking the potential of this young core would again be there to help it thrive. After two years of hardship, soul-searching, and change, the Red Sox hoped they'd emerged on the other side.

"I'm excited about the way things are looking," Ortiz said

near the end of 2015. "I think we're going to hit the jackpot for next year."

WHEN DAVE DOMBROWSKI JOINED THE Red Sox in August 2015, in the early days of Lovullo's tenure, he was given a simple mandate: fix a major league team that had become a high-priced disappointment for two years running. Dombrowski was inheriting a team with obvious assets—but one he knew needed meaningful change in order to transform from a last-place team in 2015 into a contender moving forward.

As he navigated his new organization, Dombrowski didn't hide from the fact of why he'd been brought on board or from the reality in which his new organization found itself. In some conversations with new colleagues, he was polite and respectful but direct about the notion that the team's players couldn't be as good as the Red Sox thought, given the team's two-year performance. Change had been necessary, and more change would be needed.

Yet while some members of the Red Sox baseball operations department wondered whether their new boss would take a wrecking ball to the organization—replacing longtime Red Sox front-office members with his handpicked people, or unloading players to rebuild the roster—Dombrowski defied those expectations. In his introductory press conference after the Red Sox hired him, Dombrowski said he didn't intend "to blow up" the organization, and the claim proved more than lip service.

Because he joined the Sox in August, he had a chance over the final weeks of the year to survey the organization before he considered reshaping it. He got a feel for the team's strengths, both on and off the field. He elevated Mike Hazen—the assistant GM under Cherington—to the role of general manager, and kept nearly every front-office member in place while promoting several.

And then Dombrowski got to watch the team flourish over the final weeks of the season. From the time of his introduction through the end of the season, the team went 25-18, a .581 winning percentage that, over the course of a full season, would have translated to 94 wins—a number that would have been good for first place in the AL East in 2015.

Seeing was believing. Yes, Dombrowski was now entrusted with a team that had finished in last for a second straight year, but over the quarter season in which he observed them, he saw a team capable of playing in substantial stretches like a first-place club. At various points, he identified numerous members of the team—Bogaerts at shortstop, Swihart at catcher, Eduardo Rodriguez on the mound, Betts, Bradley, and Rusney Castillo in the outfield—as potential building blocks of an elite team.

It is impossible to say how different Dombrowski's view might have been had the Red Sox struggled in the big leagues after he joined the organization. But given his mandate to reverse the organization's fortunes, and the message he at times outlined inside the front office—the team *couldn't* be that good if it was in the middle of back-to-back last-place finishes—some members of the Red Sox believe that the team's performance over those six weeks played a critical role in keeping the team's core intact.

"I think that saved the team," one team official suggested. By the end of the 2015 season, Dombrowski saw a team that wasn't as far from contention as its full-season record suggested. And more fuel was in the pipeline; the consensus view held that the Red Sox had one of the top farm systems in the game, perhaps the best. Then there were the young players already in the big leagues, perhaps Dombrowski's most valuable currency. Those with star potential who were not yet eligible for salary arbitration cost almost nothing. Xander Bogaerts would make just $650,500 in 2016, Mookie Betts just $566,000. For players at the verge of stardom, this was a pittance.

The deep farm system also offered Dombrowski a chance to make trades without compromising the team's big league roster. And because the Red Sox—a team with tremendous financial resources that perennially invested in one of the highest big league payrolls in the game—featured a big league team with so many inexpensive, homegrown talents, they could afford significant investments on established players to supplement that core. In other words, nearly every potential avenue for the improvement of the big league team was open to Dombrowski.

Dombrowski was mindful of the opportunity that awaited him, particularly after his run in Detroit. There, with an octogenarian owner, Mike Ilitch, who wanted desperately to win another title in his lifetime, the Tigers had channeled most of their resources into big league payroll while eschewing longer-term plays in areas like the farm system and the analytics department. By Dombrowski's final seasons in Detroit, players who might not be in position to contribute immediately to the pursuit of a title thus became trade powder. Ilitch did not have time to wait for promising young players to endure the uncertainty and growing pains of potential contributors. As Dombrowski put it, "We had the pedal to the metal." Until the out-of-contention Tigers sold off veterans David Price and Yoenis Cespedes at the trade deadline in 2015—days before Dombrowski was fired— the president/GM/CEO managed the system accordingly.

The Tigers thus routinely featured what was ranked as one of the worst farm systems in the game. By reputation, at least, Dealer Dave—perennially one of the most aggressive executives in the game when it came to making trades—was not Builder Dave—at least not in Detroit. But in Boston, as he talked with the

Red Sox owners, it became evident that his charge and opportunity were different. As Dombrowski's predecessor, Cherington, had noted, there aren't thirty different general manager jobs in baseball—there are thirty different jobs of general managers.

At the ownership level, the Red Sox still believed in the long view under which Theo Epstein and Cherington had operated for thirteen seasons. They just wanted someone else to be in charge of the organization's asset management, considering Dombrowski an ideal fit for what they needed at the time. The team felt urgency to recover from the embarrassment of three last-place finishes in four years, and felt that with the right decisions, it had the resources to do just that.

"There was the operating philosophy of, 'We're here to win World Series championships.' That kicked into overdrive," said Red Sox president Sam Kennedy. "The modus operandi became, all right, we're now at a point where these homegrown guys are coming into their prime. They're contributing. Let's add major league assets through either free agency or trades to complement what an amazing job the scouting and player development group has done."

Dombrowski identified two glaring areas of need for the Red Sox after 2015. The team needed an ace to anchor the rotation, and it needed to reinforce the back end of its bullpen. He planned to employ both kinds of resources—money and prospect talent—to shape the Red Sox for 2016.

MAJOR LEAGUE GENERAL MANAGERS MUST trust the evaluations of other members of their organization. The job is too vast—with roughly 200 players in each team's system, spread out among at least seven minor league affiliates, sometimes thousands of miles apart—to have an intimate familiarity with every player in the system, particularly given the other responsibilities of the job.

As Dombrowski prepared for his first off-season with the Red Sox, he recognized the need to rely upon the assessments of others. Though he'd seen some of the team's prospects in that fall's instructional league and the Arizona Fall League, the glimpses were brief. He hadn't had time to visit any of the team's minor league affiliates in 2015, when he had little more than two weeks from the time of his hiring to the end of the minor league season.

The lack of familiarity created potential danger. New general managers hired from outside of organizations frequently make mistakes in their initial trades when dealing from their prospect inventory. They simply don't know the players they're dealing well enough to understand the complete picture of their abilities, and why their performances in the minors may either underrate or overstate their potential.

Dombrowski understood in his first off-season that beyond his efforts to learn as much as he could about his new farm system by reading through the team's daily minor league reports, he'd be reliant on the evaluations of others, particularly Hazen, his general manager—the assistant GM under Cherington, and someone who'd previously served as the farm director under Epstein. Hazen, Dombrowski quickly recognized, could be trusted to distinguish between the keepers and the tradeable assets in the organization, while also offering the sort of feedback about team needs at the big league level to understand the intersection of need, opportunity, and risk.

Cherington hadn't been opposed to dealing very good prospects, but his track record nonetheless suggested reluctance to do so. His belief in player development bordered on idealism; a player's upside was almost always within reach, so long as the organization supported, taught, and nurtured that player in the right way. Dombrowski, on the other hand, was a realist. The idea of preserving the complete inventory of promising minor league players just didn't make sense for a team looking to return to the postseason. The team had to loosen its grip.

"Dave recognized that we were probably too conservative with our willingness to give up prospects," said Eddie Romero, who had been elevated from director to VP of international amateur scouting after Dombrowski's arrival. "You have to be willing to give up on some guys you like. The biggest thing is knowing where that line of demarcation is."

In a way, Dombrowski's willingness to deal was shaped by the realities of prospect attrition. It's hard to see many years into a prospect's future. There are so many elements that can derail a player before he reaches his potential ceiling. Under Dombrowski's watch, the team wasn't going to be shy about using potential long-term assets to bolster its competitive standing in the short term.

In a way, though Dombrowski had a reputation as a baseball traditionalist—someone who had lagged behind the analytics revolution in Detroit while placing greater emphasis on traditional scouting in roster building—his approach to prospects tended to align with the actual probability that they'd reach their ceilings.

Scouts spend hundreds of days a year searching the far-flung ballfields of America for a glimpse of future excellence. They have to be motivated by hope. Danny Watkins had seen something in Mookie Betts before anyone else, and he had continued to believe in his potential. Minor league managers and coaches must also be driven by promise. U L Washington had transformed the swings of hundreds of prospects who never made it; remaking Betts's made it all worth it.

Cherington had tended to hold on to speculative prospects, rather than selling and trying to recoup some value for them. It wouldn't have been unreasonable for him to see Bradley as a diminishing asset and to try to get something of value before he zeroed out. He didn't, instead giving him an opportunity that Bradley seized in 2015, earning himself a place in the team's plans. And Cherington's philosophy would continue to inform the Red Sox front office after his departure.

Still, optimism, and case studies like Bradley's, didn't alter the math. Some prospects will indeed reach their anticipated potential—and some will exceed it. But most will see their careers conclude with the dreaded questions—"What if . . . ?" and "Remember when . . . ?" Numerous studies have shown that even top-ranked prospects such as those found annually in *Baseball America*'s top-100 list are more likely to become busts than to reach their once-identified potential. Dombrowski approached his new role with the Red Sox from that empirical framework.

He was willing to court risk, believing that, while there are exceptions, most prospects he dealt wouldn't come back to haunt him. Dombrowski himself was responsible for one such exception: in 1989, while GM of the Expos, he had traded future Hall of Famer Randy Johnson for Mark Langston. Yet Dombrowski had the vision to take the long view, knowing that Johnson was but one (very unfortunate) blip in his decades-long career, in which he had mostly won such trades. At the least, if Dombrowski was confident in the big league player he was getting back, he could stomach the potential risk of parting with a future star.

The ability to distinguish between prospect groups—identifying and in most instances fiercely protecting potential cornerstones, while dealing those who offer less certainty—is perhaps the greatest skill an executive can possess. While Dombrowski had been burned on rare occasions during his career, his long-standing willingness to make deals involving most of his players while keeping a few off limits reflected the probabilities involved with such projections.

"There's a handful of guys, you don't make them untouchable but you really don't want to move unless someone forces your hand, and then everyone else is on the table," said Zack Scott, who as director of major league operations was in charge of developing the models to determine, among other things, the probability with which prospects reach their potential and the corresponding financial value that resulted.

Statistical reality, Scott recognized, almost always suggested downgrading prospects below the grades they'd received as amateurs. There were more B2 ceilings defined in every draft than there were everyday big league jobs. Properly valuing prospects required acknowledging the possibility that they could become busts—while also recognizing that some, like Betts, would outperform virtually any potential projection for their big league futures. Hence the idea of a probabilistic model that defined a value for players based on the relative likelihood of a number of career paths.

With Dombrowski clearly ready to make deals, some of the holdover members of the Red Sox viewed their charge in trade discussions fairly simply. The front office wanted to support him by giving him reasonable projections about the prospect inventory with a straightforward goal: don't trade the potential stars.

Dombrowski had seen enough of the big league players—Betts, Bogaerts, Bradley, and Rodriguez, among others—that they weren't going to be part of any trade discussions. By default, Dombrowski preferred to keep the big league team intact and to deal from prospect depth in order to avoid a scenario where he robbed Peter to pay Paul. Further, he preferred to deal from positions of strength and depth to minimize the chances of creating a long-term hole.

In mid-November, he made his first strike—a vintage Dombrowski move. He'd identified bullpen help as a priority starting in his introductory press conference with the Red Sox. He addressed that need with a top-shelf solution.

Craig Kimbrel, at twenty-seven, had forged one of the best career starts of any closer in big league history. To that point in his career, the right-hander had a 1.63 ERA, the lowest of all time by a pitcher with at least 300 career innings, with an average of 14.5 strikeouts per nine innings, the second-best mark in baseball history.

He represented the profile of player that Dombrowski loves: an established star, and a power pitcher to boot. The Red Sox were willing to pay up to get him—to a point that opened the eyes of many front-office members to the fact that the new sheriff had a different way of dealmaking.

The Red Sox could anchor an offer with a pair of premier up-the-middle prospects. Manuel Margot was a well-regarded player who projected to be an everyday center fielder but who had become expendable thanks to the emergence of Bradley and the drafting of Andrew Benintendi. Shortstop Javier Guerra, one of the tantalizing prospects in Greenville in 2015, possessed significant upside as a power-hitting, Gold Glove–caliber shortstop but there was little certainty about his future given his high strikeout rate; moreover, with Bogaerts excelling in the big leagues and Mauricio Dubon still in the system, the young shortstop seemed expendable. The Red Sox and Padres also agreed on the inclusion of Carlos Asuaje, a potential utility player coming off an unexpectedly strong minor league season.

To some Red Sox officials and even some of their Padres counterparts, that three-player package seemed like plenty. Kimbrel was elite, but he wasn't cheap—he was owed $24 million over the next two years, with an additional $13 million team option for the 2018 season. An offer of Margot and Guerra seemed likely to trump any other offer.

But that didn't stop the Padres from asking for more. They

wanted one more player, left-hander Logan Allen, a pitcher with a B2 ceiling who was just months into his professional career after being drafted by the Red Sox in the eighth round in 2015, but showed enough potential to be considered one of the team's best starting pitching prospects.

Several members of the Red Sox baseball operations department believed the deal could be done without Allen. But Dombrowski didn't want to jeopardize the deal. Allen, he concluded, was expendable.

The Padres were ecstatic.

"I can't believe," one member of San Diego's front office said, "we got those four guys for a reliever."

Even with the team landing Kimbrel, some Red Sox felt squeamish about the exchange, unaccustomed to Dombrowski's close-the-deal style that played a role in the team including Allen (potentially one of the team's better starting pitching prospects) rather than holding its ground.

Still, the deal made sense from the vantage point that the Sox wouldn't need Margot or, quite possibly, Guerra in the big leagues. With Bogaerts not yet arbitration-eligible, the Sox were set at shortstop for years to come. Asuaje had shown big league potential, but not at a level that stalled the deal. And while Allen was very well regarded by the Sox and had a chance to emerge as valuable, he belonged to a high-risk demographic—left-handed high school pitcher—that made him a lottery ticket with a far-from-certain payout.

"That first year, I was going strictly on the recommendations of the individuals," Dombrowski recalled years after the fact. "It was more difficult for me to know the ability level of the players we traded in Kimbrel because I'd just started. It's interesting, the one guy that we really thought the most of internally at that time was Guerra."

Yet Guerra's performance plummeted in the Padres system.

The upward arc of his offensive performance in the Red Sox system endured a steep reversal. Though he reached the big leagues briefly in 2018, it was as a fringe big leaguer rather than a player whom the Sox had reason to regret dealing. By early 2019, the shortstop's offensive limitations resulted in his conversion to the mound. Kimbrel, meanwhile, was an All-Star in each of his three seasons with the Red Sox from 2016 to 2018.

"It just tells you sometimes why guys are prospects," said Dombrowski.

DOMBROWSKI HAD, IN MANY WAYS, lived up to his aggressive reputation. But when it came time to address the Red Sox' most glaring need—an ace to anchor their rotation—he pumped the brakes.

For the last several years, there had been growing awareness throughout baseball of the dangers of long-term deals for pitchers in their thirties, an age where injury risk spikes and production often dwindles.

Principal owner John Henry was well aware of the data suggesting the risks associated with steep performance declines for pitchers in their thirties. Cherington, too, came to embrace the idea of acquiring an ace by alternate, less financially risky means. In the end, the team cobbled together, through trades, the farm system, and one comparatively tiny free agent signing, a rotation of Clay Buchholz, Rick Porcello, Wade Miley, Justin Masterson, and Eduardo Rodriguez.

As it turned out, they could have used Lester. The team's aceless rotation of 2015 proved a failure. The starters posted a 4.39 ERA, third worst in the American League, contributing to the team's last place finish. Box scores were littered with what pitching coach Carl Willis termed "abominations" by his starters. Still, the Red Sox didn't make any significant deals at the July 31 trade deadline.

But the front office direction seemed clearer based on the exploratory trade conversations the team conducted. They hadn't gotten a deal done, but they did have a better sense of the landscape for a potential trade that might net a front-of-the-rotation starter. The Red Sox were ready to "ante up," as Cherington put it, for an in-his-prime ace to anchor the rotation—even if it meant taking a giant ladle to the farm system pot.

In Cherington's final years, the team regularly called the White Sox about Chris Sale, but was just as regularly told that the left-hander wasn't available—a stance that remained unaltered prior to the 2015 trade deadline. But other avenues seemed slightly more open. The Sox inquired with Cleveland about Corey Kluber, Danny Salazar, and Carlos Carrasco; with the A's, ever willing to discuss trades, about Sonny Gray. San Diego was willing to discuss Tyson Ross. The Mets, rich with pitching talent including Matt Harvey, Jacob deGrom, and Noah Syndergaard, had seemed a potential match. (That match became less likely after the Mets advanced to the World Series that year.)

During the summer, with Cherington still as GM, an ace seemed within reach via trade. Dombrowski's arrival changed the conversation. As early as his initial interview with Red Sox owners, he made clear his view that the team needed to add a true No. 1 starter. In that interview, he had mentioned the name of Price—whom Dombrowski had acquired for the Tigers in a trade in 2014, then dealt to the Blue Jays shortly before the deadline in 2015—as a potentially appealing option. Price was a perennial Cy Young–caliber pitcher who could provide the talent and leadership that hadn't been evident in the 2015 rotation.

And Price, unlike the other aces the Red Sox had called about, was a free agent. The only asset that would be required to land his services was money—but a lot of money would be required. In October, the Red Sox tried to quantitatively compare the cost of a trade for an ace versus signing one in free agency. Scott oversaw the production of a sixteen-page memo, in this case exploring a hypothetical deal for the A's Gray, in exchange for a five-prospect package of Rafael Devers, Swihart, Margot, Henry Owens, and Guerra.

The team assigned a value to the prospects based on a probabilistic model of their potential careers—what paths players with the kind of scouting reports and statistical performance profiles through similar career stages typically end up taking. Based on those projections, the Red Sox considered such a trade a $230 million proposition, with the prospects carrying a projected future worth of $200 million on top of the roughly $30 million that the team anticipated it would have to pay Gray in salary over his remaining four years of control.

In that assessment, the team believed that it would cost less simply to sign a free-agent starter than it would to trade for a rotation solution—to say nothing of an alternative scenario in which the Red Sox had to deal Betts or Bogaerts for a front-of-the-rotation pitcher, whether Gray or someone else.

"I'm not ever going to say we're not going to trade someone," Dombrowski said at the time. "But gosh, there's a great core of young players here that we'd like to see grow and be part of this for a long time."

Based on that assessment, the preferred course of action became clear.

The 2015–16 free agent class was deep in elite starters. In addition to Price, Zack Greinke, Jordan Zimmermann, and Johnny Cueto were also front-of-the-rotation starters on the open market. At an October meeting of the team's pro scouting staff in Arizona, Dombrowski surveyed his evaluators about which rotation option they thought represented the best fit for Boston, with most of the conversation focused on Price and Greinke.

The clear consensus was Price. Factors that led the evaluators in that direction included the left-hander's year-over-year excellence, his dominance while pitching in the American League East, his demonstrated ability to adapt his pitch arsenal to that point in his career in a way that suggested he'd be able to keep finding ways to succeed while aging, the fact that he wouldn't require the sacrifice of a draft pick to sign (because Dombrowski, with the Tigers, had traded Price midseason, he was not subject to draft pick compensation extracted from the team that would sign him), and the belief that he was a better fit for Boston than Greinke.

The Red Sox didn't waste any time making their interest in the left-hander clear. A contingent of Red Sox officials—principal owner John Henry, Dombrowski, Kennedy, Hazen, Farrell, and senior vice president of baseball operations Frank Wren—traveled to Nashville for a dinner meeting downtown with Price and his agent, Bo McKinnis, at the Southern.

There Price surprised team officials with knowledge not just of the team's projected big league roster but also its depth beyond that. As Price approached the question of where he wanted to spend the next several years of his career, he wanted to know he was going to an organization with a promising long-term outlook. Price was looking beyond the Red Sox' struggles in 2015.

"They played really well in September," he noted. And he loved the idea of mentoring the team's promising young core in its growth. Much as the torrid Septembers of the rising Red Sox wave had ensured their own futures in the organization, they also may have helped to snag Price.

"An organization that, one, had the talent this organization had, to have the minor league system we had at the time, and then to have the funds to be able to sign any free agent, I felt like that was a pretty good recipe for success," he said.

The day after Price's dinner with team officials, on November 20, the Sox made an initial offer: seven years, $200 million. Had he accepted, it would have been the third-highest guarantee ever offered to a pitcher. Price considered his offers through Thanksgiving weekend, and viewed the Cardinals (who had made a $180 million offer while showing a willingness to go up) and Red Sox frontrunners as of November 30. That day, Greinke's agent, Casey Close, reached out to the Sox to solicit a bid for the right-hander. The Red Sox weren't ready to say if they were in or out; first, they wanted to focus on Price.

On December 1, the Sox upped their offer to $210 million. When Price and McKinnis countered at $217 million—the largest guarantee in baseball history for a pitcher—the deal was done.

The Sox recognized that they might have been aggressive in outbidding the field, just as they'd been with Kimbrel. Doing so was the cost of ensuring the outcome they wanted, a by-product of Dombrowski's leadership style.

"He's superaggressive and has tunnel vision," said one team official at the time. "He gets his guy."

Kennedy, who'd worked in the Yankees and Padres front offices before joining the Red Sox in 2002, had worked with a broad range of general managers, among them Brian Cashman of the Yankees, Kevin Towers of the Padres, and then Epstein and Cherington. On at least one count, Dombrowski had them all beat.

"I've never worked with a more decisive general manager," said Kennedy. "Dave said, 'We need a guy at the top of the rotation. We can do this and have a world-championship-caliber team. Or we can not do it and not be that.' Dave made his mark with the David Price deal."

CHAPTER 9

READY OR NOT

At FIRST GLANCE, CHRIS BENINTENDI didn't read too much into it—it just seemed like unassuming fun in the backyard after work. The Cincinnati-area lawyer would come home, grab a tennis racket, and smash tennis balls as high as he could into the air while watching his five-year-old son, Andrew, drift under and catch them. But the more he watched his son, the more he thought about his own career as a second baseman at Wittenberg University, when he'd stagger while trying to track down infield pop-ups.

"When the ball would drop literally ten feet behind me because I misjudged it, I'd be wiping my eyes, whether it was a sunny day or cloudy, like, 'I can't see the ball.' I'd ask to get the eye black on," said Chris Benintendi. "I would have won an Oscar for some of the stuff I was pulling on the field."

Andrew pulled no such shenanigans. He was an intuitive ball tracker, base runner, and, more important, hitter, with a swing that looked picture perfect virtually from the time that he started swinging a bat. His father, however, was taking no credit for it.

"I didn't teach him that swing," Chris Benintendi noted. "That was a God-given swing that he had."

But growing up, baseball wasn't even Andrew Benintendi's favorite sport; his real love was basketball. Though he'd star on the court in high school, he recognized even as a freshman that given his height, five-foot-eight, his future in hoops had a ceiling. The baseball field offered no such limitations.

But even as Andrew Benintendi pursued a Division 1 scholarship and perhaps a pro career, he tried to maintain balance in his life. He could have chosen to attend Moeller High School and play for the same program that claimed Hall of Famers Ken Griffey Jr. and Barry Larkin as alums. He chose to stay with his same close-knit group of friends by attending Madeira High School, a Division 3 program, prioritizing time with his family and friends over life inside a baseball test tube. And he skipped out on the Perfect Game showcases that have become a staple of college and pro scouting.

"If you're good enough, they'll find you," he reasoned.

Even from a smaller school, Benintendi made it easy to do so. He started for four years at Madeira, hit .542, set an Ohio state record for runs scored (199), and at one point was believed to have broken the state record for hits with 213. (Subsequent research revealed that he'd actually fallen short by nine.)

He spent his summers playing baseball for the Midland Redskins, a travel team for whom dozens of first-rounders, including Griffey and Larkin, had played. In 2011—the summer in which he turned sixteen—Benintendi was slated to play for the sixteen-and-under travel ball team. Instead, a temporary spot opened on the eighteen-and-under team, and Benintendi played so well that the two-week spot became a summer-long showcase against older competition. He joined a short list of standout players to jump ahead to the team's highest level at such a young age.

Yet even as he distinguished himself, Benintendi recoiled from accolades, cringing when someone would compare him to Griffey or Larkin. He didn't want their spectacular career paths to be used as a measuring stick for his own. The same was true of the attention coming from colleges in the recruiting process. Individual accomplishments didn't carry as much weight as the pursuit of on-field excellence.

"When he was having some successes, it wasn't like he would come home and we as his parents would tell him he's the best thing to take the basketball court since Michael Jordan or the best hitter since Babe Ruth," said Chris Benintendi. "You might be the best baseball player in Cincinnati. What does that mean as far as your objectives are concerned, to play in the major leagues? Not a lot."

Anyone who watched Benintendi play in high school came away impressed. The lightning whip of his swing featured almost no wasted motion—"A to B," in the words of both Andrew and Chris—and allowed him to square the ball with the barrel of the bat no matter the pitch velocity. His ability as a hitter, coupled with excellent speed that allowed Benintendi to make an impact both on the bases and in center field, suggested the foundation of a very good player—one ready to compete against the most advanced college competition in the Southeastern Conference (SEC), the country's best conference, an opportunity that he'd pursue when he accepted a scholarship offer to play for the University of Arkansas.

Had Benintendi been, say, six-foot-two and 190 pounds, instead of a listed size of five-foot-ten and 170, scouts likely would have flocked to him in the first couple of rounds of the draft. But like Dustin Pedroia—an excellent high school player who went undrafted before going to the University of Arizona, and who sat on the board until the second round in 2004—few considered Benintendi ready to turn pro coming out of high school.

Benintendi understood the perception. He attended a workout at the Great American Ballpark during his senior year, and couldn't help but note a glaring difference between himself and most of the other players on the field in the Reds' home ballpark.

"All the other guys were these monsters—like, six-foot-four. I was still a skinny kid," said Benintendi. "I remember everyone going up there and everybody was hitting homers. I was trying to hit line drives."

On the one hand, the willingness to work within his skill set rather than trying to force power in order to drive the ball spoke to an uncommon maturity for a high schooler. On the other hand, the fact that Benintendi wasn't in position to launch the ball in batting practice spoke to the fact that he did require further physical development.

Teams talked to Benintendi about his interest in turning pro, but he and his family told them that it would require a signing bonus of more than $1 million (a slot value reserved for the top fifty-five picks in the 2013 draft) in order to convince him to pass on his scholarship to Arkansas. Given his size and the absence of power, Benintendi wasn't viewed as a target for the top two rounds, and so with teams simply assuming that he'd go to college, he remained on the board until his hometown Reds selected him in the 31st round. Benintendi appreciated the gesture, but both sides understood he would be heading to college.

Still, Red Sox Ohio Valley area scout John Pyle had turned in a promising report on Benintendi in high school, noting a lot of traits—quick-twitch athleticism, solid defensive instincts in center field and on the bases, and obvious bat-to-ball abilities—that would make him appealing if he gained strength. That summer before Benintendi's freshman year at Arkansas, Red Sox area scout Chris Mears, who covered Arkansas to the Great Plains, got his first glimpse of the outfielder at the Connie Mack World Series. His view echoed that of Pyle: Benintendi had balance in the box, good direction, and a beautiful swing path to the ball. While players who enroll in four-year colleges such as Arkansas typically aren't draft-eligible until after their junior seasons, there is a carveout for sophomores who turn twenty-one within forty-five days of the draft. Due to his July 6 birthday, Benintendi would be such a player. As Mears filed away his interest in Benintendi during the summer after his senior year of high school, the scout recognized that he should begin evaluating him for the 2015 draft—an early identification that proved significant, particularly when his freshman production was modest.

Benintendi struggled with the physical demands of the longer college season, and suffered wrist and hamstring injuries that diminished his explosiveness. Moreover, when installed as the Razorbacks' leadoff hitter to start the year, he tried to adapt his game to the role, focusing on getting on base rather than looking to attack and drive the ball.

For most, a .278 average and .368 OBP would have represented a solid first college season in the SEC. To Benintendi, it did not. He was hard on himself throughout it, disappointed that he finished the year with just ten extra-base hits and one home run. It was the first time he had really struggled.

He vowed to use the season as a growth opportunity. Instead of playing in a wood-bat college league in the summer following his freshman year—something that could have garnered considerable attention from scouts—he went home and focused on building strength and getting healthy, determined to be a similar but better player to the one he'd been in high school.

When Benintendi returned for his sophomore year, Arkansas coach Dave Van Horn hoped to see improvement that might put the outfielder in position for early-round consideration by his junior year. Mears, however, already loved the maturity of his approach, the fact that his demeanor betrayed nothing of his struggles through injury, and considered him an early-round possibility as a sophomore. As the 2015 season dawned,

Benintendi was Mears's highest priority, starting on Arkansas's opening weekend.

But this season, too, started slowly, with Benintendi going 5-for-25 in early action. Panicked, he called home to chat with his original coach. Chris reassured his son, told him not to worry about the draft. "Things will fall in place," he said. That, Benintendi recalls, is when he "started to take off."

Benintendi emerged as a middle-of-the-order force for the Razorbacks, driving the ball to the gaps and beyond the fences with startling regularity beginning in mid-March. People started to take notice.

"I was kind of monitoring the predictions, the mock drafts, and halfway through the year I think I was in the fourth or fifth round," said Benintendi. "At the time, I was super-pumped. I was like, 'That's awesome. I'm going to have a good chance to make a little bit of money out of college and go play baseball.'"

Benintendi was destined to push his stock far higher. As a sophomore, he led Division 1 with twenty bombs while hitting .376.

Suddenly scouts were scrambling to find out more about the undersized kid from Arkansas who was putting up outsize numbers. During the SEC tournament, estimated Razorbacks coach Dave Van Horn, thirty scouts traveled to a high school to watch Benintendi take batting practice. As soon as he concluded his round, they were gone.

"It got crazy," said Van Horn.

The 2015 season would earn Benintendi a garage full of trophies, recognizing him as the best player not only in the SEC in 2015 but in the country. And it would vindicate Chris Mears's prescience from the previous year. While other teams rushed late in the season to figure out who Benintendi *was*, and where on earth his huge season had come from, thanks to Mears, the Red Sox had quietly had regional and national crosscheckers tracking him all year. So when the group assembled to discuss candidates for the team's first-round pick in 2015, Benintendi was a known commodity.

To Mears, the most impressive thing wasn't Benintendi's numbers. It was the quality of his at-bats. Benintendi had a gift for adjusting his game plan for each new pitcher he faced, whether a junkballing lefty or a hard-throwing righty. Throughout that season, Mears saw how quickly Benintendi was adapting against excellent college competition, going from someone who would make game-to-game adjustments to someone who could decipher an opponent's game plan from one at-bat to the next and, finally, emerging as a player who would solve the batter/pitcher riddle inside of a single at-bat.

"He moves at a different pace than a lot of people on the field in terms of how he processes information on the baseball field. It's just really special," said Mears. "I remember going into the pre-draft meetings saying this is the best college baseball hitter that I have ever had in my area."

For the second time in three years, the Red Sox would be picking seventh in the draft, the silver lining of their last place finish. In 2013, when they had also picked seventh, they had nabbed Trey Ball, a high school lefty from Indiana.

Ball had looked the part of a standout pitcher: six-foot-six, a wiry strong frame with room to fill out, a mid-90s fastball, and intriguing curveball and changeup. The package convinced the team to look past the fact that he came from a pool of players— high school lefties—that more often breaks scouts' hearts than rewards crushes. By 2015, it appeared likely that Ball, still stuck in Single-A ball, would fall into the former camp. By the end of the 2018 season, he was playing outfield to try to salvage his career.

Ball became yet another cautionary tale about the incredible bust rate of high school pitchers. The phenomenon became so extreme—due to injuries, level-to-level challenges, control issues, and any number of additional factors—that within a few years, the industry engaged in a dramatic shift away from such pitchers at the top of the draft, and prospect rankings systems likewise started moving pitching prospects already in the minors down on their boards considerably.

If Ball had been a high-upside long shot, Benintendi represented the opposite: a position player (inherently a lower-risk profile than a pitcher) with a standout college track record against the standout competition of the SEC (thus diminishing the risks associated with a high schooler) and a long scouting history. The group viewed him as a B1 player (an above-average everyday big leaguer) with good to excellent probability of realizing that forecast.

The team had crossed two players—Dansby Swanson, who would go No. 1 overall to the Diamondbacks, and Alex Bregman, who went with the second pick to Houston—off its draft board, knowing that both would be picked by the No. 7 selection. There was no reason to waste time in the draft room debating the relative merits of those two.

After Swanson and Bregman, the league-wide consensus was less clear, but there were several other promising options: high school shortstop Brendan Rogers, high school outfielder Kyle Tucker, Vanderbilt ace Carson Fulmer, and University of Cincinnati outfielder Ian Happ among them.

But atop the list of real possibilities on the Red Sox draft board was now slotted the name of Andrew Benintendi, with Fulmer as a respected fallback. The question was whether anyone else would take him first.

Benintendi later recalled the Red Sox and the Cubs as the two teams that demonstrated the strongest interest in him through his sophomore year. Though he couldn't have known it at the time, a three-game series in 2014 may have determined where he would be headed.

The Cubs made a rare interleague visit to Fenway Park from June 30 to July 2, 2014, and completed a three-game sweep of the Sox. Boston would finish the year with a 71-91 record, Chicago 73-89. Had the Sox won at least one of those games, the two teams would have finished the year with identical 72-90 marks—and Chicago would have had the higher draft choice thanks to the tiebreaker of the worse record of the two teams in 2013.

But instead the Cubs were picking ninth, two selections after the Red Sox—and Andrew Benintendi was on his way to Boston.

In 2015, BENINTENDI SHOWED EVERYTHING in his pro debut with Lowell and Greenville that he'd demonstrated as a sophomore at Arkansas. On the strength of his breakthrough season, he emerged as one of the most highly regarded minor leaguers in the country. *Baseball America* would peg Benintendi as the No. 15 overall prospect in the game entering 2016, and already there was speculation that the Red Sox would fast-track him to the big leagues that year.

In Greenville in the months following the start of his pro career, Benintendi joined the spectacular prospect group that had been there for most to all of the year—including Yoan Moncada. Though Moncada wasn't as polished a player as Benintendi—he struck out more than Benintendi and made more mistakes of execution—his incredible tools and rapid growth during his 2015 campaign in Greenville likewise piqued curiosity about whether he could shoot through the system in 2016.

That curiosity intensified early in spring training. Though Moncada wasn't in big league camp, he was invited to play in the organization's first exhibition game against Northeastern University. Some in the organization bristled at the fact that

Moncada, just a year removed from being signed, was being put in the spotlight so early, expressing concerns that it might fuel a sense of entitlement.

Moncada's adjustment on the field, of course, was significant. Off it, he had to adapt not just from Cuba to the States but also from poverty to sudden riches. During spring training, he had three customized cars delivered to the hotel where he and other minor leaguers were staying. Among the features was a logo on each with an interlocking "Y" and "M," a symbol that Moncada eventually had tattooed on his neck. The vehicular fleet seemed an almost garish display around peers who, in some cases, had received almost nothing to sign and were earning literally nothing but a per diem while in spring training.

Such a display struck Sox officials and others who knew Moncada well not as malicious but misguided—evidence of the unusual education he'd require in light of his sudden, substantial wealth.

"People crushed him," said Amiel Sawdaye, the team's VP of amateur and international scouting. "But he's not a bad kid. He just did what a lot of other people would do if they got thirty-one million dollars and never had money in their life."

The concern wasn't about how Moncada had spent his wealth, so much as with the broader idea that there were people who might try to take advantage of him in a number of ways. The team didn't want to seem overly judgmental—after all, given his assets, Moncada wasn't exactly spending irresponsibly when getting the cars—but the team encouraged him to try to keep a more modest profile.

Jo Hastings, one of his agents who also played the role of surrogate American parent, had similar concerns. At one point during the off-season, a nightclub in South Florida overcharged the young player by thousands of dollars, relying on his naïveté about the value of a dollar. Hastings was irate. While she was able to get the club to adjust the bill, she remained mindful of how vulnerable Moncada was amid his cultural transition, and how easily his innocence about money could be mistaken for arrogance.

"No one," she said, "likes a swinging dick."

As he tried to navigate the intricacies of clubhouse norms, Moncada was typically well liked among his minor league teammates. He wasn't standoffish, he was willing to be the butt of jokes at times, and there was a sweetness to him—particularly evident in the tirelessness with which he'd sign autographs after games, trying to accommodate anyone who crowded toward him in the stands. All of that said, Moncada commanded so much attention—both for that $31.5 million bonus, and for his play on the field, where he had risen to become *Baseball America*'s No. 3 prospect in the game—that his path to the big leagues would never be normal. For Andrew Benintendi, somewhat shielded from the expectations of his own draft slot by Moncada's presence, this was a blessing. Benintendi found comfort in the idea that he might be able to reside unassumingly in Moncada's shadow, concerned chiefly with his own improvement on the field while his teammate—the one who looked like a linebacker—dominated the spotlight. He knew that he "could just go out and play and everyone would be looking at Moncada."

Still, Benintendi couldn't slip entirely under the radar. The fact that three elite prospects—Moncada, Benintendi, and Rafael Devers (No. 18 on *Baseball America*'s list entering the year)— were all playing for the same High-A affiliate, the Salem Red Sox, to start the year demanded attention.

Salem manager Joe Oliver knew better than most what that pressure felt like for a young player. In the mid-1980s, Oliver had come up through the farm system of the Cincinnati Reds.

A catcher with huge potential, Oliver was hailed as the next coming of Johnny Bench, the Hall of Fame Reds catcher who was the heart and soul of the historically dominant Reds of the 1970s and who ranks among the best catchers in the history of the sport. The hype had been suffocating for Oliver, who, while he became a solid big league catcher for a decade, was decidedly not the second coming of Bench. He fretted that his talented young trio would wilt under the enormous expectations placed upon them.

At the same time, Oliver knew that having such an impressive cluster of prospects at a single level was a rare opportunity. Among competitive athletes, the high bar they would set for one another could push the development not just of Moncada, Benintendi, and Devers, but of the rest of the team.

It quickly became clear that Benintendi, at twenty-one, was not long meant for High-A. He opened the season with a four-hit game, and three days later, started a 23-game hitting streak during which he hit almost .400 while striking out just six times in 107 plate appearances. At one point, he went 13 days and 60 swings without a single swing-and-miss.

Much like Jackie Bradley Jr., his abilities—particularly the ability to manipulate the bat to make such frequent contact—combined with his exposure to the highest levels of amateur play permitted the team to move more aggressively with him than was the case with all but the most exceptional high school players or even an elite international talent like Moncada.

One American League scout was mesmerized. He placed Benintendi among the top four players he'd ever scouted in A-ball, putting him in a class with Mike Trout, Bryce Harper, and Betts—all players who took accelerated paths through the minors to stardom. Benintendi seemed capable of doing the same. By mid-May, less than a year after the conclusion of his college career, Benintendi was on his way to Double-A Portland.

Moncada wasn't far behind, though he was less refined. He could be careless in the field, and offensively, struck out far more than Benintendi. There were moments when, some observers thought, he seemed almost bored with an inferior level of competition, but others where he seemed hell-bent on proving its inferiority.

In the latter bursts, he showed jaw-dropping skills. In one two-day, three-game stretch in early June, he went 7-for-13 with seven doubles, and looked like a player who would hit atop a lineup for years. Periodically, he offered ridiculous shows of strength, as when he launched a baseball over a scoreboard in Salem. Oliver guessed it flew roughly 460 feet. The baseball lifer described it as one of the longest home runs he had ever seen. In 61 games, Moncada stole 36 bases, a locomotive speeding at will around the bases. And while he did suffer defensive lapses, he mixed them with remarkable defensive plays that would have fit on a Gold Glover's highlight reel.

By late June, Moncada joined Benintendi in Double-A Portland—the upper levels of the minors, driving distance from Fenway Park, and very much on the radar of the big league team for a potential promotion. On July 11, the two players enjoyed a taste of life on the bigger stage, as both were selected to start in the All-Star Futures Game in San Diego's Petco Park, with Benintendi batting leadoff for the U.S. team and Moncada hitting cleanup for the world squad.

Moncada, especially, would rise to the occasion. He made a terrific defensive play to throw out Benintendi, and later singled and stole a base. Then in the eighth, with the World Team trailing, 3–2, Moncada blasted a 406-foot home run into the upper deck of the ballpark to give his team the lead. He was named Futures Game MVP, his bat donated to the Hall of Fame.

Both Benintendi and Moncada, in the eyes of many evaluators, looked like cornerstone players. Days later, when the two players returned to Portland, Dave Dombrowski wanted to get a look for himself. In mid-July, with weeks remaining until the trade deadline, the Red Sox president of baseball operations, who'd already seen the duo play in Salem, spent a weekend watching them play in Double-A.

"Moncada went crazy," Dombrowski recalled. "Benintendi had a tough four days. He didn't play well at all."

Upon his return from Portland, Dombrowski made clear his feelings to multiple members of the organization. Moncada was one of the best prospects he'd ever seen—an untradeable cornerstone.

Members of the organization, who already anticipated that Benintendi soon would be ready for the big leagues, recognized the implications of such proclamations from a decision maker with a long-established willingness to jump prospects from Double-A and sometimes even High-A to the big leagues. As Amiel Sawdaye took stock of the game reports from Portland where Dombrowski was watching the young players, he called GM Mike Hazen.

"Well," Sawdaye said to Hazen, "I guess Moncada will be in the big leagues sometime soon."

THE RED SOX, MEANWHILE, WERE emerging as a force in the American League East. Two nights after Moncada's display at the Futures Game, David Ortiz, the constant of the Red Sox' three twenty-first-century championships, had played in his tenth and final All-Star Game amid his yearlong retirement tour. At forty, he was performing at as high a level as he'd ever displayed.

Yet a case could be made that he wasn't the best player on the Red Sox, for joining him, for the first time, in the AL starting lineup were the crown jewels of the Sox organization: Jackie

Bradley Jr., twenty-six, and a pair of twenty-three-year-olds, Mookie Betts and Xander Bogaerts. Phase Three was in effect.

Bradley's presence in the All-Star Game was perhaps most striking. One year earlier, when he was up briefly in the big leagues in late June and early July, he'd been hoping that rather than collecting splinters on a big league bench, he'd be sent back down to Triple-A so that he could take part in that level's All-Star game, to which he'd been voted by fans. Yet within weeks of the exhibition, he returned to the big leagues and by mid-August had begun a surge that hadn't stopped.

In late April of 2016, Bradley began a 29-game hitting streak, the longest streak for a Red Sox player in nearly two decades. Through his struggles, Bradley insisted that he never doubted his abilities. He remained convinced that the dismal offensive numbers of 2013, 2014, and the initial stages of 2015 weren't indicative of who he was. The hitting streak validated that outlook—while also ending any questions about whether he was coachable, whether he could hit big league pitching, or whether he could thrive in Boston.

"If I touched the ball," Bradley recalls, "it was going to be a hit. That was my mind-set."

Now that mind-set had made him an All-Star.

Bogaerts, after his 2015 breakthrough, continued to improve through the first half of 2016, a multifaceted talent who was among the league leaders in batting (.329 at the break) while showing increasing power and base-stealing abilities on top of solid shortstop defense.

But the 2016 season was most notable for the awakening of Betts. The 2015 season had given him baseline expectations—he'd hit .291, and believed that he could be a perennial .300 hitter. He'd notched eighteen home runs, proving to himself that he could clear the fences fifteen to twenty times a year.

Yet as 2016 unfolded, it appeared that Betts had set the bar too low. On May 31, he smashed three homers in Baltimore, and then as if to prove it wasn't a fluke, blasted two more the next day. Later in the year, he had another three-homer game, this time at Fenway against the Diamondbacks.

The player who hadn't hit a single homer in his pro debut in Lowell was now emerging as a slugging force atop the lineup. By the end of the year, he'd put together a stunning campaign—a .318 batting average, 31 dingers, 26 stolen bases, and 113 RBIs. Plus, he'd won a Gold Glove in right, a remarkable feat given that just two years before, he'd been a second baseman.

There weren't many historical comparisons with Betts's combination of youth and power from such a small frame. The few that did exist had become Hall of Famers, a group headlined by Willie Mays. Though it was premature to elevate Betts to such company, his ongoing display of skills in every facet of the game suggested an elite talent—a notion eventually confirmed by his second-place finish in American League MVP voting. The Red Sox were Ortiz's team in 2016, but Betts was their future.

A strong top of the rotation complemented that explosive lineup. Price gave the team stability in 2016, even as his performance proved a bit uneven and somewhat below his own remarkable standards as he adjusted to his new environs. Behind Price, Rick Porcello—after his severe 2015 struggles in the middle of the "he's-the-ace" rotation—showed remarkable, pinpoint command of a five-pitch repertoire for much of 2016, going 22-4 with a 3.15 ERA, claiming Cy Young honors. Knuckleballer Steven Wright emerged as an All-Star.

Still, as the trade deadline approached, it was the job of Dave Dombrowski to be concerned with the present. This Red Sox group had many of the hallmarks of a potential champion. In Dombrowski's eyes, they just needed a few reinforcements.

•   •   •

Moncada was off-limits. So, for all practical purposes, was Benintendi. But almost anyone else was fair game, as Dombrowski soon made clear.

During the All-Star break, Dombrowski made a one-for-one swap, landing Drew Pomeranz—a left-hander who, after bouncing between teams for most of his seven professional seasons, had flourished as an All-Star starter in San Diego in 2016—in exchange for the team's best pitching prospect, Anderson Espinoza.

The deal jolted the industry. Potential front-of-the-rotation pitchers like Espinoza rarely changed hands, unless they were the centerpiece of deals for superstars. Pomeranz, though he'd posted a 2.47 ERA through seventeen starts over a half season with the Padres, had been a journeyman prior to that year. Now, suddenly, he was fetching one of the top ten pitching prospects in the game.

The trade represented a departure. To that point with the Red Sox, Dombrowski had dealt from areas of surplus. When he traded for Kimbrel, the best prospects he included—shortstop Javier Guerra and center fielder Manuel Margot—represented redundant assets, given that the Sox were set in center field (Bradley) and shortstop (Bogaerts) for years to come.

Espinoza was different. Elite pitching prospects are almost never blocked in an organization, and Espinoza looked like the most dazzling young arm in the Sox system since Jon Lester and Clay Buchholz had moved through the system a decade earlier.

But the structure of the trade—a one-for-one deal of a pitcher who was dominating in the big leagues at that moment and who would remain under team control for two additional seasons, versus six years of control of a player who appeared at least two years away from the big leagues—challenged convention. This wasn't four prospects for one big league piece—it was one for one, with plenty of risk on both sides of the equation.

(That shared risk soon became apparent: the Red Sox discovered that the Padres had failed to disclose some medical concerns about Pomeranz's elbow; they declined an offer by the Commissioner's Office to reverse the trade. While the Sox engaged in no such shenanigans with Espinoza, he blew out his elbow in early 2017 and did so again in 2019 before he'd been able to pitch another game for a minor league affiliate.)

The deal underscored how differently Dombrowski was managing the team's minor league inventory than his predecessor. There were almost no truly untradeable prospects. The calculus had changed: there was more emphasis on the value of trying to win in the moment, while a future ceiling was discounted by its time horizon from the present.

That didn't mean that Dombrowski or the Sox didn't like Espinoza. Indeed, Dombrowski had been mesmerized by the rocket-armed righty when he'd seen him the previous fall during instructional league.

But to consummate a trade for a player he wanted, Dombrowski accepted that the price had to be painful. He was a pragmatist rather than an idealist. While some Red Sox officials had mixed feelings about the deal—Dombrowski, understanding Espinoza's value, among them—there was a logic to his calculated risk, and he'd been brought to Boston not just with the latitude but with a near mandate to make such judgments.

"Those [trades] always hurt. When they hurt, that means you've done something right," said Eddie Romero, the VP of international scouting who'd overseen the signing of Espinoza. "You developed somebody that somebody else values significantly and you are now adding a piece that will help you get to the ultimate organizational goal."

That July 14 trade marked a different way of doing business for the Red Sox—a reflection of the fact that both the competitive context for the organization's decisions and the person in charge of those maneuvers had altered. Less than three weeks later, there was further evidence of a new Red Sox modus operandi.

WHILE DOMBROWSKI MOVED TO SHORE up the Red Sox' pitching prior to the deadline with both Pomeranz and reliever Brad Ziegler, there was one other position on his wish list: left field. He had inquired with the Yankees about Carlos Beltran—though interestingly, the Red Sox owners decided that even if there was a deal to be had, Dombrowski wasn't to pursue it, since his salary (about $5 million remaining) seemed an unnecessary luxury for a team that had potential in-house solutions.

The first week of August, after the dust has settled from the deadline, frequently sees prospects on the move. Many thought Benintendi, who was crushing Double-A competition in Portland, would get promoted to Pawtucket.

In recent years, the stints Sox prospects had spent at Triple-A had grown shorter and shorter. But they almost never skipped the level altogether. But at about 10:30 P.M. on August 1, 2016, Andrew Benintendi received a call from Portland manager Carlos Febles. It was time to pack his bags, not for Pawtucket but for Seattle, where the Red Sox were playing the Mariners. In the more than fifty years of the amateur draft, Benintendi was the first position player taken by the Red Sox in the first round of the draft to reach the big leagues the next year. The surehanded fielder of tennis balls from Cincinnati would be plying his skills on a major league stage.

By that point, Andrew Benintendi was a pro at packing. Since the Red Sox had drafted him, barely more than a year earlier, he had moved from college in Fayetteville, Arkansas, back home to Cincinnati, to Lowell, Massachusetts, and to Greenville, South Carolina, in the span of three months in 2015. In 2016 he'd gone from Fort Myers, Florida, to Salem, Virginia, and then finally to Portland, Maine. His longest stay in any one place had been seventy-eight days—his shortest, just 22.

In Portland, he had finally felt settled, and was living in an apartment by himself for the first time. Now, with Febles's call, he was on the move again. He began haphazardly cramming all of his belongings into his truck. His flight to Seattle left at seven in the morning, and he concluded his packing around two. It was at that point that he remembered to call his parents to share the news.

"I woke them up," he recalled. "They went right back to sleep." Benintendi didn't fall asleep until three; then, little more than an hour later, his alarm was ringing and he was off to join his new team in Seattle.

Benintendi thought he was used to scrutiny. He'd been the best amateur player in the country in 2015, and he'd garnered prospect hype in the minors. But now there was no Yoan Moncada alongside him to deflect expectations. The spotlight of the major leagues was something else entirely.

"If you're in the outfield and pick your nose or something, somebody's going to get a picture of it," Benintendi said, laughing.

The Red Sox knew the potential perils of that transition to the big leagues all too well. After watching Betts and Bradley struggle in 2014, they sought to do everything they could to ease Benintendi's assimilation. Initially, they sat him against left-handed starting pitchers, not just to let him take advantage of the typical platoon advantage enjoyed by lefties against right-handed pitchers but also to give the rookie time to take stock of his surroundings. They would increase his playing time gradually, more similar to how the team handled Bogaerts upon his call-up in the 2013 stretch run than the deep-end plunge of Betts and Bradley in '14.

And then there was the matter of Benintendi's roommates. When Benintendi first got to Boston, he lived in a hotel room provided by the team. But when Dustin Pedroia found out that Benintendi was living in the liminal realm of a hotel, he invited the twenty-two-year-old to stay at his house for the duration of the season, at a time when Pedroia's wife and three sons had returned to their year-round home in Arizona for the start of the school year.

Benintendi thus enjoyed an apprenticeship in his first big league months from both Pedroia—almost exactly a decade removed from his big league debut—and twelve-year veteran Aaron Hill, who was already staying with the second baseman. The trio would return to the residence after games, watch MLB Network, and hang out, with Benintendi trying to absorb as many lessons as possible.

"I was almost in awe. I had never played in the big leagues, and I'm living with Pedroia and Aaron Hill," said Benintendi. "When you've got guys like that taking you in, it makes you feel a lot more comfortable."

Benintendi's play soon matched his comfort level. He hit .295 with a .359 on-base percentage and .476 slugging mark in 34 games, marks that reflected on that beautiful swing—one in which the barrel seemed to stay in the strike zone forever, increasing the likelihood of hard contact—and the advanced offensive approach that Mears had seen back when Benintendi was a freshman struggling at Arkansas. Moreover, his speed and athleticism, in conjunction with that of Betts and Bradley, turned the Red Sox' outfield into a nearly impregnable fortress that turned fly balls into outs. With three budding stars now manning the outfield, from the Pesky Pole to the Green Monster, Phase Three looked to be well under way.

WITH BENINTENDI FIRMLY ENTRENCHED AT Fenway, many eyes now turned to his old teammate in Portland, Yoan Moncada.

The Red Sox hadn't been enamored with their production at third base. Travis Shaw, whose phenomenal spring performance had allowed the Red Sox to push aside Pablo Sandoval (who would suffer a season-ending injury in the first days of the 2016 regular season, his second season of a five-year, $95 million deal) and who had been a lineup force early, had seen his production decline over the year.

Manager John Farrell steadily decreased Shaw's role, first after the Red Sox acquired Hill to face left-handed pitchers, and then by spelling Shaw with Brock Holt. As the Red Sox churned through options at the position, they contemplated other potential upgrades.

By mid-August, the Sox had moved Moncada from second to third in Double-A Portland to create a pathway for him to take Shaw's job down the stretch. But Moncada had been managing injuries and hadn't played that well, so expected he'd be heading home, not to Boston, when Portland's season ended. Indeed, he'd already purchased his plane ticket from Portland to the Tampa–St. Petersburg Airport for the day after their last game.

Then, on August 29, Moncada's agent, David Hastings, received a call from team management. The Red Sox were set to open September with a road trip to Oakland, San Diego, and Toronto. The official on the other line inquired whether Moncada had his green card. Yes, Hastings confirmed, he'd just gotten it. Did Moncada have his passport?

"No," Hastings replied, "because he loses everything."

It would have to be FedEx to the rescue. Jo Hastings called Moncada to put him on alert: it seemed he was on the cusp of being called up. Perhaps distracted, Moncada went 0-for-5 in Reading on August 31. After the game, Portland manager Carlos Febles called the most famous prospect in the minors into his office to confirm the suspicions: the Red Sox wanted Moncada in the big leagues.

Moncada was like a teenager on the first day of school. When he called David and Jo Hastings to share the landmark news, he spoke with the excitement of a kid who wanted a new outfit to make a favorable introduction to a new peer group. For the occasion of his call-up, Under Armour would send all new swag: batting gloves, wristbands, a shin guard, and cleats.

On the morning of September 1—around the time that Moncada, after unsuccessful attempts to reach his mother in Cuba the previous night, finally connected with her to share the news she'd already learned—the infielder called his surrogate American parents from the airport to confess that he was exhausted.

"Would you rather be playing in Reading, Pennsylvania, or playing with the big boys?" David Hastings asked.

Moncada, of course, wanted to be playing with the big boys. But privately, some Red Sox player development staffers doubted whether he was ready. He could destroy fastballs, but struggled to recognize changeups, and for all the comparisons drawn between his swing and that of his old idol, Robinson Cano, the violence of Moncada's cuts had the barrel of his bat flying in and out of the zone, instead of, like Benintendi, smoothly traveling through it. Those traits contributed to alarming strikeout totals, even in Double-A.

"I don't think Moncada was ready to make that jump," Febles acknowledged years later. "Moncada is a different animal [than Benintendi]. He's a guy that can have five tools. He's a guy that can be a superstar if he puts everything together. But I think it was the maturity. Benny is mature. Moncada was getting to that point. It's something you only get with time."

Moncada wasn't a polished product, and under ordinary circumstances, it would have been hard to justify his call-up. Still, while acknowledging the remaining rough edges to his game, the Red Sox didn't mind a gamble—with the notion that, if they caught Moncada at the right time, he had a chance to help propel a playoff-bound team closer to its goal of a championship, at a time when Dombrowski and Farrell had soured on Shaw.

The 2016 season was the first that Farrell and Dombrowski had worked together on a day-to-day basis. Though they got along well, they tended to amplify each other's reactions to the most recent stretches of games.

Dombrowski, who traveled to most road games with the club, was a near constant in the clubhouse and the manager's office, unusual for someone with his position. There were benefits to the ongoing conversations between the manager and president of baseball operations, among them a shared understanding of the issues facing the club and mutual involvement in decisions. But by Farrell's account, Dombrowski's presence sometimes gave added weight to short-term considerations. The two men's conversations focused the manager on trying to win each day, rather than taking a more laid-back, broader view that might have been a better fit for his players, particularly the young ones who were grappling with the scrutiny of playing in Boston's baseball bubble.

And Farrell himself couldn't escape the bubble, despite the fact that the Red Sox spent virtually the entire year in solid contention for either the wild card or division title. A segment of the fan base had soured on Farrell during the Red Sox' two last-place finishes and wasn't going to come back. The manager's serious public demeanor garnered critics, as did the lengths to which he sometimes seemed to go to shield his players from criticism rather than acknowledge shortcomings. Whenever the Red Sox lost, fans called for Farrell's firing. One team official joked about the invariable social media cry to #firefarrell after every brief downturn, lamenting the "dreaded three-game losing streak." Players tried to keep the negativity walled off inside the clubhouse, but the task wasn't always easy.

"Anything John did that didn't work right, [the fans] were against it and they wanted to fire him. They wanted him out," said Bogaerts. "He had little to no room for error."

Farrell was sanguine when it came to these outcries. He had beaten cancer; next to that, even the vitriol of Red Sox fans paled. Nonetheless, the sentiments introduced a curious element into the atmosphere surrounding a team that otherwise seemed to possess immense talent.

The existence of extreme day-to-day reactions offered the backdrop for Moncada's call-up on September 2. His next eight days would prove a case in the dizzying highs and lows of the 2016 Sox. Moncada joined the team in Oakland, where Farrell outlined a plan to ease him into playing time. He would sit that night, then start getting at-bats at third base against right-handed pitchers, essentially displacing Shaw.

That first game in Oakland, the Red Sox blew out the A's, 16–2. Shaw started at third, and, as if motivated by his new competition, had an enormous game, going 3-for-6 with a homer and two doubles while driving in five. In the late innings, Shaw moved across the diamond to first so that Moncada could enter the game and get his first two big league plate appearances—a walk and a strikeout. The next night, Moncada went 2-for-5 with a double in his first big league start. Another two-hit game followed the next day. The Red Sox looked like they might have rolled a seven . . . before one of the dice turned over from a six to a one.

He earned starts in the Red Sox's next two games. He came to the plate seven times, and all seven times he struck out. Moncada never started another game that season. He made just three more appearances—striking out late in two games and making a costly base-running mistake as a pinch runner in a game on September 10. After the game, Farrell called the lapse in concentration "elementary."

"Our primary goal is to win," the manager told reporters, while declaring that Shaw would reclaim his role as the team's starting third baseman against right-handed pitchers. "Development in this situation does not take a front seat."

Eight days had been enough to flip the team's plans—and, perhaps, to play a key role in how Dombrowski would shape the team that off-season.

MONCADA HADN'T BEEN READY FOR his moment, but the Red Sox picked up steam through September and forged a comfortable lead entering the final days of the season, rolling through an eleven-game winning streak to all but clinch the division with one week to go. With the playoffs in sight, the Red Sox looked like the consensus best team in the American League.

However, the team stumbled down the stretch, losing five of its last six (a stretch during which the nightly celebrations of the retiring Ortiz's career seemed to last almost as long as some games), and didn't regain its footing when the playoffs arrived. The Red Sox were swept in three straight games by Cleveland, a series in which they were outplayed. Members of the Red Sox concluded that they hadn't been prepared to match the intensity of their opponent.

"Sometimes you're the lion," rued Rick Porcello, "and sometimes you're the gazelle. That series, we were the gazelle."

Still, after the pain of back-to-back last-place finishes in the regular season, the Red Sox had reason to hope that with a now-established baseline for a team led by Betts, Bogaerts, Bradley, and Benintendi in the lineup, along with a rotation featuring David Price and Porcello, a bright future awaited.

As Pedroia noted, the Sox had endured a rebuild of a season and a half (mid-2014 through 2015) and had emerged on the other side to win the AL East. Given how organizations like the

Astros and Cubs had endured five miserable years on the way to a return to contention, Pedroia felt like the Red Sox had accelerated the process of creating a foundation for a potential championship group going forward. Still, it didn't make the pain of that final loss to the Indians, at home no less, any more manageable.

The game would be Ortiz's last. After a teary farewell to the fans on the Fenway Park mound, he addressed his teammates in the clubhouse. "You guys saw the best of the best playing," he told them, referring to the Indians. "You guys take a little bit of that."

At 11:44 P.M. on October 10, 2016, Ortiz drove away from Fenway Park for the last time as a player. With his exit, the Red Sox were left to determine who they'd become as they moved into a future without their icon.

CHAPTER 10

ALL-IN

Bᴀꜱᴇʙᴀʟʟ'ꜱ ᴡɪɴᴛᴇʀ ᴍᴇᴇᴛɪɴɢꜱ ᴀʀᴇ ᴀɴ annual circus, a five-day exercise in sleep deprivation masquerading as information gathering, a trade- and more often rumor-generating machine fueled in equal measure by caffeine, alcohol, and members of the baseball industry. Among the thousands of job seekers, merchandise sellers, reporters, agents, managers, major and minor league employees, and executives who convene inside a single resort-turned-baseball biosphere, few seem so at home as Dave Dombrowski.

That was certainly the case in Dombrowski's suite inside the Gaylord National Resort & Convention Center in National Harbor, Maryland, in early December 2016. There, members of the Red Sox baseball operations department—Dombrowski, manager John Farrell, other front-office members, and several of the team's pro scouts—spent two days wrestling with the present and future of the Red Sox.

The conversation wasn't merely theoretical. The White Sox were determined to move one of the game's most sought-after players, Chris Sale, at the Winter Meetings, and the Red Sox had an opportunity to be in the mix for the left-hander—so long as they were willing to pay a considerable prospect price.

The suite was set up like a classroom in which Dombrowski was the teacher. More than thirty chairs faced a broad desk where the Red Sox president of baseball operations sat in the front of the room. Over two days, the group debated the merits of a deal—the view of a future with and without Sale, with and without two of the very best prospects in the system.

Trades represent a crossroads for the present and future, a choice that highlights the priority an organization is willing to put on the group that it has in the big leagues versus the one that it sees moving toward it. Eventually, the years spent cultivating a championship-caliber homegrown core lead to a moment where a team must decide how much of its eventual potential to channel into the possibilities of the present. That moment had arrived.

"Basically what we did was talk about this a little bit philosophically," said Dombrowski. "We knew giving these guys up wouldn't make us as strong four years down the road, but it makes us stronger now."

For years, the Red Sox and other teams had inquired with the White Sox whether they might make their ace available. For years, the White Sox had demanded a massive, big-league-ready return. Not only was Sale one of the best pitchers in the game, but he also had one of its most team-friendly contracts—a five-year, $32.5 million deal, with two team options. He'd signed the deal in the spring of 2013, just before turning twenty-three.

The White Sox had turned away years of inquiries about whether they'd consider parting with Sale at all, and even as that stance softened a bit at the 2016 trade deadline, their willingness to make deals was predicated on getting not only outstanding young talents but players who were ready to contribute immediately in the big leagues. But in the early evening on Friday, December 2, that changed.

As Dombrowski prepared to leave his office at Fenway Park to head home, he received a call from White Sox GM Rick Hahn. Chicago, Hahn said, planned to deal Sale at the Winter Meetings that were scheduled to take place the next week, and their asking price had changed.

The White Sox had just seen their crosstown neighbors, the Cubs, win their first World Series in 108 years, after a five-year rebuild that was more like a gut renovation. The White Sox no longer wanted established big leaguers; they wanted what the Cubs had used as cornerstones: minor league prospects who would form a championship-caliber core who could open a window for years of contention. And so Hahn popped the question: Would the Red Sox consider parting with Yoan Moncada?

THOUGH MONCADA HAD FLOUNDERED IN his first taste of the big leagues, he was still one of the best prospects in the game. He possessed five-tool potential with a ceiling matched by few others. He had a chance to be a superstar. Even after Moncada's big league struggles and Benintendi's success in his 2016 debut, some in the organization still preferred Moncada. In the words of farm director Ben Crockett, "There was a debate."

Some, however, had become more skeptical about Moncada's future. The previous September, big league pitchers had exposed obvious holes in his offensive approach. While he could destroy fastballs, he was highly vulnerable to secondary pitches. Earlier in the summer, Dombrowski had been wowed by the twenty-one-year-old in Portland. But Moncada's sobering September, Dombrowski acknowledged, "had some effect" on his willingness to listen to offers.

Moreover, in his relatively brief professional career, Moncada had gotten banged up with some regularity. Granted, most of his injuries were minor—a hamstring, an ankle, a thumb, a wrist—but it seemed fair to wonder whether a player moving with the speed and power of a locomotive was meant to withstand his frequent crashes into the bases.

The fact that Hahn's ask didn't begin with Benintendi, meanwhile, represented a critical change in the tenor of talks. At the 2016 trade deadline, Hahn had made the potential inclusion of Benintendi and Moncada as the headliners of a package a required starting point; the Sox had declined. That package was too rich. By the end of 2016, with Benintendi having cemented himself as ready to contribute in the big leagues heading into 2017, he was off-limits.

Given that Moncada needed more time in the minors, he might be another story for the right player, particularly since it wasn't clear how Moncada fit into the team's lineup. Dustin Pedroia was on a long-term deal at second base, Moncada's primary position in the minors. At third, Moncada had appeared raw in his early look in Double-A and the big leagues. He had the athleticism to play the outfield, but Dombrowski didn't take such a transition for granted. There was enough uncertainty about Moncada that Dombrowski told Hahn that, while he couldn't offer a definite yes, the famed prospect was potentially on the table in a deal that didn't include Benintendi.

One day later, Hahn again reached out to Dombrowski, and inquired about a second name: Michael Kopech, their 2014 first-round pick with the 100-mile-an-hour fastball and tantalizing upside. Kopech, who could throw long toss from one foul pole to the other, was a scout's darling. "I don't know that I've ever scouted someone who's had this kind of arm strength," said Red Sox area scout Tim Collinsworth after the team selected the pitcher.

Kopech had at times been dominant during his first full pro

season in Greenville in 2015. But his behavior also cast a shadow. In July 2015, he was suspended fifty games for testing positive for a banned stimulant. Kopech's insistence that he didn't knowingly take the banned substance (oxilofrine), and that it may have been the result of a tainted supplement, came across as credible in the eyes of team officials. Yet even if the transgression fell short of alarming, it hinted at a carelessness that might prove costly to his future development—and in fact did the next March, when Kopech broke his pitching hand punching his spring training roommate, Tyler Hill. Kopech would miss the first two months of 2016. Though the team found that Hill had been equally at fault, and viewed the scrap as the sort of thing that isn't uncommon among minor leaguers, there was undeniable frustration that a player with one of the most electrifying arms in the game had stalled the start of his career.

"He knows he's going to have to grow up," GM Mike Hazen said.

Those who knew Kopech well believed that the two incidents didn't define him. J. T. Watkins, a West Point alum and military veteran who'd caught Kopech in Greenville in 2015, described the right-hander as "incredibly driven. He's one of the most motivated pitchers I ever had a chance to play with. He expects greatness."

That pursuit burned in Kopech while he wasn't able to pitch, and when he finally returned to the mound in the summer of 2016, he was a force, quickly changing the conversation that surrounded him. In a start against High-A Wilmington on July 13, Kopech fired a pitch that made his Salem teammate Matt Kent, sitting behind home plate with a radar gun, do a double take. Kent had seen Kopech hitting triple digits with frequency, but struggled to believe the reading on his gun: 105 miles per hour. He turned to a Wilmington pitcher likewise charting the game with a radar gun in hand. His reading was the same: 105.

The reading (probably inaccurate, as it turned out—Red Sox TrackMan data from the park registered the pitch at 102 mph) had an immediate effect. Kopech had been the guy with, in scouts' parlance, questionable makeup. Now he was a twenty-year-old standout with a magical right arm who'd thrown a pitch harder than perhaps any starting pitcher since Nolan Ryan.

"A lot of people that you could arguably say weren't fans of me," Kopech relayed with amusement, "started being a lot nicer."

Or, as one Red Sox official put it: you don't mind having a pitcher who can throw 100 and isn't afraid to punch someone in the face.

Kopech's outings in Salem became events unto themselves, with the expectation of huge strikeout totals. Dombrowski had a long-standing love of power pitchers, and two years into his professional career, the twenty-year-old embodied the term like few others.

Dombrowski got a firsthand look at Kopech—the pitcher with the Verlander-caliber fastball thanks to the near-perfect spin axis that sent his heater exploding across the plate—in the Arizona Fall League in November. He was dazzled.

"We joke about it all the time," said Eddie Romero, who'd just been elevated to assistant GM following the 2016 season. "After that game he was like, we're not trading Michael Kopech."

But Sale was another sort of prize, one who could convince a dealmaker to loosen the definition of "untouchable." As with Moncada, Dombrowski told Hahn that he'd consider it.

That outlook offered a window into how Dombrowski approached dealmaking. He often said there was no such thing as an untradeable prospect. Now that philosophy was coming to life. After his own looks at Moncada and Kopech earlier that year, he had loved both prospects. But now, for the right price, he appeared willing to part with them—to gear up for the serious pursuit of a championship in a multi-year window that started in 2017. Sale could help in that pursuit; Moncada and Kopech likely could not.

"If you have a chance to win, you try to win," said Dombrowski.

The previous off-season, Dombrowski had chosen to pursue an elite free agent (Price) rather than a trade. The Red Sox believed that the money they were willing to spend on the pitcher wasn't as valuable as the prospects they'd have to give up to acquire a very good starter to front their rotation. But the outlook after 2016 was different, for a few reasons.

First, the Red Sox wanted to sneak under the $195 million luxury tax threshold. The team had exceeded the tax line in both 2015 and 2016, and the tax rates spiked with repeated overages. The Sox recognized that they'd be surpassing the threshold again in years to come, and so in 2017, they wanted to take advantage of what might be their only opportunity in years to reset their baseline tax rate from 50 percent down to 20 percent—something that, over three years, could be worth upwards of $20 million. Sale was perhaps the only way to add multiple wins to the roster without blowing up their tax bill; his contract structure meant that he'd count for just $6.77 million toward the luxury tax threshold in 2017.

And Sale's talent was not merely considerable but extraordinary. There was no one else with his track record of perennial dominance available. The best free agent that winter, Yoenis Cespedes, had a wildly uneven track record, and he was an outfielder, an area where the Red Sox were set for years with Betts, Bradley, and Benintendi. Slugger Edwin Encarnacion seemed a potential heir to Ortiz as designated hitter after averaging 39 homers over the prior five years, but at age thirty-three, his strikeout rate had spiked in 2016 in a way that suggested risk of a considerable drop-off. And he wouldn't come cheap, meaning the Sox would have to go past the luxury tax threshold if they wanted to pursue him.

Sale, by contrast, was coming off a fifth straight All-Star season, and a fifth straight year in which he ranked in the top five of AL Cy Young balloting. He featured one of the nastiest arsenals in the big leagues—an explosive mid- to high-90s fastball, an excellent changeup, and most notably, a slider whose movement was so drastic that his Chicago pitching coach, Don Cooper, once compared it to a snitch, the elusive, winged, golden sphere of Harry Potter's magical quidditch matches. And at age twenty-seven, Sale was at the height of his powers.

"If you're trading a blue-chip prospect and you're getting an All-Star performer who gives you a chance to win for a few years, you have to really weigh what's more important," said Dombrowski. "People want to have it both ways. It doesn't exist both ways."

STILL, IF THE RED SOX were to advance talks with Chicago, Dombrowski wasn't going to make such a decision impulsively—particularly given the long-term implications of any deal.

Zack Scott, who by 2016 was the team's VP of baseball research and development, had prepared the study suggesting the Red Sox would be better off pursuing Price in free agency than trading for a starter the previous year. While the team awaited Hahn's next contact, Scott spent Sunday, December 4—the day that the Red Sox arrived at the Winter Meetings in the suburban Washington, D.C., area—comparing the value of Sale to that of the assets the team might give up to acquire the left-hander.

Scott used performance and medical data as well as the projections of the team's evaluators about what kind of players and risk levels were associated with Kopech and Moncada to create a model to estimate the future worth of their performances. If the team's evaluators viewed one or both players as superstars—if Moncada profiled to have the impact of Mookie Betts, or if Kopech looked like the second coming of his idol, fellow flamethrower Noah Syndergaard—then Scott's model would show a dramatic imbalance of the value of the prospects compared to Sale. But while the Red Sox thought extremely highly of both players, there were enough hickeys—the strikeout rate and positional question for Moncada, the development of a third pitch for Kopech—to cap their ceilings in the team's internal evaluations.

Both Moncada and Kopech were seen as future B1s (an above-average regular for Moncada, a mid-rotation starter for Kopech) with good probabilities of reaching such levels. Scott's model also assigned a value to the six-plus seasons of major league control of each player.

He compared those assessments to both Sale's projected performance and what the left-hander might be expected to command on the free-agent market to determine a surplus value for his contract. If Sale were a free agent, there's a good chance he'd clear Price's landmark seven-year, $217 million deal. It's possible a team would have to spend $250 million or even $300 million for a twenty-seven-year-old with his record of excellence. Instead, over the course of three years, he would earn just under $40 million—likely just a bit more than he'd earn for one year on the open market. Plus, there was the matter of the luxury tax.

Yet even with that added benefit, there was a confounding factor in the deal: while most of the time, a player's signing bonus is viewed as a sunk cost, the Red Sox found it hard to ignore the fact that they'd invested $63 million in Moncada. The Red Sox elected to add Moncada's bonus to the cost of Sale. Thus, while the left-hander's contract, in a vacuum, was a bargain, it wasn't quite as much of one when accounting for what the team had paid Moncada. The conclusion?

"If you look at the value of players, Chris Sale's three years was not going to add up to [the years of control of] Moncada and Kopech," said Dombrowski.

But it was close.

On sunday night, with the White Sox front office contingent stuck in Chicago due to a snowstorm, Red Sox executives adjourned from their suite at the Winter Meetings. Several team executives left the Gaylord National Resort & Convention Center to enjoy a front-office dinner. A few stayed in the hotel, heading to a ballroom to join Moncada, who was at the Winter Meetings to receive recognition as the *Baseball America* Minor League Player of the Year.

A trio of Red Sox officials—assistant GM Eddie Romero (who'd been in charge of Moncada's signing process), assistant director of amateur international scouting Adrian Lorenzo, and farm director Ben Crockett—joined him at the event, sitting at the table with Moncada and his agents, David and Jo Hastings.

David Hastings passed the player some cue cards to help him deliver a brief thank-you for the award in English, mindful that the previous year, at an awards banquet in Boston, Moncada had spent weeks practicing his delivery of remarks in English but froze in front of the audience. But as Moncada prepared to take the stage, he left his cue cards behind.

"I got this," he said, and then made his way to the front of a room filled with hundreds of baseball executives and lifers. He nailed the speech.

When Moncada returned to the table, he was beaming with a sense of accomplishment. Little did he know this would prove his final official act as a member of the Red Sox, that talks were already under way that soon would ship him out of the organization.

ON MONDAY, WHILE THE WHITE SOX fought through the weather to get to the meetings, Red Sox officials discussed the merits of a deal for Sale.

The discussion was nuanced. Sale was under contract for three years under favorable terms. If the team added him, he'd be in Boston for the remaining pre–free agent seasons of Xander Bogaerts and much of the future with Mookie Betts, Jackie Bradley Jr., Andrew Benintendi, David Price, and others. Even with a picked-over minor league prospect base, the Red Sox with Sale would look like a title hopeful for at least the next three years.

The timing of Moncada's and Kopech's development was a particularly slippery subject. As the team had seen in 2014, nailing the ETA of prospect development in the big leagues is incredibly challenging. It likely might take them another year or two or three—including a period of struggle while transitioning to the big leagues—to unlock their full powers. They needed, as Farrell put it, "more cooking time." Barring an atypical growth track, the duo's arrival dates didn't seem to line up with those of Betts, Bogaerts, Benintendi, Bradley, and the rest of the impressive roster the Sox had assembled.

Yet if the prospects hit their ceilings, their eventual emergence would position the team for perennial postseason contention for a five- to eight-year window. Sale gave them more ammo in the short term, however, even if it weakened the farm system.

The Red Sox believed in the steady work done by their amateur and international scouting departments that had led the team to Kopech and Moncada, and believed in the ability of both departments to identify other top prospects. Even trading two elite prospects wouldn't strip-mine the system if the team's talent evaluators could build upon the years of work that had created the core that had brought the team to the go-for-it moment in the first place.

"When you're a director of player development, you hold on to every young player. Your horizon is much longer," said Farrell. "This is the other side of the coin."

Not every baseball operations decision requires ownership involvement, but a decision of this magnitude did. Dombrowski took the conversation up the food chain to principal owner John Henry and chairman Tom Werner. He did not sugarcoat the dilemma.

"This is going to have to hurt to get a guy like Chris Sale," he told them.

Henry, a billionaire who made his initial fortune as a commodities trader, understood the importance of the long view. But he also believed in letting his baseball operations department direct the organization's decisions.

In 2005, under his watch, the Red Sox had traded minor leaguers Hanley Ramirez and Anibal Sanchez to the Marlins for Josh Beckett and Mike Lowell. Henry had preferred to hold on to the prospects, but trusted his baseball decision makers. The Red Sox made the trade, and Lowell and Beckett became key contributors to the Red Sox' title run in 2007, even as Ramirez emerged as a star in Florida. Then, in 2011, Henry had been reluctant to trade three blue-chippers, among them future star Anthony Rizzo, for Adrian Gonzalez. This time, his belief in the long view had been vindicated.

When it came to Sale, Henry likewise believed that the long-term play was probably the right one. Werner was on the fence. Though hundreds of millions of their dollars were on the line, they told Dombrowski that ultimately the decision was in his hands. They would support him either way.

"[Henry and Werner] are willing to be overruled I guess is a way to put it. They will go along with a decision sometimes that they may not personally support," said team president Sam Kennedy. "They can overrule a general manager, say, 'I'd really rather not do that.' But they will go along with a move if someone they really love and trust is working for them and is pushing really, really hard for something."

With the owners' consent, the debate continued inside the suite. Some team officials were against the idea of a trade involving Moncada and Kopech for Sale, though it tended to be a soft no rather than a vehement one. Others were more enthusiastic—at least with the inclusion of the first two names.

"The fact that it was one of the top three pitchers in baseball, you say, 'You know what? This is the time to do it,'" recounted Farrell.

But there was still a potential tripwire in the deal. As Dombrowski and Hahn explored what the rest of a trade package might look like, the discussions stalled. The White Sox, in addition to Moncada and Kopech, were asking for Rafael Devers. The Red Sox held Devers in high regard; he had grown considerably during the 2016 season, and had middle-of-the-order potential. Plus, he played third, which, if Moncada was on his way out, was shaping up to be a hole. Even for Sale, this seemed a bridge too far. The Red Sox told their counterparts they couldn't make that deal.

A bubble of silence floated between the teams on Monday afternoon. Yet despite rumors that the White Sox were exploring the possibility of trading Sale to the Nationals, Dombrowski remained optimistic. He didn't believe that any other team could front a trade proposal with two players like Moncada and Kopech.

That night, a Red Sox deal with the Brewers for reliever Tyler Thornburg was in its advanced stages, but Dombrowski didn't want it to jeopardize a potential Sale trade. He contacted Hahn to ask whether—if Chicago did move off Devers as a third piece—the players going to Milwaukee in the Thornburg deal—Travis Shaw, pitcher Josh Pennington, and Mauricio Dubon, Moncada's former roommate—could be dealt without preventing a trade for Sale. Hahn said that the players going to the Brewers wouldn't stop the sides from reaching an agreement on Sale.

Later that night, Dombrowski took a phone call from Brewers GM David Stearns.

"Hello, David," Sox officials heard Dombrowski say as he stepped out of the conference area of his suite and into the bedroom.

Stearns told him the medicals had checked out, that the deal was a go.

Suddenly another call came in. Dombrowski switched over. It was Hahn. Would the Red Sox do Sale for Moncada, Kopech, Luis Alexander Basabe, and Victor Diaz?

Dombrowski's answer was immediate: even though Basabe looked like he had a chance to be an everyday outfielder with a well-balanced skill set, and even though Diaz looked like he might move quickly through the minors as a hard-throwing, late-innings reliever, the Red Sox were willing to make the deal. Dombrowski didn't need to run the projections or seek the feedback of the room; he knew both were sufficiently far enough away from the big leagues that, from an analytics perspective, they wouldn't have altered the calculus significantly.

Hahn said he thought highly of that package but wanted to solicit feedback from scouts and take the night to think about what would be the first step of his team's rebuild. He believed that there was a framework for a deal but would call back in the morning to confirm whether that was the case.

Dombrowski returned to the suite. His front-office coworkers expected confirmation of the Thornburg deal, which they got—followed by the bombshell. It looked like Sale was theirs.

"A hell of a surprise," said Farrell.

The room erupted. Dombrowski tried to calm his colleagues, to slow the high-fiving by noting that the White Sox were taking the night to consider the deal, and that, of course, medicals still needed to be reviewed. Still, the excitement was difficult to contain: Sale seemed within the team's grasp.

The Winter Meetings are often a bizarre endurance test with groggy starts to many morning sessions. On Tuesday morning, an unusually bright-eyed Red Sox contingent filed back into Dombrowski's suite by 9 A.M. to pick at the breakfast offerings and await final word of Hahn's decision.

"At that point," said assistant GM Eddie Romero, "you're not leaving the room."

Hahn and his White Sox coworkers had broken for the night around midnight on Monday. Hahn hadn't slept while mulling not only the details of the potential trades but the enormity of what they represented—a kick in the gut to have to trade a potential Hall of Fame pitcher, a world of daunting possibility to start over from zero. But by 10 A.M., when he called Dombrowski as scheduled, his mind was clear: the White Sox would make the 4-for-1 deal with the Red Sox.

All that was left was the exchange of medical information and approval from Chicago owner Jerry Reinsdorf. Finally, early on Tuesday afternoon, came the news: done deal, officially. Again, the Red Sox' suite celebrated. This time, Dombrowski didn't need to temper his group's excitement.

SALE HAD LEARNED TO SHRUG off the rumors. Teams had been asking the White Sox about him for years, and still he had remained in Chicago. He didn't use social media platforms, so it had become natural to ignore swirls of speculation, particularly when he was in the cocoon of family time in his southwest Florida home.

Yet it was family, in some ways, that had placed Sale in a constant succession of rumors for years. Weeks before the 2010 draft in which Sale went to the White Sox with the tenth overall pick, his wife, Brianne, delivered the couple's first son, Rylan. While Sale had emerged as the most dominant college pitcher in the country at Florida Gulf Coast University, he was mindful of his emergence from obscurity, which had started just two years earlier.

Sale was lightly recruited and scouted out of high school. The Rockies drafted the Flat Stanley–thin six-foot-three left-hander in the 21st round, at a time when he had a mid-80s fastball from a relatively conventional three-quarters delivery. It wasn't until the summer after his freshman year with the La Crosse Loggers that, after getting hit around and showing pedestrian stuff, he accepted the advice of manager Andy McKay and pitching coach Derek Tate to lower his arm slot.

The heavens opened. Birds chirped. Choirs sang.

"Wow, why haven't I been doing this longer?" Sale wondered when, in his first time throwing from the low three-quarters slot, he saw improved velocity, movement, and command—improvements that continued through his development of one of the nastiest arsenals in the game.

The alteration put him on the path to dominance, but Sale didn't ignore his past as a fringe prospect. With a responsibility to care for his family, when the White Sox approached him with a five-year, $32.5 million deal prior to the start of the 2013 season—when Sale was about to turn twenty-three, and one year into his career as a big league starting pitcher—he jumped. If the guarantee of security meant sacrificing some money in the long run, so be it.

"Would I do it again? I wouldn't flinch. . . . I would have been an idiot to not do it," said Sale. "I was twenty-three years old. I've got a two-year-old at the house, been married two years at that point. Put thirty million dollars in front of me, I'm taking it. I had to do what was right for my family."

Yet Sale also understood the repercussions of the deal. Not only was there the possibility that he'd be leaving tens of millions of dollars on the table, but he'd also become one of the most popular trade targets in the game, someone whom every team could imagine adding to their own rotation. For that reason, as much as he'd been capable of filtering out years of rumors, there was a cumulative weariness that had set in by the winter of 2016.

"There's a lot of speculation, story after story," said Sale. "It's kind of like being the monkey in the middle."

But finally, on the Monday of that year's Winter Meetings, Sale was about to get the ball. The pitcher's agent, B. B. Abbott, had been alerted by the White Sox that this time, a deal might actually happen. Abbott informed Sale and his wife about the advancing talks with both the Red Sox and Nationals.

On Tuesday, Sale received the call from Abbott: it looked like he'd be going to the Red Sox. Sale, in a car on his way to visit the baseball program at his alma mater, Florida Gulf Coast University, erupted in profane excitement.

"In Chris's own way," Abbott said with an understated chuckle, "he said wow."

Soon after, Farrell connected with his new ace.

"He was elated in a pure way," said the Red Sox manager. "He said it was just like he got called up to the big leagues again."

For Sale, seven straight years with the White Sox had ended without a ticket to the postseason. Now the sense of possibility more than made up for the anxiety of switching organizations for the first time in his professional career.

Moncada, however, was disoriented. Shortly after leaving the winter meetings, he began getting texts suggesting that the Red Sox might trade him. David and Jo Hastings tried to explain the reality of the situation—the game is a business, players are assets who move between organizations depending on what they value at a given moment in time, and being traded for one of the game's best players was a compliment, not an indictment. Still, he was baffled. Just two years before, as David Hastings noted, "We were told, 'We think you're going to be the face of the franchise. You're going to have a long career with Boston.'"

But after the initial disbelief, Moncada came to see other sides to the deal. He would move back to second base with the White Sox, his position of greatest comfort. He would join White Sox first baseman Jose Abreu, a fellow native of Cuba who could mentor and relate to Moncada in a way that few others could. And on a rebuilding White Sox team, there would be opportunity and space to develop.

For Kopech, news of the deal chilled him to the core—or, more accurately, came while he was being chilled to the core. After an off-season training session, he went into a cryotherapy room at his workout facility. When he emerged from his three-minute spell in that arctic chamber, he found his friends smiling and waiting for him. They were the ones to break the news of the deal.

Kopech, like Moncada, was more than a little bewildered. He spent the rest of the day driving aimlessly through the vast, desolate landscape of the region of his upbringing, East Texas. When he arrived at home, he was greeted by a house that still featured Red Sox gear lying everywhere. That would have to go.

But, with time, Kopech was able to take stock of his inclusion in a deal for a perennial All-Star and recognize what that meant about how far he'd come in the two and a half years since being drafted.

"It is exciting to get traded for that caliber of a pitcher for the guys we had in our farm system," said Kopech. "It says a lot about the talent we had over there. I know we all take pride in that."

Yet the trade for Sale—along with the ones that had sent four minor leaguers to the Padres for Kimbrel, and the one that saw Anderson Espinoza likewise getting dealt to San Diego in the summer of 2016—altered the understanding for the team's minor leaguers of what it meant to be a prospect in Boston's system. As recently as 2015, the top prospects in the system saw the system as one of opportunity, a sort of meritocracy where excellence meant a future in Boston. The succession of trades— particularly those involving heralded members of the 2015 Greenville group—challenged that view. Michael Chavis, who was drafted with Kopech in the first round in 2014, acknowledged the new reality.

"You're not just playing for the Red Sox. There are scouts looking at you every day. You're playing for every team in the league because they're all looking at you."

CIRCUMSTANCE AND CONTEXT HAD ALTERED the value of prospects to the Red Sox, and thus what it meant to prospects to be a Red Sox, and likewise had altered what it meant to run the Red Sox. This was precisely the type of move that the Red Sox had hired Dombrowski to make, the hard calls of present versus future value, the open-mindedness to any kind of deal, including those that required multiple, elite prospects. This wasn't to say that those in the organization, including Dombrowski, had no qualms about the Sale trade—but they were comfortable with the logic that guided them through it.

It hurt to lose Kopech, and especially Moncada, one of the crown jewels of Cherington's tenure. Dombrowski knew that

Cherington had done so much to bring them to this point, carefully stewarding a tantalizing crew of youngsters through the farm system. But now it had been time to reexamine the organization's priorities, for Dombrowski also knew that success in Boston was defined not by potential but by the here-and-now—the likelihood of winning a championship, not five years down the line, but next year, or the year after.

"Sometimes," said Dombrowski, "you have to give up the future for the present."

CHAPTER 11

CULTURE CONUNDRUM

On MAY 1, 2017, A pair of fault lines at Fenway Park split on the same night in a way that virtually ensured that a tremendously talented team would endure a year defined chiefly by misery.

One incident came to dominate not just Boston but national news cycles. After the first contest of a four-game series between the Red Sox and Orioles at Fenway Park, Baltimore outfielder Adam Jones revealed that a fan had yelled racist slurs at him during the game, and that a bag of peanuts had been thrown at him.

Red Sox players and members of the organization universally condemned the egregious behavior. The team took swift action to announce—and then, when a fan made a racist remark about the Kenyan singer of the national anthem the next night, enforce—a zero-tolerance stance.

The incident was painful for a Red Sox organization that had worked in the twenty-first century to move beyond its history of racist behavior, most notably, its status as the last team to integrate, and wounding for the team's young African-American stars, who were pushed into an uncomfortable spotlight to discuss a painful issue.

"It's horrendous. It's 2017 and we're still kind of dealing with that," said Betts, who went on Twitter on May 2 to call on Fenway Park to give Jones a standing ovation as a signal of a rejection of racism. "For me to be here, Boston to represent me, and me to represent Boston, and to hear something like that going on, that definitely hurts me."

"It's disheartening, it really is," said Bradley. "I was in that same outfield at the same exact time A.J. was. So what made it any different that he was called out [by a racist] name, and I wasn't?"

Yet beyond those condemnations and subsequent participation in a Red Sox–organized initiative of the five major pro sports teams in the area to denounce racism, the players also proceeded cautiously on a third-rail issue. It was painful to hear how Jones—one of the game's most popular players and a mentor and friend even to his Red Sox competitors—had been treated. But Bradley, who'd encountered plenty of faceless racist invective on social media while struggling in 2014, was candid about what he described as the need to proceed with care regarding a fraught topic. A frank discussion of race—particularly in Boston, a city that had been wrestling uneasily for decades with a history of and reputation for racism—represented a no-win proposition.

"I've got a lot on my mind about that," Bradley said. "But right now I feel like less is going to be more in the current situation just because I want the focus to be on my team and I don't want any outside distractions for me, my family, and my teammates."

Even as members of the team bottled the "outside distraction" of a racist episode, on the same night that Jones was subjected to abhorrent treatment, another distraction—this one inside the Red Sox clubhouse, and thus more difficult to contain—took place.

In the aftermath of the game on May 1, before anyone with

the Red Sox learned of what had happened to Jones, the team was focused on a seismic wave occurring inside its own clubhouse. Bad blood had been boiling between the Red Sox and Orioles in the early season. In a game in Baltimore ten days earlier, Manny Machado had injured Dustin Pedroia on a hard, spikes-up slide into second base. Pedroia would land on the disabled list three times that year for knee injuries that eventually required experimental surgery that forever altered the trajectory of his career.

The team had been irate during the remainder of the series in Baltimore, with tensions escalating until Matt Barnes threw a pitch behind Machado's head. That Monday night in Fenway, the Orioles engaged in what many members of the Red Sox believed to be an act of retaliation, with pitcher Dylan Bundy drilling Betts in the hip with a fastball.

But after the 5–2 Red Sox loss, the standard postgame conversation between Dave Dombrowski and John Farrell in the manager's office—with plenty to discuss about sloppy defense and baserunning as well as debatable late-innings bullpen strategy—took on an atypical tone. The two got into a shouting match related to that night's game, particularly the team's handling of retribution, and whether the Red Sox needed to settle the score by hitting Machado with a pitch after their best player, Betts, had been drummed. The confrontation became sufficiently intense that Farrell essentially challenged Dombrowski: if the president of baseball operations took such issue with how the club was being run, then he should fire him.

The exchange wasn't confined to the office. As the shouting match echoed through the thin walls of the clubhouse, players, coaches, and other Red Sox employees couldn't help but hear it through the closed door to Farrell's office. Some scattered to more distant recesses of the players' lair, wanting nothing to do with the dispute. Others were fascinated and crowded closer to the door to gain access to the details of the blow-by-blow as simmering tension erupted in a way that had never happened before.

"That," said Farrell, "was probably the first and last major blowup that was ever gonna happen."

The two put a pin in their dispute so that Farrell could head upstairs for his standard postgame media session. Though there was an unusual edge to his discussion of that night's miscues in the field and on the bases, Farrell didn't betray any of the drama that had just transpired. With postgame press responsibilities fulfilled, Farrell and Dombrowski reengaged, albeit in somewhat more measured tones.

The blowup, Farrell later recalled, "was followed up with an opportunity to just speak from the heart, and that's when we kind of really recognized that maybe things don't align."

At the end of the exchange, the manager had a new view of his job. If there was any doubt that he wasn't Dombrowski's guy, by the end of that conversation, it was gone. From that point forward, Farrell felt that his job was tenuous, and his players knew it.

WHILE THAT BUTTING OF HEADS represented a dramatic downward turn in the relationship between the two leaders, it came atop months that already had the manager questioning his future. At the end of 2016, Farrell was two years removed from his last end-of-season media debriefing. Previously, he'd been accustomed to conducting the sessions alongside Ben Cherington, a signal of the shared responsibility and outlook of the manager and general manager. But after the 2016 season, Dombrowski followed Farrell rather than speaking with him.

Perhaps it meant nothing. But for Farrell, gears started spinning, a reminder that Dombrowski hadn't hired him but rather retained him. "That might be the first time that I thought, 'You know what? I am the guy inherited and I don't know how long this will continue,'" Farrell recounted. "Maybe he was starting to get impatient."

That speaking order created unnecessary awkwardness. All year there had been public questions about Farrell's future. He was under contract through 2017, so ordinarily, after a playoff season, it might not be necessary to answer a question about job security. But given that it had been a yearlong radio topic, it was obvious that Farrell would be asked whether he'd be back, and strange when he responded to the inevitable inquiry only by saying that he had yet to sit down with Dombrowski to discuss his future or that of the coaching staff.

It wasn't until Farrell crossed paths with Dombrowski at the end of his media session, and as the president of baseball operations was walking into his own season postmortem, that Farrell learned definitively that he'd continue as manager in 2017.

Yet even with that reassurance and with the team's subsequent decision in December to pick up Farrell's 2018 option, some corners of the clubhouse were less than thrilled with Dombrowski's decision—particularly when Torey Lovullo, who'd served as interim manager when the team enjoyed its late-2015 breakout, followed GM Mike Hazen to Arizona to become the Diamondbacks manager in November.

"A lot of people got attached to Torey and wanted him to be there. He left but John stayed," said Xander Bogaerts. "A lot of people wanted it to be the other way around."

Lovullo was magnetic; many players had a more natural, casual connection with him than they did with Farrell. Some of the young Red Sox in particular found Farrell—a six-foot-four mountain—intimidating. That style, when he was a pitching coach, had made him a natural leader of his staff—and it had helped to create order when he became manager in the aftermath of Bobby Valentine's chaos.

"We went from a clown show to structure, respect. It was what was needed [in 2013]," said Zack Scott. "But by the time of 2017, I think his intensity withdrew him from some relationships. I felt bad for the guy, thinking, 'Wow, that's a tough way to go about it.' He just looked like he was stressed out all the time, and was not someone that had the ability to hide it."

By 2016, young players rarely approached the manager's office, and felt that Farrell rarely took the initiative to communicate with them. The pressures of winning kept mounting, radiating out from Farrell to his players. In that tense atmosphere, a gap between the players and manager had opened.

Before he went to the Diamondbacks, Lovullo patched it. It was easier for the emerging core to talk through their struggles on and off the field with their bench coach. For that reason, the team's players recognized that his departure from the organization could have a significant impact on the team's culture.

"Obviously I was super-excited for Torey," said Brock Holt, "but I was like, 'Oh, man. We needed him.' He was that bridge guy."

On top of that, Ortiz—a giant in the lineup who proved capable of carrying the team offensively through stretches, as well as a father figure who provided counsel to the younger players— was no longer with the team. The Red Sox luminary made a point of keeping his distance from the club in 2017, both in order to avoid rumors that he was contemplating a comeback and to permit the team to grow into its identity without him. Yet in 2017, that identity was defined in no small part by the absence of the towering figure who'd been the team's central figure for fourteen seasons.

Farrell met with Betts and Pedroia to establish his trust in them as leaders—a message that seemed particularly important for Betts. But even though the twenty-four-year-old by that point had become more comfortable organizing team activities away from the field, no one could fill the shoes of Ortiz. The superstar, as assistant hitting coach Victor Rodriguez recalled, "took so much pressure away from everyone. He took pressure from the players, he took pressure from the manager, he took pressure from the general manager. Then he retired, and you could tell the next year how difficult it was." One other potential fount of veteran leadership, David Price, was also caught in a strange limbo. Though Price had had a strong first season in Boston, he had struggled once again in the playoffs. After giving up five runs over just 3⅓ innings in Game 2 of the American League Division Series, he had now gone nine straight postseason starts without a win. After that struggle, public skepticism about his fit for Boston and toughness for October intensified. Price spoke frequently about the idea that the only rebuttal he could offer was a postseason victory.

Then, one morning during spring training in 2017, he woke up to a feeling that inspires dread in pitchers: stiffness and discomfort in his left forearm. Though Price would not require Tommy John surgery, he spent the first two months of the year on the disabled list. The unfamiliar period of inactivity made it difficult to maintain an upbeat influence, and instead cast a pall over his corner of the clubhouse.

Between Ortiz and Price, the club entered the year defined as much by who wasn't on the roster as who was. Perhaps, then, it came as little surprise that the team struggled to take flight— particularly given early injuries that compromised the availability or productivity of Jackie Bradley Jr., Xander Bogaerts, and Dustin Pedroia.

Even when wins came, they came with an enormous degree of effort. An offense that had been explosive in 2016 was somewhere between middling and above average in 2017—but rarely exceptional. Victories came as a relief rather than a joy, and through the early months of the season, they did not come often.

Almost three weeks after the showdown in Farrell's office, the Red Sox lost three straight games in Oakland to drop to .500—an even 21-21. They salvaged the last game, but with the team returning to Boston on an off-day, Farrell wondered whether he might be fired. Had Lovullo still been with the organization, he might have been. But he wasn't, and even as some senior Red Sox officials recognized the fraying relationship between Dombrowski and Farrell, they weren't prepared to introduce massive change with unknown effects.

Still, players sensed Farrell becoming more withdrawn as his job security became a constant topic. Now that the issue was no longer just a question for talk radio but one that had confronted them inside the clubhouse, it gained life. Farrell, after the eruption with Dombrowski, knew that the genie could not be put back in the bottle. He wanted to avoid injecting questions about his job status into his interactions with the team—yet knew that it remained the elephant in the room. Players would visit his office for brief exchanges about specific topics—health, playing time, match-ups—but with a manager whose job status had become insecure, players didn't feel comfortable discussing their own personal insecurities. Farrell came to regret the impact his relationship with Dombrowski had on his players.

"The fallout of the [clubhouse blowup], I think that was always in the air," Farrell reflected. "I could've insulated the clubhouse more from the interactions that I was having and I don't want to say put up a façade, but . . . I just look at what I could've done differently and that is maybe insulate that environment a little bit differently. That would've been borne out in maybe just being a little more affable, a little more carefree, even though that may go against my personality. Sometimes I'll get too serious, and I'll get too focused and that comes across as maybe being on edge or uptight."

Now every time the two met behind closed doors in the manager's office, players wondered whether it portended a leadership change.

"Trouble, trouble, trouble," Bogaerts recalled thinking of the dynamic. "It definitely ain't good."

In the batting cage—a setting akin to a barbershop, where work is mixed with gossip—players and coaches often found themselves chatting not about the day's opposing starter but instead in search of the latest organizational scuttlebutt. What was the latest on Farrell and Dombrowski? It was a soap opera with a captive audience.

"Sometimes the players told me, 'Did you hear what happened?' They would tell me and I would say, 'I missed that?!'" said Victor Rodriguez. "They could feel it, that it was a bad relationship."

"We did what we could to keep it out," added Betts. "[But] I'm sure it definitely trickled down into our play."

So much of 2017 felt like an exercise in trying to create walls to keep a flood of uncomfortable questions and dynamics from swallowing the season. The relationship between Dombrowski and Farrell, the awkward response to Machado's slide into Pedroia, the depressing and discomfiting conversation that followed Adam Jones's treatment at Fenway all seemed to make oxygen more scarce in the Red Sox clubhouse.

So, too, did Price's health. The left-hander, seemingly unnerved by the worst-case scenarios being introduced by his elbow injury even after his return to the big leagues in late May, twice confronted members of the media in a way that invited scrutiny and embarrassment for the organization. The first incident occurred when he sought out and loudly confronted a reporter within earshot of players, coaches, and other media members in New York in early June about what he saw as unsupportive coverage of the team.

At the end of the month, more infamously, after NESN TV analyst and Hall of Fame pitcher Dennis Eckersley reacted on-air with a four-letter word—"Yuck"—to a bloated pitching line from left-hander Eduardo Rodriguez in a minor league rehab game, Price ambushed the pitching great on a team flight to Toronto. The pitcher challenged Eckersley for a style that a number of Red Sox players considered too critical.

Price insisted that he was sticking up for his teammates in both instances—an assertion of leadership for the team in its post-Ortiz reality. But if that was his intention, then the way in which he went about it backfired dramatically, contributing to a popular public meme that the 2017 Red Sox were unlikeable. That perception, in turn, introduced further tension into the environment surrounding the team.

(In hindsight, when Price reported to spring training in 2018, he acknowledged making missteps while going "stir crazy" dealing with his elbow injury. "I feel like I've always been one to lead with my actions and I didn't do that very well [in 2017]," Price said in the spring of 2018. "I know that and understand that and I look forward to getting back and being that faucet and not being a drain.")

Meanwhile, the player best suited to ease the tension was gone. In 2013, after the Marathon bombings, Ortiz had been able to stand in front of Fenway Park and find the words to restore a city's spirit: "This is our fucking city and nobody is going to dictate our freedom. Stay strong." An entire region responded. But in 2017, there was no player with that same sense of timing to give strength amid a draining year.

It's hard to say how much any of those considerations affected the young Red Sox core, but certainly, none of them helped. Whether for reasons of the atmosphere inside the clubhouse or other more traditional reasons—injuries, in particular—the positional stars failed to replicate their 2016 breakout performances.

Bradley and Bogaerts were beset by injuries. Both alternated productive runs with lengthy struggles. Benintendi, in his first full big league season, endured significant performance swings—"good month, bad month; good month, bad month," he remembered—not unlike his freshman year at Arkansas. He considered it a learning experience that would lay the groundwork for future success, and was grateful that Farrell stuck with him through it. He showed great promise, becoming just the third Red Sox rookie ever to hit 20 homers and steal 20 bases, but the fallow periods hung heavily on him. He wasn't alone.

Betts, in particular, seemed to sag amid his slip from a spectacular 2016 campaign in which he'd been the American League runner-up in MVP voting to "mere" star status. In 2017, he hit .264 with a .344 on-base percentage, .459 slugging percentage, 24 homers, 26 steals, 101 runs, and 102 RBIs. For many players, such a performance would have represented a career highlight. For Betts, it was a disappointment. He sought answers where he always had: in the batting cage.

"When you can't figure out why, it makes you stress and wonder, and just look for more and more answers," said Betts. "When you can't get to the root of the source I think that's when things really get worse. And so that was my whole season, just, 'Why am I doing this? Why am I doing this?'"

To Farrell and other Red Sox coaches, there was something admirable about Betts's desire—driven by his hope to help the team rather than personal ego—to flip over every rock in search of a solution. That sense of personal obligation, they knew, represented a sign of future leadership.

But such a responsibility was also at times too much for a

twenty-four-year-old to shoulder, and the Red Sox feared that Betts was physically and mentally exhausting himself in a way that served as a shovel rather than a ladder at times when he fell into offensive funks.

"He worked so hard that when he struggled, he overworked," said Farrell. "That's a beautiful trait, but you'd have to take it out of his hands and say, 'Mookie, I don't want you to show up for the next few days until five o'clock, give yourself a break.'"

OFFENSE DID NOT COME EASILY to Betts or the team. The Sox finished 2017 last in the American League in homers. The absence of quick-strike threats meant that most of the team's victories were hard-earned. Perhaps the lack of on-field ease contributed to the sense that, on a day-to-day basis, the clubhouse felt joyless—belying the fact that, despite their imperfections, the Red Sox emerged by the middle of the season as a very good team, albeit one that frequently had to win in unglamorous fashion.

Sale came as better than advertised, becoming the second Red Sox pitcher ever to strike out 300 batters in a season. Kimbrel, in his second year in Boston, likewise seemed capable of striking out everyone who stepped to the plate. Both looked the part of players on Hall of Fame trajectories in the middle of their career peaks. But virtually every other pitcher on the staff regressed in 2017, with Rick Porcello a particular disappointment; he recorded one of the worst follow-ups to a Cy Young season ever, going 11-17 with a 4.65 ERA.

Aside from bookend sources of dominance Sale and Kimbrel, the team had three strengths that served as the foundation of consistency and permitted the team to keep winning—even if they didn't reduce the day-to-day stress of the season.

First, the assembly of a lineup deep in hitters with elite hand-eye coordination (particularly their confluence of diminutive players—Pedroia, Betts, and Benintendi, along with Bogaerts) who could foul off nasty two-strike pitches long enough to give themselves an opportunity to collect hits presented challenges to opposing pitching staffs. The Sox didn't score easily, but they did score. Second, the outfield defense of Benintendi in left field, Bradley in center, and Betts in right excelled in turning fly balls into outs, ever more valuable as the game's hitting philosophy increasingly emphasized launching the ball in the air. Finally, the bullpen kept putting up scoreless innings when they had to. The Red Sox played many close games and won more than their fair share, going 15–3 in extra innings games.

"Extra innings were a rallying cry for us," said Farrell. "To me that was when players were most free, that's when players played their most confident."

But the stress began to take its toll. Farrell was managing for his job, making decisions as if the outcome of Game 7 of the World Series hung in the balance. Players felt pressure to play through injuries, even when it compromised their performances. Pitchers constantly were looking over their shoulders, waiting for the bullpen to stir at the first sign of struggle in a game, and took note of one particular photo from that season, which captured Farrell on the bullpen phone while watching a fly ball sail out of the yard.

Still, despite everything, the Red Sox remained in the thick of the playoff hunt. Starting with a May 21 game in Oakland—one where, Farrell thought, a loss might have meant the loss of his job—the Sox won six straight games, the start of a 29–18 run that allowed the Red Sox to arrive at the All-Star break with a 3½-game lead in the division.

Even with that strong standing, the Red Sox recognized that the uneven contributions of their team required upgrades if they wanted to maintain that position for a full 162 games. They'd

need reinforcements in the bullpen (the team traded three relievers to the Mets for setup man Addison Reed) and especially
in the lineup.

The Red Sox were already a young team, but now they contemplated getting even younger—a reflection of a player who
was emerging as a force in the minors even at an age where he
barely needed to shave.

AT A WORKOUT ON AN open field next to a horse track in Santo
Domingo, Manny Nanita didn't initially notice Rafael Devers.
But as soon as the fourteen-year-old stepped into the box to take
batting practice that changed.

Most young players Nanita saw would sell out their swing
to generate as much power as possible, doing what they thought
would impress a scout. Not Devers. Nanita watched him spray
line drives to all fields—signs both of an unusual ability to spread
the field and of atypical self-confidence and self-awareness.

As Nanita, an area scout for the Red Sox in the Dominican,
soon discovered, Devers's approach reflected an upbringing in
which hitting represented an obsession from his earliest days.

"[Devers's father] knew his son was around somewhere when
he saw a bunch of bent cans because someone was hitting them
with a stick," recounted Nanita. "He always carried that stick
with him. Anything he'd find on the floor, he'd lift it and swing
at it. That's something I'd never heard of anybody doing before."

Nanita would track Devers for two years before he could
turn pro, watching the player's steady growth—line drives becoming doubles, doubles becoming homers—and determination to prove wrong those who doubted his abilities.

Devers had been pudgy growing up. Some training programs in the Dominican, Nanita learned, had declined to work
with the young player, believing that he didn't have the athletic

physique to emerge as a true prospect. Despite the constantly smiling demeanor that had earned Devers the nickname "Carita" (dear little one), he played with a chip on his shoulder. Nanita liked that.

Nanita also liked Devers's natural gift for launching balls to the opposite field. In the middle of the scouting process, Nanita saw Devers, a lefty, clear the left-field wall in the Red Sox' Dominican academy. Nanita was stunned. Many older, more developed righties, such as Yoenis Cespedes, had struggled to pull the ball over the fence in workouts. Nanita reported back on his promising youngster. With two years until his eligibility to sign, Red Sox international scouting director Eddie Romero sent in what he described as "a militia of scouts" to follow Nanita's initial reports.

The team's international scouts agreed that Devers possessed electrifying bat speed that suggested a future middle-of-the-order slugger. Yet while some viewed him as a future first baseman—an outlook that diminished his value in the eyes of some scouts—the team came to believe that his work ethic would give him a chance to stay at third base.

"The only thing I know how to do is play baseball," Devers, through a translator, said of the constant smile that remains present even when practicing for hours in sweltering conditions. "It's what I love to do and it's what I have fun doing. That's why I work so hard."

The Red Sox believed that Devers represented a special talent, and were the first team to invite him to work out in their academy. Devers, meanwhile, was as smitten with the Red Sox as they were with him.

"I'd never been in a major league complex like that," Devers said. "I was hoping that one day they would sign me."

At the start of the 2013–14 international amateur signing period, they did, giving the sixteen-year-old a $1.5 million bonus. Though Romero and the Red Sox typically made their largest investments in up-the-middle players whose athleticism permitted the broadest number of avenues for future big league impact, Devers represented such a special offensive talent that the Red Sox departed from that pattern for the third baseman.

Once signed, Devers came under the tutelage of Latin America field coordinator Jose Zapata, the man who oversees activity at the team's Dominican academy. Zapata, a former minor league infielder, was entrusted with the responsibility of helping Devers to translate what the team's scouts viewed as the raw tools and ability to play third base into the skill to do so.

Throughout the instructional league season, Zapata would meet Devers at 7 A.M. each day to hit him grounders. He'd offer him pointers during games, and pushed him—to show up early, to run rather than walk.

"He's helped to keep me on the right path," Devers said of Zapata.

Devers would not be treated differently than the other players, but once his first professional season commenced, his abilities quickly set him apart. On opening day of the 2014 Dominican Summer League (DSL) season, Devers banged an opposite-field homer to left, the sort of blast through the dense air of the team's facility in El Toro that was nearly without precedent among Red Sox players in the Dominican academy. A couple of weeks later, Devers blasted two homers—one to left field, and one to right—emerging quickly as one of the best players in the league. Word of his deeds spread quickly as in the big leagues, Xander Bogaerts was asking about the young player's daily exploits in the DSL.

By late June, Devers had been so good that the Red Sox were prepared to do something with him that they hadn't done with

Bogaerts: promote him to the States in the middle of his first professional season. At seventeen, Devers was headed to the Gulf Coast League.

Or at least, that was the club's intention. But when members of the Red Sox DSL team learned of their popular teammate's accomplishment, they organized a celebration that got a bit out of hand, with the teenagers drinking in the academy dorms.

"We got a little rowdy," confessed Devers. "We were doing what kids do."

The next morning, by the time Zapata and then Romero found out about the misbehavior, Devers had already boarded his plane to Florida. An employee of the academy pulled him off it to take a phone call from Romero, the international scouting director turned stern (but caring) principal. Devers, Romero said, would not be promoted to the States until he paid proper penance—including cleaning shoes and running postgame—back at the academy. The implication was clear: no player, not even a seventeen-year-old with a million-dollar signing bonus who seemed destined for stardom, was above the rules of the team.

Indeed, for many teenagers at the academy, adjusting to its rigid daily routine—the rules and detailed schedules not just of practices and games but also meals, classes, and off-field activities—was tough. The Red Sox recognized that, given the ages of the players in the lowest levels of the minors, "player development" couldn't be extricated from personal development. Staff members were not only baseball instructors, but also had to fill the roles of teacher, mentor, even parent.

"You have to remind yourself of [how young the players are] all the time," said Romero.

Devers spent roughly two additional weeks in the DSL before he was moved up to the States. That relatively brief postponement, however, made a lasting impression. "In the moment, you think it's terrible for obvious reasons," said Devers. "Thankfully I was able to have Eddie there to pull my ear a little bit and to make sure it's a learning experience."

The misstep was a blip that did little to diminish what Devers was accomplishing on the field. When he reached the Gulf Coast League, he continued to stand out against older, more experienced players. While his aggressiveness at times worked against him ("As soon as the ball leaves the pitcher's hand, [Devers] wants to swing," said GCL Red Sox manager Tom Kotchman), he showed uncanny power to all fields. He batted third and starred for a Red Sox team that beat the Yankees' Rookie Ball team in a best-of-three series to win the league championship.

The following spring, 2015, Devers headed to full-season Greenville as an eighteen-year-old. Devers got off to a scorching start and became the youngest Red Sox player ever to be named to the All-Star Futures Game. Though he faded somewhat later in the summer—the full 115-game season taking its toll—he finished 2015 with a .288 average, .329 OBP, and .443 slugging mark along with 11 homers and 50 extra-base hits. All the signs suggested a rare young talent. Crockett, who at the time was in his sixth season in player development, described Devers's all-fields power at such a young age as "certainly unique with the players I've seen. . . . It's not necessarily someone we've had in our system."

Though large for his age, Devers moved well at third and on the bases, showing the athleticism to be more than a one-trick, power-hitting pony. One scout surmised that within a few years, he would either shed weight and gain strength in the mold of Adrian Beltre, or would end up more like Pablo Sandoval. Still, that range of outcomes—a World Series MVP who'd been a key contributor to three champions in San Francisco, or a Hall of Fame talent who represented one of the greatest third basemen in big league history—was special. On a loaded Greenville team, Moncada was considered to have the highest ceiling, and Benintendi the most certain bet to enjoy a long, successful big league career. But some evaluators pegged Devers as having the second-highest ceiling of the trio—ahead of Benintendi—and the second-highest likelihood of reaching it—ahead of Moncada.

In Salem in 2016, Devers was again paired with Benintendi and Moncada at the start of the season on one of the most-watched teams in the minors. Yet while his two older teammates flourished at the level and ultimately moved up to Double-A Portland in the early months of the season, Devers endured a prolonged struggle.

Members of the organization felt that the weight of trying to prove he was the equal of his well-known peers had compromised his offensive approach. At his best, Devers would allow pitches to travel deep into the strike zone and smash them to the opposite field. That approach allowed him to recognize pitch types as well as whether they were likely to land in the strike zone or out of it, the gift that had so impressed Manny Nanita back in Santo Domingo.

But in Salem, Devers sold out his swing for power in hopes of clearing the fences in a park, Salem's Lewis Gale Field, that was commonly referred to as a hitter's graveyard. The results were dreadful, with the nineteen-year-old hitting .180/.268/.293 through 40 games. That Devers struggled, however, didn't come as a complete shock to the Sox. He was moving aggressively through the system, playing against much older competition in an environment that zapped one of his foremost strengths.

Minor league coaches and officials frequently invoke the mantra that "player development isn't linear," that struggles are expected at some stage of a player's career. In many ways, teams want their prospects to endure—and overcome—difficult periods in the minors so that they have such an experience to use as a reference point when they invariably struggle in the big leagues.

In Salem, Devers could lean on hitting coach Nelson "Pepe" Paulino—the Dominican native who'd been his hitting coach the previous year in Greenville, and who'd helped him emerge from his second-half swoon. The relocation of Paulino from Greenville to Salem was no accident, as the Red Sox wanted to keep the hitting coach with Devers and Moncada, prized pupils whose trust he'd earned. Over the final three and a half months of the season, the nineteen-year-old reestablished his commitment to driving the ball to all fields, hitting .326/.365/.507 over his final 88 games.

By the end of 2016, Devers had posted almost identical statistics in High-A Salem to the ones he'd amassed the previous year in Greenville. Yet the similarity of those numbers failed to capture the young player's growth and improving self-understanding, traits that—along with major defensive strides at third base—suggested a player who'd taken a considerable step toward the big leagues.

In 2017, Devers was no longer part of a prospect peloton. Benintendi was in the big leagues. Moncada and Kopech were in the White Sox system. Anderson Espinoza had been traded to the Padres. Devers was riding alone, the remaining jewel of the Red Sox farm system. He entered the year with Double-A Portland determined to become a better, more consistent player.

Portland manager Carlos Febles and hitting coach Lee May saw a succession of lightbulbs go off that year. During a brief early season struggle, Devers asked May to meet him early in the cage to work on his swing. May said he'd meet Devers, but that the two wouldn't change a thing about the young slugger's swing.

May flipped Devers five balls below the knees. Devers hit all of them into the ground. The hitting coach then threw him five in the middle of the zone, each obliterated. Instantly, Devers understood: the problem wasn't his swing but his pitch selection. That feedback from May and Febles echoed teachings from Paulino in the previous two years; now Devers was mature enough to apply such messages in days or even hours rather than weeks or months.

The result was a breakthrough. In 77 games in Double-A, Devers hit .300 with a .369 OBP, .575 slugging mark, and 18 homers. Febles described him as "way more advanced" than Moncada had been in Double-A the previous year due to his ability to do damage against all pitch types—roughly two-thirds of his homers in Portland came on breaking balls—and the comfort he showed at third base. In his excellence and particularly his on-field exuberance, Devers reminded May of another young star with whom he'd grown up in the Cincinnati area: Ken Griffey Jr.

Devers earned a second invitation to the All-Star Futures Game. It served as the backdrop for a fascinating reunion, with Devers rejoining Moncada and Mauricio Dubon (now with the Brewers) on the World Team. Fellow 2015 Greenville Drive and 2016 Salem Red Sox alum Michael Kopech pitched for the U.S. team. The quartet got together for breakfast the morning of the game, stepping back to appreciate how far they'd come in two years and how special a group they'd had while coming up together through the Red Sox ranks.

"We had a great team in Greenville," said Devers. "To find ourselves in this position, going to the Futures Game together—even though we're not in the same organization—it is kind of crazy."

For the Red Sox organization, it was a moment to reflect on how far Devers had come in the four years since signing. That he stood on the cusp of the big leagues in that time represented a remarkable development—Devers would join Bogaerts as just the second twenty-year-old position player to reach the big leagues with the Red Sox since 1980—yet also underscored how drastically different baseball is from other professional sports.

"The NFL you're going from playing in the college game, a bowl game, next year [in the NFL] you're starting game one," noted Romero. "[In baseball], you look at it like, oh my God, it's been three years. It's so crazy. It takes so long, but it's really not long in terms of regular [development] curves, but I get so impatient."

After the Futures Game, Devers was promoted to Triple-A Pawtucket. Benintendi and Moncada had had mixed experiences skipping Pawtucket in 2016, and the Sox wanted to give Devers time to round the edges of his development—particularly facing more breaking-ball-heavy pitch diets and adjusting to the more challenging defensive pace of the game—in Triple-A. Devers had other ideas.

In his first game with the PawSox, against Syracuse, Devers—making a midyear move to a higher level for the first time since 2014—delivered an electric performance. From the moment he took the field for batting practice, he looked like he belonged—certainly in Triple-A, perhaps in the majors. Devers opened the game with a single to left, then followed that with a two-strike line drive single to right. His third time up, he slammed a one-hop double off the wall in right. Finally, in his fourth and final plate appearance of the night, Syracuse summoned thirty-seven-year-old left-hander Neal Cotts—a veteran of ten big league seasons—to face the left-handed slugger.

Cotts missed the strike zone with two straight breaking balls, then got Devers to overswing and chase a neck-high fastball. On the next pitch, Cotts tried to double up with another fastball. Devers launched the ball into the light tower. To punctuate the night, he made a tremendous defensive play—fielding a slow tapper barehanded and making a perfect off-balance throw while falling to his right—that conjured thoughts of Beltre.

"In my time in the minor leagues," said PawSox broadcaster Will Flemming, then in his ninth year calling minor league games, "no one who looks like this doesn't get to the big leagues and become a badass."

The Red Sox rapidly arrived at the same conclusion. Devers spent just nine games in Triple-A—hitting .400 with two homers—before the team summoned him to Seattle in late July, the same city where Benintendi had made his big league debut almost exactly one year earlier.

THERE WERE NO GUARANTEES WHETHER Devers, like Benintendi, would be ready, or whether like Moncada he'd be in over his head. Debate existed within the organization as to whether it was in the interests of both the big league team and the player's development to call up Devers. But with the Red Sox offense amid a yearlong struggle to claw for runs, the team was willing to take the risk.

After an 0-for-4 debut, Devers blasted a 427-foot homer just to the left of dead center in his second career game, becoming the youngest Red Sox player to homer since 1965. That was the first of a series of landmark homers by Devers, who delivered a power show with little precedent in major league history for a twenty-year-old at the inception of his big league career. On July 31, he went 4-for-4 in a win over Cleveland, joining Ted Williams and two others as the only twenty-year-olds in the previous one hundred years to amass four-hit games for the Red Sox.

On August 3, with the Red Sox facing Moncada and the White Sox, Devers flicked a pitch on the outer half of the plate over the Green Monster for his third homer in eight games. Moncada, meanwhile, was struggling, with four hits in forty at-bats since his own call-up, and advance scouting reports identified multiple giant holes in Moncada's swing that were easily exploited for strikeouts.

Had the White Sox asked to build the Sale trade around Devers and Kopech rather than Moncada and Kopech, Boston almost certainly would have happily complied. But now, even as onlookers continued to acknowledge Moncada's sky-high future ceiling, it was becoming quickly apparent that Devers was the one who was positioned to make an impact in more immediate pennant races.

On August 13, Devers made that case in front of a national audience. With the Red Sox trailing the Yankees, 2–1, in the ninth inning in Yankee Stadium, Aroldis Chapman— the hardest-throwing pitcher in baseball—put Devers in a one-ball, two-strike hole. But on the next pitch, Devers smoked a 102.8-mph fastball over the fence in left-center for a game-tying home run in an eventual 3–2 Red Sox win. It was the first home run Chapman had ever allowed to a left-handed hitter in a two-strike count, and the hardest-thrown pitch in ten seasons of pitch-tracking data to be drilled over a fence.

Victor Rodriguez, the assistant hitting coach, had just one thought. "Whoa—this guy is not a normal kid."

Devers hit two more homers the next night and another two the following weekend against the Yankees back at Fenway Park, making eight dingers in his first twenty big league games. A look to the record books for similar starts by twenty-year-olds drew up names like Babe Ruth, Ted Williams, and Frank Robinson—all-time luminaries, even if Devers had never heard of most of them.

Eventually, however, the league caught up to Devers, who hit .241 with a modest .642 OPS over his last six weeks. As that struggle took hold, evidence of the atomized Red Sox environment started to become visible.

After the third baseman had come up in July, he was often left to sit by himself at his locker rather than drawn into more animated exchanges—the sort that had become increasingly rare for the Red Sox in 2017. Indeed, the person who became Devers's mentor in 2017 wasn't one of the team's familiar mainstays but instead Eduardo Nunez, who'd come to the Sox in a trade with the Giants on the same day that the team had decided to promote the twenty-year-old to the big leagues.

As Devers tried to make sense of his struggles down the stretch, he counted on Nunez and Victor Rodriguez. Bogaerts lent an occasional hand and periodically invited him out on the road—not that such outings were frequent.

"They play their Fortnite," Raquel Ferreira noted of the changing extracurriculars of up-and-coming players, a contrast to the more mischievous players of previous generations. "It's kind of better. I'd rather have them playing Fortnite than going out . . . as long as they don't get carpal tunnel."

Devers was far more understated in the big leagues than he was in minor league clubhouses. He felt reserved about approaching other veterans, who seemed lost in their own struggles. And in contrast to Benintendi, who'd been invited to live with Pedroia, Devers—who was living without a teammate for the first time—first had his father (also named Rafael) stay with him, and then spent the conclusion of the year living by himself. He didn't seem integrated into the Red Sox clubhouse so much as he'd parachuted into it.

Nonetheless, the initial surge produced by the precocious power hitter offered a gust in what had been a windless sail on the Charles River. Though the Sox slipped a half game behind the Yankees in the division at the end of July, a stretch starting on July 31 of sixteen wins in twenty games put the team in relatively comfortable position.

But the players never felt they could enjoy their first-place status, a notion perhaps best encapsulated by the blowback that the team's outfielders experienced in reaction to how they observed victories. In 2016, Red Sox outfielders had started to converge following wins for a celebratory ritual: "Win, Dance, Repeat." The three outfielders would meet on their way toward the postgame handshake line and bow toward one another, then engage in a brief choreographed dance. At the conclusion of that exchange, whichever outfielder had made the largest contribution to the victory performed a solo dance move while the other two outfielders squatted and pantomimed the operation of a hand-cranked movie camera.

As Bradley explained, "It was like, 'All right, I'm going to have a better day than you, and I'm going to have a better day than you.' I think that made us play better together."

It was a simple expression of joy in a victory. But as the 2017 season wore on, the outfielders sensed that their efforts to treat their profession, even just momentarily, with childlike levity were not appreciated. The delight that had followed, for instance, Bradley mimicking a ski jump or Benintendi's demonstration of dance moves made famous by Michael Jackson had worn off.

"We're getting criticized for having fun after we won a game," said Betts. "I wasn't really sure I could understand why."

That puzzling sense of omnipresent severity hovered throughout the year. The clubhouse was often quiet, and younger players were cautious about seeking the advice of veterans and coaches. Wins felt exhausting, losses unbearable. Even though the team finished the year with a 93-69 record—identical to its mark in 2016—there was little satisfaction.

"It was really a grind year, despite how good the team was," said bullpen coach Dana LeVangie. "Especially here in Boston, if you're not having fun and winning all those games we won, it wears you down."

The Sox looked the part by the time the playoffs arrived. For the second straight year, the Red Sox won the AL East, but opened the Division Series on the road against the Astros—a team whose own core had taken shape and emerged as a force. Houston crushed the Red Sox in the first two games, and though the Red Sox rallied to win Game 3 at Fenway, the Astros overcame an eighth-inning deficit in Game 4 to claim a 5–4 victory and advance to the American League Championship Series.

It was a game that was emblematic of the Red Sox season. The team enjoyed a glimpse of possibility and a reminder of the talent on its roster when Bogaerts, Devers, and Benintendi all homered, one of just five playoff games ever in which three players who were twenty-five years old or younger did so. Yet it hadn't quite been enough.

"They were not playing the game like they were capable," observed Rodriguez. "Even though we won the division, we were still missing something."

After Game 4, there was a brief postgame meeting involving Farrell—who'd been ejected in the second inning for arguing balls and strikes—and Dombrowski in the manager's office, a standard discussion of medical reports and health updates. Dombrowski didn't linger.

"He said, 'You know, I've got a lot to do. I'll be in touch,'" Farrell recalled. "I thought, 'Geez why don't you just fire me now?'"

Two mornings later, on October 11, Dombrowski called Farrell in for a meeting at Fenway Park to do just that.

"I said, 'I'm not surprised. . . . I'll have my shit out of here by the end of the day,'" Farrell recounted telling Dombrowski. "'But I do have one question for you. After we clinched against Houston in the final series of the year, you walked in here and you congratulated me and said, "Great job with all we went through this year." So my question is, what happened in the last week?'

"There was no answer. I said, 'I get it. Don't worry about it. I'm outta here.'"

At a press conference later that day to discuss the decision, Dombrowski avoided specifics. ("I think change is good for the organization," he said. "I'm not going to share facts.") That said, few pushed back against the notion that it was time for a different voice.

Farrell had been the perfect antidote to Bobby Valentine a half decade earlier.

But five years can feel like a lifetime—or several lifetimes—in Boston. Players change, team dynamics change, and over time, managers change—with the outcome that eventually, the team changes managers.

"I think everybody that sits in that chair, particularly in Boston, they're going to go through stages in their own path. They're going to get hardened and I think begin to lose some of that personal touch," Farrell reflected in early 2019. "While I maybe didn't realize it was happening all the while, I look back now like, 'Holy fuck, that job fucking killed you'—in my case," he added with a laugh of a cancer survivor versed in the art of gallows humor, "almost literally."

CHAPTER 12

A NEW LEADER

For all that the red sox accomplished the previous two years, the consecutive rapid exits from the postseason raised questions. Both years they had won 93 games, both years they had won the division, both years they had been defeated, soundly, at home in the American League Division Series. As they entered 2018, Dave Dombrowski had a decision to make. Another executive might have been tempted to shake up the team's roster, believing that a mix at risk of stagnating needs stirring. But Dombrowski "never even thought along those lines."

Dombrowski believed in the larger sample of the regular season as a measuring stick. Winning the American League East in consecutive years showed a team with an exceptional talent base. He saw a group that was gifted, and had been toughened by the successes and challenges of the previous year.

With the influence of the right voices, it could hold its own against any competitor. Still, though, he acknowledged that something was missing.

Alex cora had come into an unsettled Red Sox clubhouse situation before. In 2005, Cora was with Cleveland in the first season of a two-year deal he'd signed as a free agent. The twenty-nine-year-old had come to Cleveland with a modest offensive profile—a career .246 average, .314 OBP, and .351 slugging mark—but with sterling reports of his baseball IQ, leadership, and defense. Both the player and team reached the deal with the expectation of supplying Cora with regular playing time. Instead, his role was squeezed. Cora told the team he was uncomfortable with the changed job description and in early July was dealt to the Red Sox.

The Red Sox, coming off the franchise's historic first championship in 2004, had a clubhouse renowned for its closeness and free-spirited nature. But that's not what Cora found when he joined the team in Baltimore just before the All-Star break.

"Holy shit! What is this?" Cora recalled thinking of his first exposure to the Red Sox.

It was July 7, 2005. One night earlier, outfielder Jay Payton—like Cora, unhappy with a reserve role after a career as a regular—had refused to enter a game in the late innings of a blowout, precipitating a dugout row with manager Terry Francona. Payton was designated for assignment the next day, the same one on which Cora joined his new club.

On top of that, Francona was dealing with hostility from his players about who was being selected for that year's All-Star roster. Though Francona—the American League manager of the midseason showcase owing to the Red Sox' presence in the World Series the prior year—had little flexibility to select his own players, the clubhouse fumed at his inability to add reliever Mike Timlin to the AL roster. On top of that, key veterans from the 2004 season bristled as their playing time dwindled in 2005 in the face of declining production.

Then Cora found out that his playing situation wouldn't be much better; the Red Sox, like Cleveland, viewed him as a reserve rather than an everyday player. Dave Wallace, the Red Sox pitching coach who knew Cora from a previous stint together in Los Angeles, asked Cora to choose his future.

"Do you want to be an everyday player on a second-division club or do you want to really be part of winning and a winning culture?" Wallace recalled asking Cora.

Cora contemplated those options during that series in Baltimore and while he packed his house in Cleveland during the All-Star break. He returned with clarity: embracing a support role—excelling in it—would make him a valuable player who could have many more seasons in the big leagues in the pursuit of championships.

"I accepted my role and moved on," recalled Cora.

Cora emerged as a revered teammate, someone trusted not only to contribute when called upon but also to aid the development and growth of other players. In 2007, Cora had gotten off to a scorching start, while the Red Sox' promising rookie second baseman, Dustin Pedroia, had struggled mightily. Another veteran might have reveled in his competition's growing pains, but Cora mentored Pedroia. He made clear that the position would soon belong to the rookie once he got his big league footing.

As the season progressed, Cora delighted in seeing his younger teammate emerge as a top-of-the-lineup force, helping him with lessons on and off the field whenever possible. Over time, Pedroia became comfortable in the big leagues, and proved a wildly entertaining, mile-a-minute trash talker who contributed to what Cora saw as the team's swagger. In that atmosphere, the bilingual Cora served as a bridge builder to different sides of the clubhouse—a rare player who won the trust of English and Spanish speakers, position players and pitchers, young players and veterans, stars and role players—and a trusted confidant of Francona. Invariably, for anyone who asked, he could offer unusually sharp insights.

Over parts of four years as a player in Boston, Cora started to see the game from the perspective of a manager, and indeed, Francona took him on as something of an apprentice. During Francona's favorite time of the night—the twenty to thirty minutes before the start of the game, when quiet descends upon the dugout—he often gave Cora brief tutorials about managing, among them principles for bullpen usage and the division of labor with a coaching staff.

Cora never forgot Francona's generosity. And he loved the Boston baseball experience. His big league career would span fourteen years, with stops in Los Angeles, New York, Arlington, Texas, Washington, and Cleveland. But none could top Boston, with its sophisticated, passionate fan base whose investment in the game, Cora felt, finally matched his own.

NINE YEARS AFTER THE END of his days as a Red Sox player, Cora, in his new role as bench coach of the Astros, had emerged during the 2017 postseason as what Houston manager A. J. Hinch called "the hottest managerial candidate on the planet." The Red Sox, after firing Farrell, were one of several teams contributing to that status.

As members of the front office surveyed the remaining playoff field, particularly the Houston team helmed by Hinch that had just vanquished them from the postseason, they saw a manager who seemed very different from Farrell. He was upbeat and young enough to relate to his players about their lives away from the field while also versed in new analytical approaches that allowed him to make use of the Astros' considerable intellectual firepower.

The Red Sox recognized that they'd need someone from that mold to coax more production out of their young stars. The 2017 team was different from the one that Farrell had been hired to manage entering 2013—younger and greener, in need of direction, instruction, and perhaps even a hint of cockiness to nudge them beyond their characteristic humility.

The Red Sox felt that the demographics of their roster—millennials who had grown up in a different era of technology and social media than prior baseball generations—required a different voice to connect with their players.

"I can't parent the same way my parents parented. Not that it was wrong; it just doesn't fit for today's world," said Dombrowski. "It's the same way when it comes to managing people."

Cora represented an obvious candidate to address that changing landscape—and not just to the Red Sox. Several teams expressed interest in him, including two of his former teams, the Nationals and Mets. But Cora wanted to see if he and the Red Sox would be a match.

"Here was kind of the perfect fit," said Cora. "This is the place I wanted to be."

And the Red Sox wanted him. The team engaged in a limited search, talking to Cora, former Tigers manager Brad Ausmus, and former Twins manager and Diamondbacks bench coach Ron Gardenhire.

But Cora quickly emerged as the favorite—not just because of his ties to some who remained in the organization but also because of how perfectly his personality along with the skills he'd developed in Houston aligned with what the Red Sox needed.

"I'm not saying I know a lot," said Pedroia, Cora's teammate with the Red Sox from 2006 to 2008, "but that one, I was like, 'If we get him, a lot will change.'"

On October 21, the team issued a press release announcing Cora as the forty-seventh manager in team history. Eleven days later, he won the World Series with the Astros—and almost immediately, he got to work in redefining the dynamics inside the Red Sox organization.

THE POST-2017 OFF-SEASON WAS QUIET around the league, and the Red Sox were no exception. By the start of spring training, the team had made just one move involving the major league roster: re-signing first baseman Mitch Moreland to a two-year, $13 million deal. But the coaching staff was all new, apart from Dana LeVangie, who'd been promoted from bullpen coach to pitching coach.

"People have talked about how we haven't made a lot of changes in the last year," Red Sox owner John Henry said—at a time when the team had not yet reached agreement on a deal with J. D. Martinez. "In my mind, we've made significant changes."

Over the winter, the new manager bounced around the country in order to get to know members of his team in informal settings, sitting down with most players face-to-face. In his introductions, he dazzled.

David Price—who joined with fellow rotation member Chris Sale, catcher Sandy Leon, outfielder Jackie Bradley Jr., and Cora for lunch at B. J.'s Brewhouse in Fort Myers in January— instantly sensed that the Red Sox had their Joe Maddon, the manager under whom Price had reached the big leagues with the Rays in 2008.

Maddon, though one of the older managers in the league, married an ability to relate to young players with a perhaps surprising willingness to see the game through a modern prism. Under his oversight, an inexperienced Rays team had flourished. Cora likewise put the players at ease and related to them casually (discussions of changing the diapers of the manager's infant twins will do that) while also framing expectations boldly, telling his new players that he recognized a championship-caliber team that had yet to realize its potential.

Andrew Benintendi had dinner with Cora in Boston in January. Benintendi had appreciated Farrell for maintaining faith and keeping him in the lineup even through unexpectedly prolonged slumps. Still, upon sitting down with Cora, Benintendi was struck by how different it was to relate to a younger manager. Cora, after all, had been a Red Sox player just a decade earlier; he had been teammates with several players currently on the roster.

A Winter Weekend event at Foxwoods Resort in late January assembled much of the team for a couple of days and nights. While the day featured several events involving fan interactions, outside of that part of the schedule, Cora and the coaches got to hang out informally with the players. The ease of the interactions was evident to all. Bonds of trust were being built even before the start of spring training.

The players were getting a read on their manager, but Cora likewise found the character study of his team fascinating. As he got to know his new group, there was a trait that was distinct from the players on the two teams with whom Cora had won titles, first as a Red Sox player in 2007 and again ten years later as the Astros bench coach in 2017. This group was humble.

"For how talented they are," Cora recalled, "they don't brag about it, they don't dress that way, they just love to show up here and play. For how young they are, they're not caught up on the whole stuff that goes on at that age. If they wanted to, they'll be rock stars in Boston, but . . . it's not in their DNA."

Cora wanted to be respectful of their personalities, but also thought it necessary to let the players know that they need not hide from their talent. The manager projected an air of confidence—one of Henry's only concerns about him was that he seemed, if anything, too confident in the interview—and wanted his players to do the same.

In Fort Myers, during spring training, Cora invited Betts, Bogaerts, and Bradley to a meal at Connors Steak & Seafood, an upscale restaurant in the Gulf Coast Town Center, a sprawling outdoor mall that offered an array of restaurants where Cora invited team members that spring. His message was twofold. First, he wanted to reiterate how good those three players were, that other teams viewed them as possessing elite abilities—a valuable reminder after the long, doubt-instilling slog through 2017. Cora reminded Betts he had the talent to be the best player in the game, told Bogaerts that he belonged in a conversation about the game's top shortstops, and encouraged Bradley to think of himself as a standout all-around player.

And second, he let them know that they hadn't spent the previous year carrying themselves accordingly. Cora had seen the Sox up close in 2017; the Astros and Red Sox played the last four games of the regular season against each other and then four more in the ALDS, with the Astros winning six of the eight contests. As Bradley recalls, Cora was candid: the Astros had respected the talent of the Red Sox in 2017, but they knew based on body language alone that they would roll Boston.

"He just kept saying, 'Y'all are damn good, so make sure everyone knows that when you come to the ball field, and make sure the other team knows that when you're playing against them,'" said Bradley. "It felt really good for him to make that statement. He knew."

Cora had served as the general manager of Team Puerto Rico in the 2017 World Baseball Classic. In that role, he'd seen a talented group rise to excellence by playing the game with flair and passion. He witnessed something similar when the Astros emerged as the last team standing in October.

Cora loved seeing his players show emotion on the field, loved seeing players who weren't afraid to display fire and excitement in games. The prior Red Sox coaching staff, Bogaerts felt, had wanted the team to play a buttoned-up, traditional brand of baseball. Cora sought something else.

As Bogaerts remembers, Cora himself put it succinctly: "Play like you're a badass."

As the team got to know Cora better during spring training, it became clear he was more than talk. He regularly emerged from his office to interact with players by their lockers and in their space, in turn making it more comfortable for players to reciprocate and come into his office—a considerable contrast to Farrell, who rarely lingered in the players' space. Lines of communication easily followed, with bench coach Ron Roenicke observing that players were choosing to sit next to Cora in the dugout for baseball discussions during exhibition games.

In drills and spring work, Cora valued quality over quantity. Rather than ask players to take endless ground balls in the spring, he shortened the drills but demanded precision—something that seemed a better fit for the attention spans of millennials, and that served the dual purpose of limiting the physical demands on players in February and March in hopes of keeping them performing closer to their peaks in September and October.

For similar reasons, he and LeVangie scaled back the workloads of the Red Sox' starting pitchers during spring training. The pitching staff, especially, had felt burnt out by the time they got to the playoffs in 2017; Cora wanted to ensure it wouldn't happen again.

Mentally, too, he wanted his team to cultivate a healthy relationship with the game. High on the wall of the Red Sox clubhouse at JetBlue Park, the team's spring training home, is a quote from Red Sox legend Carl Yastrzemski: "I think about baseball when I wake up in the morning. I think about it all day and I dream about it at night. The only time I don't think about it is when I'm playing it."

Certainly, such an outlook made Yastrzemski great—a Hall of Famer who had arguably the greatest individual season in Red Sox history in 1967, when he carried the team to a pennant in "the Impossible Dream" season that put baseball back on the map in Boston. But more than fifty years removed from that time—and with the social media rabbit holes truly making it possible to think about baseball during every waking moment— Cora wanted his players to have the ability "to disconnect from the game."

"You can be mad all you want after the game," Cora said. "But once you shower up, you're headed home, that's it. Think about tomorrow."

Cora wanted his players to enjoy themselves. After the previous year, when joy in victory had rarely carried forward and when losses left behind a sulfuric residue, this was a refreshing departure.

IN ONE MORE WAY, CORA'S approach was new, and needed. While the Red Sox had once been considered at the vanguard of the game's information age, over time, they'd slipped in that regard. Other teams had more robust analytics departments, with managers and coaching staffs more adept at using new forms of data and relaying them to players.

Cora came from the Astros, a team that had become one of the most progressive in the game in terms of integrating data into decision making. With the Red Sox, Cora wanted to create something similar, a notion he made clear to VP of baseball research and development Zack Scott during Cora's interview process.

Scott hadn't gone into the managerial search expecting to find someone who wanted to be involved with the front office's data efforts. Nor had he really sought one. But Cora changed that. "I came away from that process thinking, 'Wow, he's really invested in this stuff. He's really all-in,'" said Scott.

In other eras, managers grudgingly put up with input from the analytics department. Cora, from the first day, saw his as a useful tool. He wanted the team's analysts to design more efficient defensive alignments. He asked them to develop both offensive and pitching game plans for opponents (which were then compared against the coaches' own thoughts on how to attack other teams), and sought data to inform decisions about, among other things, lineup construction and when to play the infield in.

In very little time, Cora changed both the flow and types of information being made available to players. His team was young enough that it welcomed a new way of doing things. His immediate closeness to the players created a foundation for discussions of new concepts—sparking curiosity that extended not just from the manager to his players, but subsequently from player to coach, and player to player. The environment created the framework for a renovation of the offense.

THE RED SOX IN 2017 had clear offensive strengths, in particular a number of players (including Betts, Benintendi, Bogaerts, and Pedroia) with elite hand-eye coordination that suppressed strikeout totals in an era where power pitchers routinely made contact next to impossible. Moreover, the team featured impressive speed throughout its lineup.

But while those traits helped the Red Sox to produce solid offensive numbers, ranking sixth in the American League with 4.85 runs per game, the team had shown almost no power. The

Red Sox cleared the fences just 168 times, last in the American League—an almost unfathomable ranking for a team that enjoyed the cozy left-field wall at Fenway Park. Partly this was a function of personnel. In contrast to the Yankees, who featured a team of NBA-sized sluggers, many of the Sox' everyday players were under six feet tall. Yet Cora wondered whether size was the real reason behind the power outage.

In 2017, the Red Sox had swung at first pitches 21.1 percent of the time—less frequently than any team in the majors. In other hitters' counts—three balls and a strike, two balls and no strikes, two balls and a strike, etc.—the Sox consistently ranked among the most passive teams in the majors. For players with at least 400 plate appearances in that season, Betts (12.1 percent) and Bogaerts (11.9 percent) had swung at the sixth- and fifth-fewest first pitches in all of baseball. This disciplined approach wasn't new in 2017. For years, it had helped make the Red Sox one of the most productive offenses in the big leagues by driving up the pitch counts of opposing starters and then slicing through the soft underbelly of opposing staffs, the middle relievers.

But by 2017, Cora knew, bullpens were different. The explosion of mid- and high-90s throwers—a trickle-up effect from the amateur ranks to the big leagues—meant that teams featured waves of power arms in the middle and late innings. The drop-off from starter to reliever was no longer pronounced, if it existed at all; indeed, the increased employment of bullpen games and relievers handling the initial outs of the games *before* giving way to more traditional starters (the strategy of "the opener" popularized by the Tampa Bay Rays in 2018) suggested that for some teams, the opposite had become true. The effective counter was not to wait out opposing pitchers in a rope-a-dope strategy, but instead to be ready to attack whenever a pitcher made a mistake in the strike zone, particularly in hitters' counts.

Cora sought a team that would, in his parlance, "do damage" when pitchers made mistakes in the zone. Jumping on first pitches and driving them in the air was part of that strategy. To fully implement, he knew he needed fresh hitting instructors.

Tim Hyers had been the Red Sox minor league hitting co-ordinator between 2013 and 2015 before going to the Dodgers for the 2016 and 2017 campaigns. He had the trust of the players from his prior relationships with them, yet he had a new message to offer after his time in the data-driven Dodgers organization. Hyers worked with players—most notably Betts—to swing through the ball. Instead of a direct path of the bat down to the point of contact with the ball, he encouraged Red Sox hitters to swing on the plane of the pitch with an uppercut that had been espoused a half century earlier by Red Sox legend Ted Williams but that, puzzlingly, hadn't taken hold until the last few years.

In 2017, the Red Sox had lagged behind the game's Launch Angle Revolution. One of the team's coaches, in fact, showed little love for what he referred to as "that launch angle shit," believing that the foundation of hitting remained an all-fields, line-drive approach.

The team's hardest-hit balls that season tended to result in hard grounders or low line drives—good, perhaps, for singles and doubles, less so for home runs. Under Cora and Hyers, the Sox wanted more of those long fly balls that cleared the fences.

In the middle of spring training, that pursuit was aided by the addition of a player who preached the gospel of Launch Angle.

In 2013, J. D. Martinez had seen a once-promising professional career sputter. Just a 20th-round pick in 2009, he had dominated the minors and made the Astros' big league club in two years. But after initial success in the majors, he'd settled into mediocrity and didn't know why. There was no one on the Astros—a team committed to a teardown-rebuild process—to help provide answers.

"I never had an older veteran player to talk to," said Martinez. "I remember just searching for answers, searching for ideas."

Finally, Astros hitting coach John Mallee offered a blunt appraisal. Martinez's swing wasn't going to allow him to be an impact player in the big leagues. He was chopping down at the ball—the direct path that had been taught for generations, but that almost guaranteed groundballs at a time when pitchers were pounding the bottom of the strike zone with fastballs thrown ever harder.

The counter to this fascination with the bottom of the strike zone was to feature an uppercut swing on the plane of the pitch. What had been taught as a successful outcome—a hard ground ball or line drive up the middle—was no longer what Martinez should try to do if he wanted to be a game-changing hitter.

"It was," Martinez recalled of the epiphany, "an out-of-body experience, like, 'This is so crazy. Everything I've been taught for so long has been so wrong.'"

Everything in Martinez's swing had been constructed to achieve the wrong outcome. He employed an early stride that removed the strength of his base from his swing—by the time he actually hacked at a pitch, he was relying solely on his upper body, thus stripping a considerable amount of potential power from his swing. And before the pitch, rather than starting his hands high and swinging with one fluid motion, Martinez started with his hands low, brought them up, and then swung down on pitches.

As Martinez studied a number of the game's elite sluggers over the duration of the 2013 season—Mike Trout, Miguel Cabrera, Ryan Braun, Joey Votto—he realized how different their swings were from his, how different their offensive approaches were from his. In the off-season following 2013, Martinez went to work with Craig Wallenbrock and Robert Van Scoyoc, private hitting instructors in Santa Clarita, California. It was as if he'd gone on a hitting vision quest, embracing the annihilation of his former hitting self as a precursor to offensive rebirth.

"You take a million swings one way and all of a sudden you've got to tell your body you can't do that anymore and have to take a million swings [another] way," said Martinez.

He overhauled his swing both physically and philosophically. But the Astros failed to appreciate the metamorphosis. Houston gave him just eighteen plate appearances in spring training in 2014 and released him shortly before the end of camp. Martinez quickly signed a minor league deal with the Tigers, and days after his release, in a Triple-A game, he launched three homers against an Astros minor league squad—one to left-center, one to center, and one to right-center. Over the next four years, Houston would realize the magnitude of its mistake, as Martinez established himself as one of the game's top hitters with the Tigers and, after a mid-2017 trade, the Diamondbacks, posting a .300 average with a .362 on-base percentage, and .574 slugging mark while walloping 40 homers per 162 games.

The Red Sox viewed him as the preeminent offensive player on the free-agent market after the 2017 season, a presence who could fill the Ortiz-sized void that had opened in the middle of the order the previous year. Martinez represented an established run producer who could allow the younger Red Sox to be comfortable in their own abilities rather than feeling a need to compensate for the absence of their longtime lineup cornerstone. Yet after Martinez reached agreement on a five-year, $110 million deal with the Red Sox shortly after the start of spring training, it soon became apparent that his impact would not be limited to what he did in the batter's box. His reputation as a self-created star and student of hitting preceded him.

To his new Red Sox teammates, Martinez represented evidence that players had untapped abilities that they might be able to harness with the right approach and hard work. (Once asked to name his favorite superhero, Martinez identified Iron Man. Why? "Self-made," he said.) Throughout spring training, players frequently stopped at his locker and got into their batting stances, exchanging notes and ideas. Martinez had rued not having veterans to ask advice from early in his career. Now he became that veteran, and delighted in sharing his insights. One pupil, especially, was fascinated.

Mookie Betts had a long reputation for being remarkably inquisitive and curious, dating to the days when he'd shadow his uncle, Terry Shumpert, at Herschel Greer Stadium in Nashville. Coaches would joke affectionately about how he wore them out with questions about every detail of the game. That trait, in tandem with an unrelenting work ethic, offered evidence of a constant quest for improvement in all aspects of the game that resided at the heart of his brilliance on the field.

Betts had lots of questions, and Martinez's answers were unlike any he'd encountered before. Given that Betts was in the process of overhauling his swing to get more on the plane of the pitch—the philosophy of Hyers and Martinez—rather than down and direct to the ball, the timing of their partnership proved serendipitous.

Day after day, Betts would emerge from the batting cage alongside Martinez, the duo usually beaming as if having solved a riddle. In many cases, they had.

Red Sox officials had believed throughout 2017 that Betts, Bogaerts, Benintendi, Bradley, and other members of the team had the capacity to explore new dimensions of their game, to turn a very good team into a powerhouse. By the start of the season, the team believed that it had a chance to do something remarkable.

"The supplementation [with Cora and Martinez] really

changed everything," said Jared Banner, Red Sox VP of player personnel. "Bringing them in was a cultural change for the organization."

On March 27, lefty starter Eduardo Rodriguez gathered the team for a dinner in St. Petersburg, Florida, two nights before the start of the season. Fifty-six players, coaches, and staff convened.

Different members of the team stood and addressed their teammates. Cora detailed what he'd seen in the 2017 Astros that had fueled their title run. Longtime Red Sox captain Jason Varitek, who'd been a part of all three Red Sox championships (in 2004 and 2007 as a player, in 2013 in his new role as a front-office special assistant), spoke passionately about what it meant to play and win championships in Boston. Price, coming off his controversial season, spoke about how much he cared about his teammates, and how badly he desired a championship after his hellacious 2017 campaign.

Appropriately enough, given his job description, closer Craig Kimbrel spoke at the end. He had missed much of spring training to be in Boston with his newborn daughter, who'd undergone heart surgery in Boston. He talked about his job, what it meant to be trusted to secure the final outs of a win and what, in turn, it meant to him to reward that faith.

"It was emotional," Cora said of the dinner. "It was a great moment for us."

The Red Sox had entered the off-season convinced that their club possessed the raw materials of a champion. In the way that the group started to connect even in spring training, under Cora's influence, that vision started to take shape.

•   •   •

Officially, alex cora's tenure as Red Sox manager began
with a thud. In possession of a 4–0 lead in Tampa Bay through
seven innings after an excellent performance by Chris Sale, the
Red Sox bullpen endured a six-run, eighth-inning meltdown
that resulted in a startling 6–4 loss to the Rays that prompted a
litany of social media snark.

Yet even in defeat, the Red Sox seemed changed. Despite
having just one player, Martinez, on Opening Day who hadn't
been in the organization at the end of the previous season,
this was a different team than the one that Cora's Astros had
drummed out of the postseason in four games the previous year.

That first game, Bogaerts went 3-for-4 with a pair of
doubles—and after a seventh-inning two-bagger, he positioned
his thumb and index finger on his forehead in the shape of an
"L" while dancing back and forth. It was a performance of the
"Take the L" dance in the video game Fortnite that signaled the
humiliating defeat of an opponent. Bogaerts never would have
considered such a display prior to 2018; but under Cora, having
fun was mandatory.

Elsewhere in the clubhouse, too, Cora's message was taking.
In an introductory dinner meeting with Betts, Cora told the star
right fielder that he'd be the Red Sox' lead-off hitter, and that
he wanted him to swing with bad intentions at the first pitch of
the season—which the manager expected to be a fastball down
the middle from Rays starter Chris Archer.

On Opening Day, Betts did just that—crushing a pitch 406
feet to the fence in center field, where Kevin Kiermaier made a
spectacular catch while slamming into the wall. The outcome
wasn't exactly the home run for which Cora had hoped, but it
was close—close enough to suggest that Betts and the Red Sox
were buying into concepts being espoused by their new manager
and his staff.

And then there was Cora himself. Bullpen blowups are the

low-hanging fruit of public managerial second-guessing. Yet Cora was more concerned with his decision-making process than the results, which in this case meant taking a longer view of the season and not rushing reliever Craig Kimbrel into the eighth inning after the closer had missed most of spring training looking after his daughter. Francona, during their early evening seminars years before, had often told Cora to manage with a larger purpose in mind, not to chase wins. Despite a disappointing outcome, Cora hadn't panicked and was pleased he had remained true to his plan, even if some fans and media were not.

"The sky was falling right away," Cora said, laughing.

The next day, when the Red Sox eked out a 1–0 win over the Rays, the players celebrated Cora's first managerial win by stuffing him in a laundry cart and pushing him into the shower, where they doused him in beer. Cora was sticky, but touched. "It was cool for them to do that for me, and it was the start of something cool."

Many more celebrations soon followed, starting the next day, when Joe Kelly—two days removed from his Opening Day, eighth-inning meltdown—got a dousing after he recorded the final three outs of a 2–1 victory for his first career save. The Red Sox reeled off nine straight victories. That run came to a halt in a 10–7 loss to the Yankees on April 11, yet even that defeat highlighted the newfound unity of the 2018 Sox.

During that contest, Yankees first baseman Tyler Austin slid with his legs up into second base, clipping Brock Holt. Benches and bullpens emptied, words were exchanged, and players from both teams congregated around second base. Cooler heads seemed to prevail. But when Austin stepped to the plate later that game, Kelly drilled him in the back with a 98-mph fastball. Austin stomped toward the mound, Kelly encouraged him to charge, and punches ensued. A wild-eyed Kelly, shirt ripped and neck bleeding from scratches, emerged from the fracas.

Rather than fracturing the clubhouse as had been the case with the messy handling of the Machado-Pedroia incident the previous year, Kelly's handling of the Austin/Holt incident unified it. Players wore "Joe Kelly Fight Club" shirts throughout the year. In the visitor's clubhouse, the Wi-Fi password was changed as an homage to the Red Sox right-hander.

The next day, the Red Sox beat the Yankees—taking the first series of the year between the two teams—and resumed dominating the league. In a much-anticipated match-up against international rookie sensation Shohei Ohtani and on the same field as Mike Trout, the consensus best player of his baseball generation, Betts led off the game with a homer and then added two more. Two days later, he closed out the Angels series by leading off another game with a homer. If there had been any question about whether Betts still belonged among the league's best, they had vanished by the beginning of May.

The Red Sox improved to 17-2 before running over their first pothole of the season, a three-game losing streak in Oakland and Toronto bookended by Sean Manaea no-hitting the Sox and Craig Kimbrel giving up a walk-off homer to Curtis Granderson. The team would never suffer a longer losing streak all year.

This time it was Betts once again who halted the team's skid. It seemed as if every time he made contact, he threatened to leave the yard. He went deep twice against the Blue Jays on April 25, one night before his emerging partner in crime, Martinez, somehow got on top of a neck-high fastball and lined it over the fence in right field for a three-run homer and a 5–4 win over the Blue Jays.

By the end of April, the Sox' offense had scored the second-most runs per game in the majors; their pitching staff had allowed the third fewest. It felt as if the team had fused the best parts of its 2016 and 2017 clubs, with Martinez and the homegrown position players dominating offensively, and the key pitching acquisitions of recent years—Sale, Price, Porcello, and Kimbrel—leading a run of pitching excellence, aided by one of the game's best defensive outfields.

But Cora was wary of complacency. The Sox lost to the lowly Royals on May 1, and nearly did so again on May 2 before Betts and Martinez, combining for four home runs, came to their rescue in a come-from-behind, 5–4 win. The Sox were 22-8, having just won two of three from Kansas City. Yet on their way out of town, Cora assembled his players for his only team-wide meeting of the regular season. He reminded them of their ultimate purpose: to be the best team in baseball on the way to a championship.

"We won a few games, but we weren't playing well," said Cora. "We needed to be better for us to get to where we wanted to go, and they understood."

THEY UNDERSTOOD IN PART BECAUSE of some atypical elements of the team that tended to sharpen the group's focus. Typically, teams meet once before the start of a series to go over a game plan for an opposing team's pitchers. In 2018, Martinez suggested to Cora and Hyers that the Red Sox meet on a daily basis to establish a plan of attack against opposing pitchers. The manager and hitting coach immediately loved the idea of a daily open exchange among players and coaches as part of the team's routine preparations.

The meetings of all of the position players as well as a handful of coaching staff members tended to be brief, starting roughly ten minutes before the scheduled time for batting practice. That structure was intentional, with Cora and Hyers believing in the value of brevity to achieve attention to detail.

At times, the meetings featured video of the opposing starter.

Yet often the low-tech reports were the most valuable. Players who had faced the starter before would describe what his stuff looked like from the batter's box—a two-seam fastball from a righty that looks like it's starting over the middle of the plate but veers inside to a righty; a four-seam fastball with such a high spin rate that it crosses the plate two ball widths higher than a player would anticipate—and what part of the strike zone an opposing pitcher liked to attack.

That level of detail served several purposes. They focused players on that night's game, helping to wash away any residue of the previous contest. They helped establish a culture where details *mattered,* a prerequisite, Cora and Martinez knew, for outstanding execution. And they also served as a sort of tribal bonding experience, allowing players not just to talk about the game but also to enjoy each other's company.

Sometimes, when they'd recently faced that day's starter, the players might skip the baseball conversation in favor of some laughs. Advance scouting assistant J. T. Watkins might queue up some short clips of recent bloopers committed by the Sox. But even when they were having fun, it was clear that something had shifted. The players saw that their best players, Martinez and Betts, weren't coasting along on talent; they hungered for any information they could get. If Betts and Martinez cared so much about spin rate and pitch sequencing and the intricacies of that day's infield shift, their teammates reasoned, they had better care, too.

"CARITA!"

On June 11, J. D. Martinez walked into the visitor's clubhouse in Camden Yards to summon Rafael Devers by his commonly used nickname. Devers was struggling. Martinez wanted to help.

Martinez had become a sort of extension of the hitting coaches. From time to time, when Hyers and assistant hitting coach Andy Barkett had a message to communicate to players but wanted to present it in a different voice—from a peer, rather than a teacher speaking to a student—they turned to Martinez, something that they were now doing in Baltimore.

With Devers and Martinez, the team felt that task became a bit easier a little more than two weeks before Martinez called Devers into the Camden Yards batting cage. On May 25, after returning from a road trip, the Red Sox made a dramatic decision to walk away from Hanley Ramirez and the roughly $15 million remaining on his contract.

On the surface, the decision had been made because the Red Sox needed a roster spot for Dustin Pedroia, who was returning from the disabled list. Initially, the team considered dealing Blake Swihart. But at a time when Ramirez could only play first, the same position occupied by another player—Mitch Moreland—who was on an early-season tear, and when the DH spot was occupied largely by Martinez, the Sox started to ponder how well Ramirez—who'd started the season well, providing some key hits in early season victories, but who'd become easy prey for pitchers by May—would take to a reduced role.

Already, Ramirez's clubhouse influence had offered the closest thing that the 2018 Red Sox had to a false note. He wasn't malicious toward fellow players or members of the coaching staff, but there were times when, in the company of Devers and catcher Christian Vazquez, he'd make light of the game-planning-intensive approach that was coming to characterize the team. The influence on Vazquez appeared considerable, with the catcher employing some of Ramirez's hitting habits—particularly a pronounced leg kick while swinging for the fences—ill-suited for his skill set. The team worried that Devers might similarly be led astray. And some detected an element of jealousy on Ramirez's part directed at Martinez, the team's emerging hitting alpha dog. Even if not, Martinez seemed to find his voice in a different way after Ramirez was released.

"I think when Hanley was around, because of his presence, I think J.D. might have been a little bit more hesitant to take that type of [leadership] role just because Hanley is an established major league player, an established Red Sox player," said assistant hitting coach Andy Barkett. "J.D. was very respectful. I think being around Miguel Cabrera [with the Tigers], he knew to kind of stay in his lane. He got more vocal, especially in meetings, when Hanley was gone."

On that day in Baltimore, Martinez showed Devers a drill to maintain a better swing path and keep his bat head through the strike zone rather than trying to yank the ball for power so frequently—a problem Devers had the first couple of months of the season. But that day laid the groundwork for an alteration of the work that Devers did, as it became part of a new daily routine. Every day, instead of spending his time on the field during batting practice, he remained indoors in the cage with Barkett and a rolling cast of other Red Sox—Martinez and Mitch Moreland were regulars, with drop-ins from Cora and Betts—who wanted to get some of their own work done, but also wanted to spend time with their young teammate to discuss drills, hitting philosophies, and plans of attack against other pitchers.

The group wanted to help advance his hitting education, a sign of nurturing that stood in contrast to what Betts felt he'd encountered as a young big leaguer four years earlier. The Red Sox had created a culture concerned with player development at the big league level.

From across the field, Orioles manager Buck Showalter could sense the changed dynamic around the Red Sox post-Ramirez. Showalter saw a team in which every member of the roster seemed focused in the same direction.

"When they made that move," he recounted later on MLB Network, "I remember saying to myself, 'Uh-oh.' That was a defining moment."

WHILE THE DEPARTURE OF RAMIREZ seemingly benefited the team's culture, his absence further exposed the lineup to one of its most significant vulnerabilities: left-handed pitching. By the end of June, the team felt it had to upgrade. Enter Santiago Espinal—in a way.

In the draft room, the Red Sox give each scout the opportunity to identify a "gut feel" player, someone who, though not a blue-chip prospect, the scout believes has a chance to emerge as a meaningful big league contributor. On the draft board, each "gut feel" guy earns a star next to his name.

In the spring of 2016, South Florida area scout Willie Romay had little question about the player who deserved his star: Santiago Espinal. The shortstop at Miami-Dade College hit .432, and though he had almost no power, he combined several intriguing attributes: the ability to hit for average, the ability to play defense on the left side on the infield, and decent speed. Romay saw his overall skill set as worthy of a B2 player—an excellent utility player if he wasn't an everyday option at one position. The Red Sox snagged him in the tenth round in 2016.

Espinal had a solid first full pro season in 2017, hitting .280/.334/.358 with 20 steals in Single-A Greenville, but in 2018, he came back as an offensive threat, hitting .313/.363/.477 in High-A Salem. Though Espinal had been relatively obscure in college—he signed with the Sox for just $50,000—he now had a skill set that earned the notice of other teams.

On June 28, the Sox traded Espinal to the Blue Jays for Steve Pearce, a right-handed hitter with a long track record of demolishing lefties. From the time that he arrived in Boston through the end of the season, Pearce hit over .300 with an OPS over 1.000 against southpaws. On August 2, Pearce blasted three homers in a game against the Yankees, kick-starting a four-game Red Sox sweep that helped turn a taut division race into a runaway down the stretch. Though Espinal, Romay's find, hadn't been directly a part of that, Pearce's contributions remained a source of considerable pride to both the scout and the scouting department down the stretch, another reminder of the way that their work could contribute to the machinery of a dominant team.

Two days after Pearce's landmark game, another Red Sox newcomer offered his own mark in the series against the Yankees. On August 4, in his second start since being traded to Boston from Tampa Bay, Nathan Eovaldi delivered eight shutout innings in a tidy 93 pitches.

In one sense, Eovaldi highlighted the uneven development of the Red Sox' homegrown talent base. When Alex Cora filed his lineup card each afternoon, it was a safe bet that most of the names on it were Red Sox lifers. Mookie Betts. Andrew Benintendi. Xander Bogaerts. Rafael Devers. Christian Vazquez. Jackie Bradley Jr. But it was virtually assured that the last name on the card, the night's starting pitcher, was not. Chris Sale, Rick Porcello, Eduardo Rodriguez, and Eovaldi all had been added via trades. David Price had been imported as a free agent.

A number of factors played into what had been a scouting and player development disappointment for the Red Sox for several years, dating to an era in the middle of the previous decade when the organization introduced pitchers like Jon Lester, Jonathan Papelbon, and Clay Buchholz from their ranks.

Pitching is inherently more volatile to predict than position players, given the significant injury risks that exist when hurling

95-mph comets toward the plate. Yet beyond that industry-wide concern, there were perhaps other ways in which the Red Sox had struggled in their talent evaluations.

The team's focus on size and clean deliveries that were thought to diminish the likelihood of injury had been misguided. For years, prior to the arrival of radar-based TrackMan data to understand the physics of amateurs' pitches, they'd struggled to identify pitchers who featured true swing-and-miss secondary pitches that would be able to overwhelm not just Triple-A hitters but also big leaguers.

Moreover, there was an entry barrier problem. Because the Red Sox were typically contending, they only rarely had opportunities to commit to young, back-of-the-rotation starters through their uneven performances while trying to break through to the big leagues. It's far easier to live through the developmental bumps of a position player—whose impact on the game is limited to a few at-bats or defensive plays—than to a pitcher, for whom a bad night creates a high likelihood of a loss with repercussions (taxed bullpens) for other days.

"It's harder to be patient with guys if they're not coming up and performing right away," said Ben Crockett, the farm director. "I think it's harder for us generally to break in a middle- or back-of-the-rotation guy because most guys aren't ultimately going to be [that] in their first year in the big leagues."

The Sox weren't alone in their struggle to create a pitching pipeline. The Astros relied heavily on imports Justin Verlander and Charlie Morton in their 2017 championship run, the Cubs relied entirely on starting pitchers who'd been developed in other organizations on their way to a title, and the Royals featured just one homegrown starter during the 2015 postseason. Across the board, pitching prospects flame out at a higher rate than position players, leading to the famous TINSTAAPP acronym formulated by Baseball Prospectus founder Gary Huckaby: There Is

No Such Thing As A Pitching Prospect. The terminology was exaggerated for effect—of course there are pitching prospects—but highlighted the vulnerability of the demographic.

Even so, industry-wide trends weren't a complete justification for the Red Sox' abnormally high bust rates, and in 2015, starting at a time when Cherington was still GM and continuing in the months following Dombrowski's arrival, the team began to overhaul its approach to amateur pitching, most notably with the naming of former pitcher Brian Bannister—who'd long been at the vanguard of pitching analytics even in his big league career—as a director of pitching analysis and development. Yet he wasn't the only personnel member added to that effort.

One of the critical figures in the overhaul of the team's approach to evaluating amateur pitchers was the same person who'd been in charge of scouting Benintendi. Chris Mears, a former big league pitcher who'd been scouting for the team, was named a national pitching crosschecker in late 2015 who would fly around the country to help with draft-room comparisons of different arms.

That promotion came one year after Mears had discovered an arm who, like Santiago Espinal, emerged from obscurity to become a difference-maker. In 2014, Mears affixed his gut-feel star on the draft board to one of Benintendi's teammates at Arkansas: left-hander Jalen Beeks. At a thick five-foot-eleven, Beeks didn't look the part of a prototypical starter, but the Red Sox—after years of whiffing on pitching draft picks in part because of a premium they'd placed on size; bigger, it turned out, did not always mean better—didn't mind. Mears believed that Beeks had a three-pitch mix and the competitive toughness to become a valuable big leaguer. By day three of the 2014 draft, he couldn't suppress surprise at the pitcher's ongoing availability.

"I just remember saying, 'How the heck is this dude still here in the twelfth round?'" Mears recalled.

The Red Sox made sure that he didn't stay on the board for the thirteenth, plucking the lefty with the 374th selection. Yet Beeks didn't travel a direct line to the big leagues. In some ways a pitcher's equivalent of J. D. Martinez, he had to open himself to changing virtually everything he did on the mound, overhauling every pitch that he threw.

With the benefit of vastly improved pitch data and a very open-minded pitcher, the Sox' minor league coaches reshaped his entire arsenal—not because he'd failed, but instead because they recognized that the bad contact he elicited in college and the lower minor league levels might give way to loud contact in the upper levels. To become a big leaguer, he'd have to generate movement that allowed him to miss bats. In Single-A Greenville, Walter Miranda encouraged him to shift from a two-seam to a four-seam fastball. In High-A Salem, Paul Abbott helped him develop a curveball that played off the four-seam fastball and also helped him refine his changeup grip. And in both Double-A Portland and Triple-A Pawtucket, Kevin Walker helped Beeks develop and refine a cutter that turned him into a strikeout machine, leading to a big league debut with the Red Sox on June 7.

The outing went poorly, with Beeks allowing six runs in four innings, and he was sent back down to Triple-A. Four weeks later, he made another appearance for the Red Sox, this time allowing three runs in 2⅓ innings out of the bullpen.

Red Sox officials believed that Beeks could, in time, develop into a valuable contributor, a potential B2, back-of-the-rotation starter. But they also knew that in Dombrowski's looks at the left-hander, he hadn't seen someone who was either ready to contribute immediately or irreplaceable.

"Those," said Zack Scott, "are tough to be patient with."

Tampa Bay could better afford to be patient. The Rays had been intrigued by Beeks for some time, inquiring about his availability early in the summer. The verdict at the time was clear: Beeks was off-limits. But in mid-July, after that second big league outing, Tampa Bay called again. Suddenly Beeks was on the table. He was dealt straight up for Eovaldi—a moment of considerable satisfaction for the team's amateur scouts and player development department, which had helped the Sox identify and shape a player who brought back a significant contributor at the deadline.

One day after Eovaldi's dominant performance against the Yankees, the Red Sox rallied from a 4–1, ninth-inning deficit against Yankees closer Aroldis Chapman, tying the game, 4–4, and setting the stage for a walk-off single from Benintendi in the tenth. The Red Sox were jubilant, armed with the confidence of a team that never saw itself as being out of a game—quite reasonably, given that opposing teams blew nearly as many late-innings save opportunities against the Red Sox (21) as they converted (22) in 2018—and that had effectively planted a flag atop the American League East for a third straight year.

This was a runaway train. The team ended up leading the majors in runs, batting average, on-base percentage, and slugging. The lineup represented a versatile nightmare for opposing pitchers, capable of ambushing pitches early in counts while also proving the toughest team in baseball with two strikes and the most prolific in the game with two outs. They could hit homers and steal bases. The pitching staff allowed the second-fewest runs per game in the American League and proved incredibly efficient at turning leads into wins. It was the formula for dominance.

By the end of that four-game set at Fenway, the Red Sox were 79-34, up 9½ games in the division. They were only chasing history. They had a chance to become the first Sox team since 1946 to win 100 games, even to eclipse the 1912 team's franchise record of 105 victories. But the big question for Alex

Cora's team was whether they could exorcise the demons of the last two Octobers past.

SEPTEMBER PROVED A MARCH TOWARD milestones. A 7–2 win on September 11 guaranteed the team a postseason berth. One day later, David Price—who'd reinvented himself midsummer, adapting both his position on the mound with a move from the third-base to the first-base side of the rubber and his arsenal to emerge as one of the most dominant pitchers in the majors in the second half—pitched the Red Sox to a 1–0 victory over the Blue Jays, Boston's 100th of the year. The 2018 Red Sox were the winningest team the franchise had seen since 1946. They weren't done.

On September 20, the Red Sox again torched the Yankees bullpen, wiping out a 6–4 deficit en route to an 11–6 victory that was punctuated by an upper-deck Betts home run down the left-field line hit so high that it seemed to pose against the Yankee Stadium façade before its descent. The win clinched the AL East title for the Red Sox, who partied in the visitor's clubhouse of Yankee Stadium for the second time in three years.

The game also all but locked up MVP honors for Betts, who was closing out a season in which he led the big leagues in average, became the second player in Red Sox history with 30 homers and 30 steals in the same season, and displayed what Orioles manager Buck Showalter called the greatest right-field defense he'd ever seen.

Betts was just one of many Red Sox players who propelled their careers to new heights in 2018. Benintendi became a steadying presence behind Betts in the second spot in the order, a player who hit a ton of doubles (41), got on base frequently (a .366 on-base percentage) in front of the middle-of-the-order hitters, and had less extreme performance swings than he'd endured in his rookie year. He looked like the player who had fascinated Mears back in 2015.

Martinez was brilliant, earning a reputation as perhaps the best pure slugger in the game, a hitting professor who blasted 43 homers, drove in 130 runs, and hit .332. Bogaerts became a middle-of-the-order presence behind Martinez, hitting .288 with career-highs in on-base percentage (.360), homers (23), RBIs (103), and extra-base hits (71), thus fulfilling Cora's hope that he would thrust himself into the conversation of the best shortstops in baseball.

And the pitching staff, led at different points by Sale—who in the middle of the season enjoyed one of the most dominant runs in baseball history, a seven-start, 44-inning span in which he allowed just one run and struck out 79—Price, and Porcello, mixed consistency with dominance. The Red Sox were brimming with talent that ran more than twenty-five players deep, and given the culture that elevated their collective performance, it was unsurprising to see the group not only claim a third straight division title but to do so in such remarkable fashion.

Just one milestone remained. On September 24, back at Fenway Park, the Red Sox beat the Orioles 6–2 behind a dominant Eovaldi, who struck out ten Baltimore batters in five innings. With the final out, the scoreboards at Fenway flashed the number 106. The 2018 Red Sox had won more games than any other in franchise history.

In Cora's office, amassing victories created a physical challenge. Prior to the start of the year, the manager—in hopes of remaining true to his mission of taking the time to celebrate every win—asked team photographer Billie Weiss to put a picture on the wall of his office that captured the essence or key moment of each victory.

But there was a problem: the original wall selected by Cora behind his desk had room for only eleven columns of nine pictures each. Once the team surpassed 99 wins, a second wall to the left of Cora's desk had to be appropriated. By the end of the season, 108 photographs would hang on those walls. It was a mind-boggling accomplishment: more regular-season victories than any team in baseball since 2001.

Yet the man who had sat in that office all summer, literally surrounded by images of triumph, wasn't satisfied. At the beginning of the season, he had told his team that its success would be defined by whether it won a championship—nothing less. The 108 wins were nice, but unless they could amass 11 more, the photographs in Cora's office would be ultimately unfulfilling. Their historic regular season would mean nothing if it wasn't backed by a better postseason performance than those of the previous two seasons.

But this time, the Red Sox vowed, would be different.

CHAPTER 13

OCTOBER READY

By OCTOBER 2018, THE RED SOX core was no longer emerging. It had reached maturity.

A span of a few years had offered a baseball lifetime of shared experiences that ran a remarkable gamut: an education in professional life; a prospect's infinite sense of possibility and then certain lesson in humility; the weight of collective failure embodied by the big league team's two last-place finishes; massive leadership change inside and outside the clubhouse; the collective breakthrough that had propelled the Red Sox from that organizational nadir to three straight first-place finishes in the American League East, the last a historic trampling of opponents.

In an ordinary year, one might have looked at the Red Sox' 108-54 regular season record and .667 winning percentage—the sixth best since the introduction of the 162-game schedule in 1961—and concluded that they were almost surely better than whomever else they'd encounter in the playoffs. But 2018 wasn't an ordinary year.

The American League featured three juggernauts—the Red Sox, an Astros club that had followed its 2017 title season with 103 wins, and the Yankees, who won 101. It was the first time in baseball history that three teams in the same league had won 100 games.

The separation between the Red Sox and their postseason peers seemed surprisingly narrow, especially given that Boston had struggled against the other AL playoff teams. They had posted an 18-21 mark against the Yankees (10-9), Cleveland (3-4), Houston (3-4), and Oakland (2-4). Yet within the organization, the Red Sox did not view their extraordinary regular season as somehow misleading. To the contrary, the steady steamrolling of opponents had confirmed traits that had been evident throughout the season, dating to its earliest days.

"These guys are good and they know they're good," Raquel Ferreira recalled thinking in spring training. "It wasn't in this cocky way that they thought they were better than everybody else. They were just like, 'Yeah, we're gonna win. We can do this.'"

When the Yankees won their wild card game over the Athletics on October 3, it set up a match-up that for much of the season had seemed inevitable. The Sox' road to a championship would go through New York.

While Boston was seen by Las Vegas as the likelier team to advance, the team sensed doubt in the eyes of the public—particularly in its own market, as suggested by the "prove it" tone that emanated from local media outlets and sports radio. The memory of the two swift exits at the hands of the eventual American League champions—Cleveland in 2016, Houston in 2017—placed the burden of proof on the Red Sox to show that they could win amid the heightened stakes and scrutiny of the playoffs. That lack of prior postseason success was one of multiple perceived flaws in 2018.

So, too, were a lack of bullpen firepower to match that of postseason competitors such as the Yankees and Astros and a rotation that collectively had never won a postseason start. The uncertainty about the team's starters was growing entering October, at a time when Chris Sale had been erratic in the few weeks he'd pitched since returning from shoulder inflammation.

But in the face of perceived slights, the team felt emboldened.

"We're not the favorites. Who gives a shit?" Bogaerts thought. "We have the best record. We're supposed to [win]."

Cora sensed the brimming confidence of his players and loved it. Their attitude reminded him of other homegrown player groups that had emerged as champions in recent years. The prior four World Series winners—the 2014 Giants, 2015 Royals, 2016 Cubs, and 2017 Astros—all featured incredibly talented foundations that, over years of playing together and at times struggling through the minors and the big leagues, had formed into puzzle pieces that interlocked perfectly. He could only hope that this group, as well, would prove transcendent on the game's biggest stage.

BEFORE THE START OF THE ALDS against the Yankees, Mitch Moreland hosted a handful of teammates at his house. Moreland had been a member of the Rangers in 2011, when they endured one of the most heartbreaking World Series losses ever. In Game 6, the Rangers, up 3–2 on the Cardinals and seeking to close out the series, entered the ninth inning with a two-run lead and their trusted closer, Neftali Feliz, on the mound. Feliz had St. Louis down to their last *strike* when David Freese tied the game with a triple. In the tenth, the Rangers again took a two-run lead and again needed just one more strike in the bottom half of the frame. This time it was Lance Berkman who came through for St. Louis with a game-tying single. The Rangers would lose the game, and then, the next night, the World Series.

Moreland and his former Rangers teammate, Ian Kinsler, were there, along with Rick Porcello (another World Series loser, in 2012) and Benintendi, among others. As they pounded beers ("Seven, eight, fifteen . . . ," recounted Porcello), they reflected on why their past postseason experiences had ended in disappointment, and on the need to control the emotions that inevitably accompanied the raised stakes of the playoffs so that they could allow their abilities to show on the field.

Pitching coach Dana LeVangie likewise wanted his pitchers to enter the postseason with conviction, to understand that despite all the questions about the Red Sox bullpen, the team had more than enough talent to win a championship. Typically, before the start of a series, LeVangie led a detailed breakdown of opposing hitters to devise plans of attack. Prior to the start of the series against the Yankees, however, he broke form.

The Red Sox had played the Yankees nineteen times that year; they already knew this lineup of mashers. Instead of scrutinizing hot and cold zones that had already been committed to memory, LeVangie had advance scouting assistant J. T. Watkins prepare a video of Red Sox pitchers striking out one Yankee hitter after another.

"It was probably a ten-minute clip of everybody on our staff punching guys out, punching guys out," said Porcello. "And [LeVangie] basically was like, 'You guys just saw it. You're more than fucking good enough to dominate these guys. So let's go out there and do it.'"

In the first inning of Game 1 of the ALDS against the Yankees, amid a steady roar at Fenway Park, Sale struck out three Yankees, and the Red Sox lineup immediately built on that strong beginning. Benintendi shot a single through the left side and stole second base. Steve Pearce drew a walk. Then J. D. Martinez blasted a three-run homer off lefty J. A. Happ to give the Red Sox a 3–0 lead, which the Red Sox successfully navigated—thanks to critical bullpen contributions from Matt

Barnes and Porcello—to a 5–4 victory. For the first time, this Sox group could play from ahead in a series.

Still, the tenor of the series shifted dramatically one day later, when the Yankees crushed a pair of homers off David Price, chasing him in the second inning. The Yankees would win, 6–2. The idea that New York—which owned a 7-0 postseason record at Yankee Stadium in 2017 and 2018—could close out the series without returning to Boston filled Fenway Park with a sense of dread. As Yankees slugger Aaron Judge strolled through the Fenway concourse to his team bus that night, Frank Sinatra's "New York, New York" blared on his portable speaker—a playlist selection that was caught by a passing camera phone, released into the Twitterverse, and exploded as a social media phenomenon.

The Red Sox didn't say much publicly about the fact that the Yankees' traditional home victory anthem had echoed in their park, or that the series now was being treated as New York's to lose. But certainly, they noticed.

"Everything here is Yankees winning in four, Yankees in four. I'm like, 'What is going on?'" wondered Bogaerts. "How can we have 108 wins and they'll be like the Yankees are going to win in four? I don't understand."

Again, external doubt became competitive fuel. When Game 3 opened in New York, the Red Sox emerged as the aggressors. Just as he had in the first game of the season, Betts set the tone, jumping on Luis Severino's first pitch of the game—a 96-mph fastball down the middle—and blasting it to straightaway center field. Though the ball expired in the glove of Brett Gardner just over 400 feet from the plate, the boisterous Yankee Stadium crowd immediately was quieted by the near-homer on the game's first pitch.

"It didn't go out," said Cora, "but it kind of let them know, 'Hey, we're here.'"

From that point forward, the Red Sox lineup had Severino, the Yankees, and their crowd on the defensive. In the second inning, a pair of two-strike hits, the second a two-out, run-scoring knock by Christian Vazquez, suggested that signature elements of Boston's league-best regular season offense would persist into October. Two more two-strike hits—one by Benintendi (who reached base four times in the game), one by Bogaerts—contributed to two more runs in the third.

A punch-drunk Severino returned to the mound for the fourth, already having thrown 64 pitches. The Red Sox did not let up, loading the bases and forcing him out of the game. They would drop seven runs that inning to open a 10–0 lead and set a blowout in motion.

Eovaldi, the prized July addition, dominated, vindicating those in the Red Sox organization who made the case to add him rather than an established bullpen option prior to the trade deadline. Through seven overpowering innings, he allowed one run on five hits, walked none, struck out five, and simply overwhelmed the Yankees with a fastball that clocked regularly in the upper-90s, which he complemented with a cutter and slider.

The 16–1 victory was punctuated when Brock Holt, already in possession of a single, double, and triple, laced a homer down the right-field line in the ninth to become the first player ever to hit for the cycle in the postseason. Holt, who had one hit in fifteen career at-bats against Severino entering the game, hadn't even expected to be in the lineup before he got a text from Cora the night before.

"Are you sure?" Holt replied.

The decision highlighted how Cora, in tandem with the Red Sox' analytics staff, employed data to inform decision-making. Fifteen at-bats simply didn't constitute a meaningful sample size. Instead, Cora focused on career-long patterns for Severino and how Holt's left-handed swing matched up with the right-handed pitcher's slider. Cora took some amusement in the success of his logic.

"Play the Powerball tomorrow, and hopefully I can get it," he said.

Holt, one day removed from history, then was absent from the lineup for Game 4 against Yankees lefty C. C. Sabathia. Again, Cora's lineup choice paid dividends. Ian Kinsler (acquired at the deadline from the Angels in exchange for a pair of minor league relief pitchers) hit a run-scoring, two-out double to left as part of a three-run third inning that helped stake the Sox to a 4–0 lead.

With the Sox still ahead, 4–1, in the eighth inning, Cora elected to summon Sale out of the bullpen. The left-hander's perfect frame brought the Red Sox within three outs of advancing past New York. Still, even though many franchise demons had been exorcised in 2004—when the Red Sox beat their archrivals in Yankee Stadium in Game 7 of the American League Championship Series on the way to the team's first title in eighty-six years—a wobbly appearance from closer Craig Kimbrel in the ninth conjured darker memories.

Walk. Single. Strikeout. Walk. Suddenly the bases were loaded, with one out, and Neil Walker striding to the plate. Kimbrel's first pitch clipped him in the ankle: 4–2. Gary Sanchez, the Yankees' powerful catcher, was up, with the winning run on first. He crushed a ball to left that appeared to have a chance to leave the park and give the Yankees the walk-off victory.

Instead, Andrew Benintendi settled under the moon shot and caught it on the warning track for a very loud second out. But Didi Gregorius scored from third on the sacrifice fly, whittling the Red Sox' lead to one.

More than six months earlier, at the team dinner organized by Rodriguez just before the start of the season, Kimbrel had told his teammates how much he valued their trust, how great a responsibility he felt to respect the work that went into building a lead by securing the last outs of a victory. All that stood between him and rewarding it was twenty-one-year-old Gleyber Torres.

On the fourth pitch of the at-bat, Torres tapped a slow grounder to third. Eduardo Nunez charged, gloved it, but then fired wide of the bag. Steve Pearce—among the shortest first basemen in the game—used every inch of his five-foot-ten frame to sprawl like a hockey goalie and reel in the throw for the final out.

Or did he? Instead of celebrating immediately, the Red Sox were forced to endure sixty-three seconds of suspended emotion while waiting for replay to determine whether Torres had indeed been beaten by the throw. The call was affirmed, and the Red Sox swarmed to the middle of the field.

After two years of frustration, their core had finally won a series together. The first summit had been conquered.

"We were stuck here for a while," Bogaerts said of the Division Series round. "It's about time. It's about time. It was tough in this first round for a while but I think this group we have is pretty special."

The champagne-soaked clubhouse—made somewhat perilous by the plastic sheeting not just protecting the players' lockers but also the carpet, with pools of champagne turning the surface into a skating rink—featured a playlist with a message. Interspersed among tracks from New York native and hip-hop icon Jay-Z, "New York, New York" blared, an act of reciprocity for Judge's perceived taunt in Fenway Park three nights earlier.

Barkett took to Twitter as he prepared to exit Yankee Stadium.

"Speaker is charged," he pronounced.

•   •   •

Wᴵᴛʜ ᴛʜᴇ ʏᴀɴᴋᴇᴇs ᴅɪsᴘᴀᴛᴄʜᴇᴅ, ᴛʜᴇ Red Sox now faced a fa-miliar foe. To advance to the World Series, the team had to go through Houston in the American League Championship Series—the same Astros team that had bounced them from the playoffs the year before.

But the dynamic had shifted. In 2017, Houston had entered the postseason at full strength, while the Sox seemed ready to collapse by the time they pushed past the regular season finish line. And indeed, that's largely what had happened in the Astros' four-game series win over the Sox. Still, the series hadn't been so lopsided. After all, the Sox had a lead in the late innings of Game 4, at a time when a victory would have sent the series to a winner-take-all Game 5. At times, some members of the Red Sox wondered how different the world might have been had the team advanced past Houston. Would they have been able to justify firing Farrell if they'd won a postseason series? And if he'd been brought back for 2018, would the team have been able to achieve the same kind of alchemy under him as it did under Cora?

But they had lost, Farrell had been fired, and Cora—the Astros' bench coach in 2017—had imported many of the best practices of the team that had vanquished the Sox. The supe-rior integration of the work of the analytics department into game planning, an improved offensive approach, and workload and playing time management: all were designed to have Red Sox players performing at their physical peaks in October.

Houston, meanwhile, was depleted. Shortstop Carlos Correa had fought oblique and back issues throughout the season. Sec-ond baseman Jose Altuve, the 2017 MVP, was playing on one leg in the postseason, the result of a knee injury that would require surgery at the conclusion of the year. Still, Houston's offense remained impressive, and their pitching staff was historic. It had allowed just 3.3 runs per game during the 2018 regular season—

the fewest allowed by an American League team since the introduction of the DH in 1973.

The top of the Astros' rotation, so important in any postseason series, was formidable, led by perennial Cy Young contender Justin Verlander and a pitcher who'd emerged as one of the best in baseball in 2018, Gerrit Cole. Their bullpen, meanwhile, reinforced by the trade deadline acquisitions of Roberto Osuna (a controversial reliever who'd been suspended seventy-five games under MLB's domestic violence program) and Ryan Pressly (a former Red Sox draftee who, years after leaving the team's minor league ranks as a pitcher with nothing but a fastball, had developed both a slider and curveball to become an elite late-innings option), was now equally capable.

"There were sleepless nights for a hitting coach," acknowledged Red Sox hitting coach Tim Hyers.

In Game 1 of the ALCS, he wasn't the only member of the Red Sox who looked weary. Sale—who for two months in the summer had been overwhelming, mixing a 96–100 mph fastball with an unhittable slider and changeup—looked jarringly vulnerable. He'd lost his velocity—suddenly he was struggling to hit 90 on the gun—and his command.

At one point, in the second inning, he could locate only one pitch in one spot—that pedestrian fastball to his glove side, meaning the inner edge of the plate against right-handed hitters. He showed remarkable grit in pitching through his limitations and limiting Houston to two runs on one hit in four innings—but his outing raised questions about what kind of postseason contributions, if any, he might be expected to make moving forward.

Verlander likewise endured an unexpected struggle with his command, thus dimming the luster of what promised to be a special match-up of two of the most dominant pitchers of the twenty-first century. While he'd been handed a 2–0 lead in the fifth inning, the Astros ace lost the strike zone, walking three straight batters with one out to force in one run.

But with Verlander reeling, Betts was tardy on a first-pitch, 98-mph fastball down the middle with the bases loaded and one out, tapping it to third baseman Alex Bregman, who threw home for an out. Though the Red Sox tied the game that inning on a wild pitch, their opportunity to open an offensive geyser had sputtered with Betts's missed moment, and the Astros eventually claimed a 7–2 win.

"You can't miss that pitch," Betts lamented, some frustration bubbling amid a third straight postseason of limited offensive production. "I need to do my part. I haven't been doing it."

The defeat, in which the Red Sox lineup had been punchless, again raised questions about whether the Red Sox might be outclassed by the defending champions. With the series ready to shift back to Houston after Game 2, it felt like the Red Sox' season faced a crossroads in the second contest of the ALCS, with the much-scrutinized Price on the mound against Cole.

Cole, whom Houston had acquired from Pittsburgh in a trade prior to the 2018 season, had enjoyed a breakthrough with the Astros thanks to some adjustments to his arsenal and pitch mix that had been encouraged by Houston's analytics department. Among the most important was his near-abandonment of his sinking two-seam fastball in favor of a four-seam fastball at the top of the strike zone, one that he was capable of throwing with well-above-average spin that limited the degree to which it sank as it traveled across the plate.

Visually, a high-spin fastball at the top of the zone appears to almost rise, staying elevated above where the hitter anticipates it. The Sox, however, devoted considerable attention among their hitters to understanding how an opposing pitcher's spin affected the flight of the ball. Hyers and the Red Sox advance scouting team and analysts would study spin data and translate it into digestible terms for hitters, letting them know, for instance, to adjust their sights by the width of a baseball or two to get on top of a specific pitcher's fastball at the top of the zone.

When it came to Cole, the Sox were prepared. In the bottom of the first, Betts jumped on a 96-mph fastball and smashed it off the fence in center for a double. One pitch later, Benintendi jumped on another fastball—this one up in the zone—and lined a single to drive in Betts and wake up Fenway. Rafael Devers did the same, staying on a 99-mph fastball later in the inning to shoot a single through the left side of the infield that delivered a second run.

But Price couldn't lock down that early advantage, giving up one run in the second inning and two in the third to put the Red Sox in a 3–2 hole. The Red Sox, however, needing to muster a rally to keep hold of the game and the series, loaded the bases with two outs in the bottom of the third. Up to the plate stepped Jackie Bradley Jr.

By 2018, THE DOUBTS ABOUT Bradley's personality and makeup had long since vanished. Over time, members of the Red Sox organization had come to understand him as a rarity—an incredibly well-grounded person who maintained a consistent outlook on both his baseball career and life regardless of his recent performances. Bogaerts and especially Betts could live and die on the last week's box scores.

"Mookie's kind of a roller coaster. He goes oh-for-eight, we gotta get the Kleenex box out," said Dustin Pedroia.

Over the years, Bradley had endured by far the most extreme performance swings of the three, the sort of slumps that would have driven Bogaerts or Betts to despair. Yet he remained strikingly self-assured.

"He's a rock," said Pedroia. "I think he helps those guys more than anybody in just the way he acts and carries himself."

Early in 2018, Bradley had withstood one of the more drastic slumps anyone on the Sox could recall. Over a roughly four-week stretch in late April and early May, his ability to hit major league fastballs suddenly and alarmingly vanished. Over 64 at-bats, he managed just 6 hits—and 32 strikeouts. The Sox, for a period, scaled back his everyday role, having Bradley sit for six of eight games in mid-May.

He responded to the benching by hitting the ball as hard as just about anyone in the big leagues, with only one problem: he kept making outs. By late June, he was still hitting well below .200. The rumblings, like those from late 2014, began: Even given his elite defense, was he still capable of starting for a contender?

Fortunately for Bradley, the man whose opinion mattered most never wavered on that question. Alex Cora understood that new measures of the quality of contact—exit velocity, launch angle, swing-and-miss rates—offered a more accurate picture than traditional numbers such as batting average, a number heavily dependent on luck and fielder positioning. In June, Bradley had moved beyond his swing-and-miss issues, and had ranked among the big league leaders in average exit velocity—an indicator that he was hitting the ball extremely hard on a consistent basis. He just wasn't finding holes. Bradley was still below the Mendoza Line, but Cora knew he had figured something out.

"We trust where he's at," Cora said in late June. "Everybody feels that he'll go through stretches and get hot for a month and a half. Maybe this is the year that it's August, September, and October."

Over the final three-plus months of the season, Bradley's production started to fall in line with how he was hitting the ball. He hit .282 with a .349 OBP and .502 slugging mark over his final 76 games—approaching the performance level that had netted him an All-Star start in 2016. By the playoffs, he was no longer overwhelmed by fastballs—he was hunting them.

Such was the case against Cole with the bases loaded and two outs in the bottom of the third inning of ALCS Game 2. Cole missed the strike zone with a pair of pitches, then blew a fastball by Bradley. The pitcher tried to double up on his heater, but Bradley got his bat inside of a 98-mph fastball down in the strike zone and on the inner-third of the plate, golfing it down the left-field line and off the Green Monster to give the Red Sox a 5–3 lead in an eventual 7–5 victory.

In the early season, Cora had taken the longer view with Bradley. He'd overlooked short-term struggles with the notion of an October payoff. In Game 2, that forward-looking perspective had been rewarded.

Credit for the victory went to reliever Matt Barnes, who, with Bradley, had been at the front of the emerging wave of Red Sox prospects in 2012. While the Red Sox' view of Barnes as a mid-rotation starter hadn't been realized, by 2018 he'd emerged as a critical late-innings presence out of the bullpen.

Back in A-Ball, Barnes had been able to blow away opposing hitters solely on the strength of an explosive fastball that registered in the mid- and upper 90s. As for his breaking ball . . .

"If you needed someone to throw a curveball in the left-handed batter's box, I was your guy," Barnes joked.

Yet he found one—in a way that illuminated how player development isn't just a function of instruction from coaches and managers and front offices, but instead can be a cultural product of peer-to-peer bonding. In 2013, Barnes spent much of his time with Anthony Ranaudo and Brandon Workman, pitchers who'd been drafted one year before him. Both had the consistent ability to spin curveballs for strikes. It was the grip, they finally suggested to Barnes during batting practice one day before a game against the Yankees' Double-A Trenton affiliate.

"Have you ever thought about spiking it?" they asked Barnes, suggesting that he bend the knuckle of his right index finger before placing the fingertip on the seam of the ball, thus creating a pressure differential that would allow him to spin the ball but with finger placement that might allow him improved command. Suddenly the curveball became a reliable weapon, as Barnes rose to Triple-A and then to the big league club, where over time he came to excel at throwing the pitch over parts of five seasons.

In Game 2, with the Sox clinging to a 5–4 lead in the fifth and Price having walked two batters, Barnes entered the game. He threw Marwin Gonzalez a curveball, then another. Four pitches, all curveballs—strikeout. Barnes returned for the sixth and set the Astros down 1-2-3, throwing 10 curveballs in 11 pitches.

As in the ALDS Game 4 clincher against the Yankees, Game 2 against the Astros ended with Benintendi securing an out on what would have been a game-changing hit. With a man on first and two outs in the ninth, Alex Bregman lofted a deep fly ball to left off Kimbrel. A capricious gale caught it, and Benintendi, who'd initially drifted back and to his right against the scoreboard, suddenly had to reverse directions and charge to his left. Benintendi's familiarity with the expect-anything mandate of playing left field at Fenway helped him to track a ball that seemed to change directions numerous times during its game-ending descent into his glove. The series was tied.

IN GAME 3, THE RED SOX turned again to Eovaldi, who overpowered the Astros over six innings, allowing two runs. In the top of the sixth, Pearce broke a 2–2 tie with a solo homer and

Bradley, who had just one hit in seventeen regular season at-bats with the bases loaded, delivered his second such game-changing knock of the ALCS, jumping on an elevated fastball from Osuna and sending a rocket into the stands in right for a grand slam in an 8–2 win.

In many ways, the next contest served as the most critical of the postseason for the Red Sox as well as the embodiment of the full extent of the talents of their homegrown group. Seven runs were driven in by players who'd come up through the Red Sox' ranks, with Rafael Devers putting the team on the board with a two-run single in the first, Xander Bogaerts delivering a pair of run-scoring hits, and Christian Vazquez hitting a sixth-inning, two-out double to extend the inning in front of Bradley, who once again gave the Red Sox a lead by blasting a two-run homer to turn a 5–4 deficit into a 6–5 lead. Yet somehow, in a game in which fourteen runs scored, offense became almost an after-thought. Instead, the game was shaped by the extraordinary defensive gifts of the Red Sox' outfield, particularly Mookie Betts in right and Andrew Benintendi in left.

The Red Sox had often prioritized athleticism in their early-round, high-dollar picks, believing that great athletes have the ability to adjust to the game as it becomes harder while moving up across levels.

"It's a game of inches," noted Red Sox VP of amateur scouting Mike Rikard. "The more athletic players you have on the field, the more of a chance you have to come out on the right end of it."

In Game 4, Betts and Benintendi validated Rikard's approach, from the first inning through the last. In the bottom of the first, with the Sox in possession of a 1–0 lead, the Astros had a runner on first for Jose Altuve, who lofted a fly ball to the opposite field. Initially, it seemed routine, but the ball kept carrying to the warning track. Betts followed it there, then leapt with perfect timing—only to have his glove punched closed by a reaching fan.

Umpire Joe West determined that Betts would have caught it but for the spectator's efforts, and ruled Altuve out on fan interference. West's call hardly inspired universal agreement, even if Betts was "one hundred percent positive" that he'd have made the catch. But the mere fact that West could assume the same was a testament to the right fielder's phenomenal athleticism and sense of timing, traits that had been evident to Watkins back on the Overton High basketball court.

Betts further brandished his Gold Glove credentials in the eighth, when Tony Kemp—a friend dating to Little League in Nashville—opened the inning by shooting a liner down the right-field line. Kemp has tremendous speed; the play seemed like an almost-certain double.

But Betts took a perfect angle to cut off the ball before it reached the wall, and with a second baseman's balletic footwork, spun, and with a lightning release, fired a perfect throw to Bogaerts, who had merely to drop his glove to retire Kemp—an almost certain leadoff double that might have served as kindling for a significant rally instead transformed into an out.

Still, the play wasn't enough to guarantee victory on a night when Kimbrel was struggling to deliver a six-out save. Kimbrel, it turned out, was tipping his pitches through his glove position and the timing of when he turned his head toward the plate— tells relayed to Cora later in the series by his close friend and former teammate, Eric Gagne.

The Astros knew when to anticipate Kimbrel's high-90s fastball and when he'd be spinning his power curve. Houston scored a run in the eighth to narrow the deficit to 8–6, and threatened to wipe out the deficit completely when Kimbrel issued three walks to load the bases in the ninth.

With two outs, Bregman stepped to the plate, in position to

tie the game or even give the Astros a series-tying victory with a hit. If the Astros could have picked a player to send to the plate at this moment, it would have been Bregman. He ranked among the best hitters in the majors with runners in scoring position in 2018 and possessed the sort of cockiness that often characterizes players who excel in such moments.

In 2015, Bregman had been the only player whom the Sox might have contemplated ahead of Andrew Benintendi in the draft. And now, in left field, a relatively shallow 293 feet from home plate, Benintendi was poised for the game-deciding moment.

Benintendi and Bregman had been college rivals at Arkansas and Louisiana State University, respectively. On the diamond, they shared a similar approach, but off it, they could not have been more different. Bregman was outspoken and loved being the center of attention. Benintendi was more reserved; he had enjoyed playing in the shadow of Moncada in the minors, and now happily took a supporting cast role under Betts and Martinez.

But on the field, Benintendi was as self-assured of his skills as Bregman was of his, a fact that became apparent in a span of roughly three seconds when the Astros star jumped on a first-pitch fastball from Kimbrel and hit a soft liner that seemed destined for the turf in shallow left field. Benintendi had to cover forty-five feet from where he stood to where the ball would hit the ground, a distance that left virtually no margin for error.

Left fielders make that play only about 21 percent of the time, according to Major League Baseball's Statcast calculations. If the ball fell, it would mean a tie game; if it got past Benintendi, the Astros would win.

Benintendi didn't hesitate. He went into a dead sprint and dove, extending his right arm to snare the ball just before it hit the turf, then leapt with a barbaric yawp in celebration of the dramatic game-ending catch. Bradley rushed to his teammate and lifted him in celebration; Betts ran all the way across the outfield to join them. Holt gave Benintendi a kiss on the cheek. The Red Sox were within a win of the World Series.

For Rikard, this was affirmation. "Athleticism plays," he said. "Guys that can do things just naturally seem not to be quite as affected by the stresses that come with big, big games. It's amazing."

CHRIS SALE HAD BEEN HOSPITALIZED briefly after his Game 1 start due to a stomach issue, one that he joked was related to an infected belly-button ring. The illness left him unable to start Game 5, and so the Red Sox turned back to Price on three days of rest. The ask seemed even larger due to the fact that Price had spent a significant chunk of Game 4 of the ALCS warming in the bullpen (and occasionally taking a rake to tend to the mound dirt) in case the Red Sox needed him as an emergency relief option.

But during that work in the bullpen, Price had figured something out. He'd slightly altered his posture to create more back-to-front tilt in his delivery, resulting in greater velocity and a slightly higher release point of his pitches. In Game 5, he would attack the top of the strike zone with that newly lively fastball, using it to set up a changeup that proved particularly nasty, dipping barely below the zone—and the bats that were swinging over it. Price would dissect the Astros for six shutout innings in which he struck out nine.

The Sox, meanwhile, beat Verlander even on a night when he was sharp. J. D. Martinez kept his hands inside of an elevated curveball to blast a solo homer in the top of the third inning, and Rafael Devers—with an understanding that Verlander would try to attack him with that riding fastball at the top of the zone—got on top of one of those offerings and drilled it into the left-field Crawford Boxes at Minute Maid Park for a three-run homer in an eventual 4–1 Red Sox win.

The Red Sox exulted, blasting champagne and beer all over the visitors' clubhouse and surrounding hallways in a landmark victory for the group. No footnote would be necessary for the 108-win regular season. Yet reaching the World Series didn't just represent the fulfillment of the 2018 season but instead the outgrowth of seven years together for many of those players, dating to those days hanging out in Betts and Bradley's dorm room in the instructional league seven years earlier.

Bradley claimed ALCS MVP honors, eliciting particular joy from those who'd seen his performance roller coaster over several years. Hitting coach Tim Hyers recalled the time he spent with Bradley in late 2014, after he'd been demoted back to Triple-A following his all-consuming offensive struggles in the big leagues.

"It was worth it," said Hyers.

The front office had kept its faith in Bradley, and had been rewarded. Teammates saw a player whose unflappable demeanor had allowed him in 2018 to work through a period when poor numbers would have driven most of them crazy—and long before that, had allowed him to overcome the brutal struggles of 2014, when his future in Boston seemed uncertain.

"Jackie was with me every step of the way. There were so many people trying to drive a wedge between us in '14 when he was struggling, and people saying I was taking his spot. But me and him remain the best of friends," said Betts. "We've been through the ranks together. I can look next to him and know that we've been together kind of every step of the way. I knew what kind of player he is. He's proven it. He can do it all."

The team likewise felt that it was operating without limitations as it stood four wins from a title.

THE RED SOX WEREN'T MERELY competing for a title. They were an evolving photo album of growth that was, for many, seven years in the making. Still, as was the case on Alex Cora's wall, there were more pictures to assemble.

Tim Hyers had spent the previous two years as the assistant hitting coach for the Los Angeles Dodgers, whom the Red Sox would be facing in the World Series. J. D. Martinez had spent the second half of 2017 with the Diamondbacks, the Dodgers' division mates, and had seen plenty of their staff. Hyers knew the strengths and weaknesses of Dodgers pitchers in a way that allowed the detail-oriented Red Sox lineup to prepare in meticulous fashion; Martinez had a long history against Dodgers ace Clayton Kershaw that helped to inform the team's planning for Game 1.

The Red Sox immediately jumped the Dodgers left-hander in the first inning of Game 1, with Betts leading off the game with a single, stealing second, and scoring on a Benintendi single. Benintendi later scored on a Martinez single as the Red Sox took an early 2–0 advantage.

Though neither of the top two hitters in the Sox lineup had ever faced Kershaw before, they knew from Hyers and Martinez where to focus—pitches up in the strike zone, in to righties, away from lefties. A culture of information allowed exceptional talent to thrive on the field, and though the Dodgers twice tied the game, they never led, as the Red Sox won Game 1, 8–4.

The next night, thanks to six sharp innings from Price and three perfect frames from the no-longer-maligned bullpen— with scoreless innings from Joe Kelly and Craig Kimbrel as well as Nathan Eovaldi, who played the role of "rover," a tactic Cora employed to use starters out of the bullpen to entrust the greatest number of innings to his most dominant pitchers—the Red Sox claimed a 4–2 victory for win number 117 of the year. Just two victories separated the Red Sox from one of the greatest seasons of the modern era.

Still, that proximity to a championship was no guarantee of securing it as the series shifted to Los Angeles. Upon arriving in Dodger Stadium, the Red Sox lineup in particular seemed somnambulant due to the combination of the rigors of travel, the body-clock adjustment, and the presence of Dodgers rookie Walker Buehler on the mound. The right-hander overwhelmed the Red Sox through seven shutout innings, preserving a 1–0 advantage for Los Angeles.

But with Dodgers closer Kenley Jensen summoned for the eighth inning, Bradley blasted yet another game-changing homer, this one a solo shot to tie the game, 1–1. Thus began nearly another game's worth of extra innings. In the twelfth inning, Cora—who'd already summoned seven relievers, including rovers Price and Eduardo Rodriguez—into the game, called for Eovaldi to enter, at a time when the right-hander looked like the most dominant pitcher standing in the postseason.

Eovaldi had been slated to start Game 4. But Cora sniffed a chance to lock down the series right then. Even though summoning the right-hander—who'd retired all three batters he'd faced in the eighth inning of Games 1 and 2—likely meant turning to another starter in Game 4, Cora was all-in on Game 3, and Eovaldi's overwhelming arsenal of pitches justified that faith.

The Red Sox scraped a run across the plate in the top of the thirteenth inning, but with two outs in the bottom of the inning, second baseman Kinsler lost his footing fielding a routine grounder and threw wildly to first. What should have been a game-ending play turned into a game-tying mishap that ensured the continuation of a contest that now felt endless.

Eovaldi kept coming back to the dugout with a message for Cora: He was good for another inning. And another. And another. His pitch count soared—69 pitches by the end of the fifteenth inning, 80 after the sixteenth, 90 after the seventeenth—yet the right-hander kept firing pitches in the upper 90s in an epic show of pitching fortitude.

Yet while Eovaldi kept holding Los Angeles at bay, the Red Sox offense mustered nothing. With the game being played under National League rules and without benefit of a DH, several key lineup members were long gone as the game progressed through frame after frame. And the two offensive mainstays who remained in the game, Betts and Bogaerts, combined for a historically hideous 0-for-15 line.

Finally, in the bottom of the 18th inning, Dodgers slugger Max Muncy drove Eovaldi's 97th pitch of the game over the fence in left for a walk-off homer. After 18 innings, 561 pitches, 7 hours, and 20 minutes of baseball, the Red Sox had left Game 3 with nothing to show for their troubles. Dejected, Eovaldi and his teammates trudged off the field, a sickening mix of exhaustion and emptiness prevalent in the clubhouse.

WHEN ALEX CORA WAS A junior at the University of Miami in 1996, his team went on a magical run through the College World Series. In the tournament's final game, against LSU, they were one out from winning the title. Cora was stationed at shortstop when Miami closer Robbie Morrison gave up a walk-off homer to LSU's Warren Morris. Cora had fallen onto the infield dirt and wept as Morris circled the bases.

He wasn't alone. The entire Miami team felt shattered by the gut punch. Their coach, Jim Morris, couldn't find words to break the funereal silence in the Hurricanes' locker room.

Cora recognized the team's heartache and knew that someone had to speak. He was just twenty years old, and speaking in his second language, but it didn't matter. He told his teammates that he loved them, that he appreciated all that they'd achieved together, and that Robbie Morrison was the pitcher they all would have wanted on the mound with a chance to win the championship.

Now, in the Red Sox clubhouse after Game 3, Cora similarly took the team's grief and reshaped it into hope. He celebrated their effort, reserving particular praise for Eovaldi, whom he asked to stand up. The entire clubhouse stood and gave the pitcher a standing ovation—a monumental transformation that allowed the team to leave Dodger Stadium not under a cloud of defeat but instead eager for the games to come.

Laz Gutierrez, the Red Sox' mental skills coach who was in the clubhouse following Game 3, had been on Cora's Miami team in 1996. Instantly, he recognized the parallels.

"His innate ability to know when to deliver a message, how to deliver it, and what the context of the message is—I've never been around anyone who does it better than him," said Gutierrez. Cora had become the perfect voice for this team. He had fashioned a culture of focus on the field and closeness off it. His decision making in games connected the detailed work of the analytics department with the feel-based emotion of a given moment in a way that repeatedly in the postseason seemed to elicit the most of his players' performances. So, too, did his ability to look beyond the present and to identify the long-term best interests of his club.

Agent Scott Boras, who'd represented Cora during his playing career, had heard from current clients on the Red Sox such as Bogaerts, Bradley, and Martinez about the manager's gift for helping his players fulfill their potential. Boras dubbed it "Coralytics."

"Coralytics understands that you have to have the synergy of analytics plus the psychology of a player," Boras said. "Coralytics is worth something far more than analytics, let's put it that way. We know where analytics come from. The thing is, someone can bring you all the ingredients for the cake. But if you don't know how to bake it . . ."

THE AFTERMATH OF GAME 3 was more soufflé than cake. Cora prevented his team from caving at a moment of peril. Yet early in Game 4, the offense was overmatched against former Red Sox pitcher Rich Hill. Through six innings, Hill had shut out the Sox, staking the Dodgers to a 4–0 lead. Chris Sale had seen enough.

Prior to the top of the seventh inning, the starting pitcher erupted in the dugout—and it wasn't to tell his teammates that he loved and appreciated them. Sale shouted at them to wake up, to stop embarrassing themselves, to play their game.

It's not clear whether the speech produced excitement or just fear—no one in the Red Sox dugout made eye contact with Sale during his rant.

"I didn't want to look at him, that's for sure," recalled Barkett. "He's an intimidating dude and he was pissed."

Whether a coincidence or not, the offense did indeed explode after Sale's speech.

The Red Sox scored three runs in the seventh when Mitch Moreland—masterful as a pinch hitter, particularly at anticipating and jumping on first pitches from relievers—attacked the first offering he saw and drilled a three-run homer deep into the right-field bleachers at Dodger Stadium. An inning later, Steve Pearce blasted a solo homer to tie the contest. The game was now within the Red Sox' grasp.

While veterans Sale, Moreland, and Pearce had been chiefly responsible for the surge to that point, the Red Sox then asked the baby of the roster to succeed in a role in which he'd had no prior success. Following a Holt, one-out double, Cora sent Devers to the plate as a pinch hitter.

Pinch-hitting is a task more often entrusted to veterans than to young players. The role is the equivalent of parachuting onto a running treadmill, an undertaking that easily can throw its practitioners off-balance unless they have a firmly established clock for the game—a trait that often requires years to develop.

Entering Game 4 of the World Series, Devers had been sent to the plate as a pinch hitter seven times in his big league career. He hadn't once put a ball in play, striking out six times and walking once. But by the ninth inning of Game 4 of the World Series, Devers's understanding of the game had advanced.

In a way, Devers had delivered a very impressive performance in 2018, considering that at twenty-one years old, he would have been the youngest position player on the Red Sox' High-A Salem affiliate. With 21 homers, he joined Tony Conigliaro and Ted Williams as the only Red Sox players ever to hit at least 20 homers at his age.

Still, his .240 batting average, .298 OBP, and .433 slugging mark had been humbling. During his uneven season, Devers could sometimes be defensive in response to well-intentioned critiques, compounding his struggles. He hadn't been able to keep pace with the league's adjustments, his rough stretches made worse by injuries—a sore shoulder and a hamstring injury—that he'd tried to play through. When Devers went on the DL twice in the span of three weeks for his hamstring injury, the Red Sox recognized an opportunity for Devers to recalibrate.

When he was ready to return to the field, the team sent him on a rehab assignment to Triple-A Pawtucket—a level he'd all but skipped on the way to the big leagues—not for a game or two but for six. And when he returned to the big leagues, he did so in a part-time role, sometimes going three or even four days between starts. "Hopefully this is a wake-up call for him, like it was for Mookie and Jackie [when they were optioned to the minors in 2014]," said third base coach Carlos Febles, who'd managed Devers in 2017 in Portland. The reduced role stung. But as Devers returned to more regular playing time in late September, the Red Sox saw more focus in his at-bats and a better job of applying game plans.

"Honestly, it was very tough for me," Devers said of his struggles. "I said to myself that if I get another opportunity, I'm going to give one hundred percent."

Pre-injury, with Holt on second base and a chance to take the lead in the ninth inning, Devers likely would have stepped to the plate, swung from his heels three times while trying to pull a homer, and struck out. In Game 4 he remained disciplined, first in taking a pair of pitches that missed the strike zone and then, on a 2-0 count, grounding a sharp, run-scoring single up the middle—the first of five ninth-inning runs as the Red Sox claimed a 9–4 advantage.

In the bottom of the inning, he helped to quell an incipient Dodgers uprising with a terrific defensive play to his right to rob Manny Machado of extra bases, playing a significant role in the Sox' 9–6 win. His opportunity had come, and as he'd vowed, Devers had taken advantage of it, a coming-of-age at the most important time.

As the red sox stood on the cusp of a championship, those who'd watched the group develop paused to appreciate not a moment but a process. The waves that had passed through Salem in 2012 and Greenville in 2015 had intersected in a fascinating way, a rising tide not just of talent but of interpersonal commitments—sometimes seen in the form of player-to-player advice, sometimes simply in the supportive atmosphere that had taken shape in the minors and flourished under Cora.

The foundation had been laid through failures and then successes that nonetheless remained incomplete. A homegrown group—Betts, Bogaerts, Bradley, Benintendi, Barnes, Devers, Vazquez, and others who were on the roster—had taken shape, struggled, developed, learned, improved, and ultimately ascended. Then an additional raft of talented players—Kopech, Moncada, Guerra, Margot, Beeks, Espinal, among others—had been deployed in trades that, in concert with some big-dollar free-agent signings like Martinez and Price, along with the right managerial voice, created the supplementary components to round out a group that finally, truly deserved the title of "championship caliber."

"It's like a bunch of puzzle pieces. You've got to put the pieces together. Now," surmised Bradley, "the puzzle is done."

And so it was. On October 28, in Game 5 of the World Series, it was mostly the players acquired by Dombrowski as finishing pieces—along with some contributions from Benintendi (who scored the game's first run) and Betts (who finally hit his first career postseason homer)—who punctuated the Red Sox championship.

Pearce blasted a pair of homers, including a two-run shot in the first off Kershaw; Price delivered seven dominant innings and allowed one run; Martinez launched a solo homer; and, finally, Sale literally left the Dodgers in the dust, striking out the side with a relentless succession of overpowering sliders.

At 11:17 P.M., Dodgers slugger Manny Machado corkscrewed himself into the dirt in futile pursuit of one of Sale's signature offerings. Vazquez secured the ball, raised his arms in triumph, and sprinted to the mound, where he jumped into his pitcher's arms following the final out of the World Series.

"I felt like I was flying," the catcher said. "It was the best moment of my life, that jump."

As the players, coaches, and front-office members embraced and celebrated on the field, on the stage during the World Series presentation, and in the clubhouse afterward, most did so not just with a sense of having completed a great season but of having finally arrived at a destination toward which they'd been striving for years.

"When you go through the minor leagues with guys, you grind with them on twelve-hour, overnight bus rides eating shit food because you don't have another option at three o'clock in the morning, and you grind through a minor league season with those guys, you just have a bond that's just different," said Barnes.

"It's cool being kind of like homegrown talent, instead of just putting pieces here and there," concurred Bradley. "It's special, getting to see everybody kind of just . . . grow—grow from who they were, learning what we possibly can be."

The front office, too, felt as though they had been through something special. The organizational effort—scouts driving or flying tens and sometimes hundreds of thousands of miles in the unending search for talent, coaches who'd arrived early and stayed late in order to teach and help the players grow, front-office members who'd been part of the effort to forge a culture of development—inspired an almost parental joy throughout Dodger Stadium that night.

It was not a hastily assembled championship team but instead one that had been painstakingly and sometimes painfully forged. There had been doubts, there had been last-place finishes, there had been failed prospects and failed strategies. For many people in Dodger Stadium, the sense of elation was nonetheless also mixed with awareness of those who'd been crucial in assembling the group but who were no longer with the team.

Still, on that night, amid the sense of triumph that accompanied 119 wins and the conclusion of one of the most dominant seasons in baseball history, the hardships of the past all became worthwhile. If anything, they added to the sense of accomplishment. The Next Great Red Sox Team had arrived.

Tom Kotchman will never forget his sixtieth birthday, the day that he and dozens of Red Sox minor leaguers—including several of the team's most promising prospects—nearly died.

On August 14, 2014, Kotchman—the manager of the Rookie Level Gulf Coast League Red Sox—and his team were traveling on a bus from Sarasota to Fort Myers following their 3–2 loss to the Orioles' Rookie Level affiliate. About halfway into the drive, as they barreled down highway I-75 at roughly 70 mph, a tire blew out.

The bus, as Kotchman recounted, started swerving from its position in the left lane. Pitching coach Dick Such was sitting behind the driver with his visiting teenage grandson, whom he instinctively grabbed, while the driver wrestled the wheel and tried to save the lives of everyone on board.

Roughly thirty-five passengers—including seventeen-year-olds Rafael Devers and Luis Alexander Basabe, eighteen-year-old shortstop Javier Guerra, and 2014 draftees Michael Chavis and Jalen Beeks—had just enough time to process the terror of the moment.

"At first, it was the confusion of what happened. Have you ever been on a roller coaster when you take the turn? It kind of jerks and hits you real hard. That's what it felt like at first," recalled Chavis. "I thought, 'Maybe it was something on the road.' But then it kept fishtailing."

Somehow, the driver kept the bus upright and avoided any

collisions as the vehicle slid. She managed to pull off the left shoulder of the highway and onto the downward slope of the grassy median. The door faced the whooshing highway traffic—which at one point included Kotchman's wife, who was on her way to meet her husband for a birthday dinner—forcing everyone to remain aboard the tilting vehicle for an hour until a replacement bus arrived.

As relieved passengers disembarked carefully, some put their hands on the earth to confirm with relief that they had emerged unscathed.

"That team, you remember for many reasons," Kotchman recounted four years later. "When we get on that interstate, sometimes I still think about that day."

The road to homegrown did not get derailed by that terrifying moment, yet the near-accident underscored the central role played by risk and uncertainty—even chaos—in the quest to develop a championship team.

Assembling the 2018 team was an exercise in managing the known unknowns—and, more dauntingly, the unknown unknowns—that make it challenging to achieve a yield of even a few standouts at the big league level. To become a championship nucleus, even an immensely talented group of prospects must withstand an asteroid field.

"There are so many variables, different things that are scary," acknowledged longtime Red Sox farm director Ben Crockett.

Teams factor the notion of attrition into their farm systems all the time. The number of prospects who fail to make it dwarfs those who achieve big league success. The Red Sox knew that well.

One of the most gifted Red Sox prospects in recent memory, Rhode Island native Ryan Westmoreland, required life-threatening surgery in early 2010—just over eighteen months after being drafted and months after being named the team's top prospect, a potential five-tool superstar—to remove a cavernous malformation from his brain stem. In 2013, when it became clear, months after a second brain surgery, that he'd never regain the motor coordination to play a game that had once come to him effortlessly, the outfielder announced his retirement.

"It's still hard for me to talk about," Raquel Ferreira confessed six years after his retirement.

In the spring of 2013, outfielder Bryce Brentz—a 2010 supplemental first-round pick about whom area scout Danny Watkins had been just as excited as he was for Mookie Betts the next year—shot himself in the leg while cleaning a gun. One of the club's most highly regarded prospects at that time thus had his invitation to big league spring training camp rescinded and never got called up during a championship season.

Henry Owens, the final draftee signed in the rush to midnight in 2011, went from a pitcher viewed as a potential rotation linchpin to one who couldn't throw strikes. He was waived in 2017.

His longtime teammate and fellow 2011 first-rounder Blake Swihart looked like an untouchable after a strong big league run in 2015. But after the Red Sox lost four of his first six starts of the 2016 season, the team replaced him behind the plate with Christian Vazquez and sent Swihart to the minors to start playing left field. He suffered an injury at that position that forever altered his development schedule, and by early 2019, the Red Sox designated him for assignment after seeing his role dwindle.

Left-hander Brian Johnson, a first-round pick in 2012, had his pro debut that summer truncated when he got hit in the face by a line drive back up the middle at the Futures at Fenway Game at Fenway Park, suffered nerve irritation in his left elbow that prevented a big league call-up and rotation audition in late

2015, was a victim of a carjacking that winter, and during the 2016 season took months away from the game and nearly quit baseball to seek treatment for anxiety.

"Everyone probably goes through their own depths— whether it's a lot or not much at all. I think it's just how you deal with it. It's not easy," said Johnson. "Football, other sports, you go out and take your anger out on the field. Baseball is not like that."

And on . . . and on.

The players who squeezed through the bottleneck to become championship contributors for the Red Sox had seen so many of their peers fall by the wayside that they tried to savor a magical season. Baseball careers are short, transcendent success fleeting. Someday not far off, trades or free agency almost inevitably would break up the group.

"You never know what can happen," Bradley reflected in October 2018. "That's the thing. We definitely try to make the best of every single moment that we have together."

In the wake of the championship, some wondered how credit should be divvied up between Cherington and Dombrowski. But on reflection, team officials resisted the idea that one or the other had "been right" in managing the core. *Both*, in a way, had been, depending on the circumstances—Cherington in clinging to players to see which would emerge from the pack, Dombrowski in his constant willingness to reassess his projections of prospects and his aggressiveness to supplement a near-championship-caliber group with the players who would give the team its best chance to win. And, of course, both had made missteps at different points of their tenures.

At the winter meetings following the 2018 season, Dombrowski and Cherington—by that point, the Blue Jays VP of baseball operations—briefly crossed paths in the lobby of the Delano Hotel in Las Vegas. The two spoke cordially for a few minutes, with Dombrowski particularly eager to deliver a message of gratitude.

"I thanked him for the players we had who were here," said Dombrowski. "He was a part of it. I appreciate everything that he did."

Yet the fact that Cherington was no longer a part of the Red Sox organization also offered reminders—about the expectation to win in Boston that can make patience so difficult to maintain; about the need to remain philosophically flexible in the management and assembly of an elite group of young talents; about the remarkable intersection of circumstances necessary to produce a season as charmed as 2018; and finally, how drastically the team's resources had been shifted from the future under Cherington to the present under Dombrowski.

The Red Sox, after 2018, were ranked by *Baseball America* as having the worst farm system in the game—a byproduct of the fact that the team had graduated several elite prospects to the big leagues, where they'd become contributors to the title, while trading several others. While some team officials bristled that the farm system was underrated, the Red Sox entered 2019 with few players in the upper levels who were perceived by the industry as combining above-average ceilings with high-probability floors. There were potential contributors, but the flow of the pipeline seemed more likely to occur in drips than floods.

The Red Sox elected to keep their World Series–winning team largely intact entering 2019. Only one player—middle reliever Colten Brewer—on the team's Opening Day roster had not been a part of the organization in 2018.

Yet even with the decision to bring back the band for another year, the Red Sox understood well that there were no guarantees that the conditions that had permitted their players to thrive in one season—not just talent, but also health, a culture of remarkable on-field focus, several players performing at or near the peaks of their abilities at exactly the right time of year, and the avoidance of the asteroid field of unknown unknowns—would persist into the next.

After all, the franchise had seen firsthand evidence in 2014 of the fragility of success. Players who excel in championship campaigns—even those in their primes—cannot necessarily replicate such performances from one season to the next. Nor is it the case that pieces of a team that interlock perfectly in one year will enjoy such a fit in another.

For that reason, the success of a homegrown core is perhaps best defined not purely by championships but instead by having opportunities to pursue them year after year—"bites of the apple," in the parlance Theo Epstein used in discussing that famed 2011 draft—and the growth of a group in attempting to seize them. Yet growth also points to the inevitability of change, and with it, the need to keep scouting for and nurturing the next Red Sox cornerstones.

ACKNOWLEDGMENTS

In 1982, my cousins the Goldners took me to a minor league doubleheader in Rosenblatt Stadium to see the Triple-A Omaha Royals—the first baseball games I'd ever attended. I had no idea where the hell I was or what the hell I was watching. John Goldner, my father's first cousin, proved immensely patient in answering an endless array of questions to try to give me some semblance of a clue about the action taking place in front of us.

Thirty-seven years later, I have a somewhat improved understanding about what transpires on a baseball field, thanks chiefly to the people who have continued to humor my interest in and curiosity about the sport and who have remained patient in the face of a well of questions that has yet to reach its bottom. This book is a reflection of the thousands of people who have taken the time to explain the game to me: players, managers, coaches, scouts, executives, fellow reporters, broadcasters, and baseball lifers, particularly those who have allowed me to understand the game as a developmental process. More important, it is a reflection of the family members, friends, teachers, and colleagues who supported and nurtured me in more ways than I can delineate.

I would need another book, longer than this one, to thank all of you. To those of you whom I do not thank by name: my bad, but please know that I've thought of all of you during this six-month journey to the remote mental region of Dagobah.

Nick Amphlett of HarperCollins, my book editor, was a veritable Yoda during these months: calm, reassuring, and encouraging. At a couple of instances in which I was close to losing my mind, he restored my tenuous grasp on sanity. For that, and for the willingness of William Morrow Books to publish this book, I'm grateful.

The original idea for this book was coaxed out of me by Joy Tutela of the David Black Literary Agency, who assured me—as I talked with her about the 2015 Greenville Drive—that a long-term examination of an elite group of prospects could indeed yield a worthy topic for a book. Joy then helped me recast the idea for the book when it appeared that the events of 2018 warranted doing so.

The support offered by my bosses at the *Boston Globe*— Matt Pepin, Joe Sullivan, and Brian McGrory—has been little short of astounding, as has the collegiality of the incredibly talented writers, editors, and photographers at the *Globe*. Dan Shaughnessy offered much-needed and invaluable counsel for a first-time book writer and the reassurance that I could actually finish the project. The indefatigable Peter Abraham kept volunteering to assume an enormous workload on the beat, without which I never would have had time to finish this book. Those are just a few of the people who have made clear that I am extremely fortunate to work at the *Globe*—a remarkable institution, with remarkable people.

One of those remarkable people, Nick Cafardo, passed away this spring. During the heartbreaking months since then, I've been grateful to reflect on the examples set by Nick and the late John Martin of NESN, both of whom exhibited pride in their pursuits of excellence and, more important, unabashed delight in all that they did both on and off the job.

As I've done so, I've been able to appreciate the exceptional people and colleagues around me on the Red Sox beat. Every day that I go to work, I am surrounded and supported by friends— while also pushed to exhaustion by the need to keep up with the tremendous work being done by my coworkers and competitors. I wish I'd told Nick more often how much I appreciated working with him; I will not make the same mistake with all of you.

In particular, John Tomase and Rob Bradford have mentored

me from the time that I arrived on the Red Sox beat with absolutely no formal training as a journalist. As appreciative as I am for the incredible guidance offered by John and Rob, I am even more grateful for their friendship.

Ian Browne, my fellow alum of the third row of the Fenway press box, Mike Silverman, a five-star driver to J.P. and a veteran of the 4 train, Julian Benbow, Tim Britton, Steve Buckley, Evan Drellich, Chad Jennings, Scott Lauber, Brian MacPherson, Chris Mason, Jason Mastrodonato, Sean McAdam, Jen McCaffrey, and Jonny Miller are among the many amazing peers who have offered me wisdom and encouragement, particularly during the months spent working on this book.

Keith Law, a pub quiz force, offered a vast array of scouting and player development lessons. So, too, have the colleagues whom I've encountered through the years at *Baseball America*, whose passion for minor league coverage and constant discovery of new layers of it led me down this path. Peter Gammons delivered constant reminders about the human dimensions of young players on their trajectories, and why it's more enjoyable to examine the world through a prism of possibility. Howard Bryant and Seth Mnookin offered time, wisdom, and perspective that made the book better.

Chris Price and Vin Sylvia gave me my earliest opportunities as a baseball writer, when I was entirely unqualified for the task, to which I say: Thanks, and what were you thinking?!

I am overwhelmed by the generosity of so many people who offered their time and insight for the book. Many of them are named somewhere in the pages of this book; many are not. But to all whom I have had the pleasure of interviewing over the years, I thank you for the opportunity to learn.

Many of those interviews occurred only because of the tireless efforts of media relations staffs: foremost the Red Sox media relations staff members who have been exceedingly helpful over the years, with particular gratitude to Kevin Gregg, Abby Murphy, Justin Long, and Daveson Perez for their assistance this spring, as well as those with all of the minor league affiliates who somehow manage to find time to lend a hand to curious writers while juggling a million other tasks. Good luck with your tarp pulls.

Of course, before I had the good fortune of encountering so many wonderful people in this professional field, I had family members who, despite only a passing interest (and at times an avowed disinterest) in baseball, stoked my passion for the game, tolerating the invariable detours during summer vacations to get to ballparks around the country. What were diversions—the long drives accompanied, suitably enough, by the soundtrack of books on tape—became a destination.

I treasure the memories of those times with my parents, Richard Speier and Sandra Speier, and my sister, Susanna Speier, all of whom provided unfailing support for me even as they challenged me to grow and learn, and even on those occasions when I behaved like a jackass (hopefully fewer now than on some of those road trips). Mathilde Speier has encouraged me as a writer virtually from the moment that we met. Sharon Knotts has put the "ama" in "amazing," and I have no idea how our family would have functioned without her during this time.

My sons, Max Speier and Gavin Speier, displayed remarkable patience with me during the months of work on this book—and offered more encouragement, enthusiasm, and joy than I could have dreamed, as well as inspiration with their boundless energy, creativity, thoughtfulness, and love. I am such a proud, lucky father.

Most important, Alyssa Speier is a delight, a wonder, a marvel—the best person and partner I could imagine, someone with whom I am so lucky to share so much. Despite my sesqui-pedalian predilections, I have yet to find words that adequately capture my appreciation and love for you, but I'm happy to con-sider it a life's mission to keep looking for them.